C000241084

TNT

The New Theatre

TNT

The New Theatre

Paul Stebbings & Phil Smith

lessons, techniques and ideas for making new theatre for a changing world from the most widely travelled theatre that ever packed a bag

Published in this first edition in 2020 by:

Triarchy Press
Axminster, UK

www.triarchypress.net

Copyright © Paul Stebbings and Phil Smith, 2020

The right of Paul Stebbings and Phil Smith to be identified as the authors of this book has been asserted by them in accordance with the Copyright, Designs and Patents Act, 1988.

All rights reserved.

No part of this publication may be reproduced, stored in a retrieval system or transmitted in any form or by any means including photocopying, electronic, mechanical, recording or otherwise, without the prior written permission of the publisher.

A catalogue record for this book is available from the British Library.

ISBNs:
Print: 978-1-911193-83-8
ePub: 978-1-911193-84-5
pdf: 978-1-911193-85-2

tp

Contents

This book is dedicated to all the TNT artists and administrators who should have been acknowledged in this book.

Preface

By Paul

I am Stalin. This is Leningrad. A sea of eyes catch the light. The eyes focus on me, this is my element. I reach into a pocket of my great grey coat. I remove a sugar jelly baby. Raising the strawberry sweet into the light I announce: "Ah, an old Bolshevik!" I bite the head off the candied child and toss the mutilated body into the audience. The theatre gasps. I swivel my blood red eyes inside my melting white make-up and twitch my clown's nose. I skip across the stage, tilting my head from side to side so the untied flaps of my fur hat waggle spaniel-like. I am monster, dictator, betrayer, clown and Doctor. *Dottore.* On my operating table lies a shivering Harlequin. Beautiful Columbine, chained and gagged, is forced to witness this brutal operation. Her rose red cheeks are stained with tears. I produce a plastic knife and cut into Harlequin's chest, pulling out his rubber guts. I speak the words of Stalin as reported in *Pravda* in the year of the Terror: 1937. Finally, I extract from Harlequin his Bolshevik heart: a water filled balloon. Harlequin is cured. I applaud myself. But to confirm his good health Harlequin must renounce his love for Columbine and the True Revolution: all things closest to his discarded heart. But Harlequin, moved by the sight of his chained lover, calls out words that tumble the poets Pasternak and Mayakovski into one long howl:

> In everything I want to reach the real essence,
> In the search for the way, in the heart's turmoil, to catch a thread of fate
> To live, to think, to feel, and to love.
> Sweet Columbine, I love you.

I shake my head with a medic's professional sadness and speak:

> In the opinion of your Doctor, you are living on borrowed time, laddie: about thirty seconds to be precise.

Harlequin goes to the audience and shakes the hands of the front row. I tie his wrists with a red flag. Blindfolded, he kneels at my rasped command and speaks his final words:

Horse, listen to me, Horse,
Dying in this life is not so hard, building a life is harder.
So, Horse, don't cry.
Do you think you are any worse than anyone?
Dear child, we are each a bit of a horse, of course,
We are each a dumb horse in some sort of way.

I take a football rattle from my Doctor's bag and whirl it above my head. Rat tat tat. Rat tat tat. Harlequin falls, felled by a hail of bullets. Blackout.

Lights up. I bow. Applause... that dies, because Harlequin does not rise to take the curtain call. His corpse remains onstage until the last audience member files away into the cold Russian night. Harlequin is Meyerhold, murdered by Stalin for his life and art. He remains dead and this is his memorial. So, Horse, don't cry.

This play was TNT's manifesto piece. The performance in Leningrad took place ten years after its premiere in Britain. It was given on the stage of the Leningrad State Comedy Theatre – an institution whose members had been persecuted and murdered during Stalin's rule. And now here we are in Gorbachev's Soviet Union as it wobbles like Harlequin's red balloon heart.

TNT theatre started with 'Harlequin' (1980) and the vision of the Russian director Meyerhold. TNT started with nothing but three unemployed actors in my mum's little car. Decades later TNT has become the most popular touring theatre in the world. How that came about, and maybe why, is the subject of this book. Which, like 'Harlequin', is dedicated to the marvellous yet murdered Meyerhold who wanted to make the New popular. Inspired by that idea, we built TNT: The New Theatre and we made his motto ours: "Tragedy with a smile on its lips".

How to Read this Book

TNT's largest production was a dramatisation of Herman Melville's epic novel 'Moby Dick'. It was a production that combined equal numbers of dancers, musicians and actors in a performance that came close to the essence of the company style for which we continually search.

The novel itself sings like a whale with some of the finest prose ever penned. Herman Melville was also a master of structure. What is seldom recalled about 'Moby Dick' is that half of the book has nothing to do with Captain Ahab and his doomed pursuit of a white whale. Every other chapter concerns the nature of whaling, the voyages of the hunters, the biology of the leviathans and the minutiae of life in a whaling port. Since the story of TNT, the most travelled of theatre companies, is by its nature a travelogue, a voyage of artistic and geographical discovery, many of the narrative chapters that follow the Introduction will be like parts of the tale of a journey. Sometimes the journey will loop back on itself and you may read the same story from a different angle. These chapters can be read for pleasure (we hope); just to enjoy the travellers' yarn. Taking our lead from Melville, however, between the chapters of the travellers' tale, there will be sections of more specialised interest that address how and why the company makes theatre and reflect on this curious art form that has illuminated humanity for longer than almost any other.

Finally, the life of any theatre company is the life of its productions. They do not stand separate from their journeys. Instead, some of the countries and cultures where we have toured for decades have imposed their own narratives on the ones we have performed. So the story of TNT is not to be told in an entirely straight line. Instead, our history is told in the uneven and sometimes tumultuous stories of its productions, its countries and its ideas. It is told through blinding flashes of discovery, slogs and setbacks; wild seas in which we have swum and on occasions floundered only to reach the surface once again and strike out, not for the shore, but further into the endless ocean.

Introduction

By Phil

In his Preface, Paul describes how in 1990, in the dying days of the Soviet Union, he stood on the stage of the Leningrad State Comedy Theatre and performed to a packed audience in the role of *Il Dottore*/Stalin. I was there to see him. I would never have imagined that such a thing were possible as I sat in the audience for the first performance of the same show ten years before. 'Harlequin' opened in a coalminers' welfare hall in Nottinghamshire. The final rehearsal was watched by three small local (and, happily, rapt) children. Yet this remarkable journey turned out to be possible. As would be the case with many subsequent tours, where our productions tangled with major cultural upheavals across the world. While good fortune has often played a key role, there also had to be a theatre company ready to respond to opportunity. What follows is the story of that company.

Mark Heron (left) and Paul Stebbings (right) in 'Harlequin'

Our purpose is partly to give an account of TNT for those who come to see our performances, or who have heard about the company and want to know more. We hope to pass on to a wider readership some of the principles and techniques that have served us well. We hope these may inspire and inform anyone wanting to make their own new theatre in a changing world.

But this is also a research report. The past forty years have been a very long experiment and it is about time we reported our findings, drew a few provisional conclusions and made some claims for our contribution to original knowledge in the field of popular experimental theatre. Those two words – 'popular' and 'experimental' – are very important to us and our project. They are not found together as often as they should be in the worlds of art and performance. Their confluence marked a very significant moment in the early life of TNT.

The second performance of 'Harlequin' was given at Penzance Arts Centre, 350 miles from the Miners' Welfare Hall at Calverton (long ago demolished). By our good fortune, Allen Sadler, a regional critic, reviewed this performance for *The Guardian*, a national newspaper. It was a very enthusiastic review and it helped us to sell the show to many venues over the coming year. The review summed up the show as "experimental, with popular appeal". There it was! The provincial reviewer had grasped what lay behind our manifesto performance: a speculative combination of experimental and popular theatre. An experiment made not under laboratory conditions, but in all the mess of theatre touring in the austere and riven 1980s.

The experimental concoction of that first production had been some time in the mixing, reflecting both our love of popular performance and an understanding of an almost forgotten innovation in the making of performance. In regard to the former, both Paul and I had been drawn during our formative years to forms of live entertainment generally regarded as non-artistic or 'common'. My father was a fan of music hall and variety and told me stories of the performers he saw; often very poor, according to him. We were both taken to annual Christmas pantomimes; Paul in Nottingham where his father was the Theatre Royal's doctor, and me in Coventry where my Nan (maternal grandmother) was a close friend of Nan Eggington who ran the stage door at the theatre. This allowed me to meet the performers: Mister Pastry (a sensationally good physical comic) gave me a toy that I would later donate to the props table of our production of 'Lord of the Flies', I was kissed by singing star Janie Marden, and I was able to examine closely the machine that dragged the rats of Hamelin across the stage.

Paul met top variety comedians – the inheritors of music hall traditions – like Leslie Crowther and Ken Dodd. We both attended (often violent and riotous) football matches in our home cities, and rock concerts – for me it was Bowie, Roxy Music and Mott the Hoople; for Paul, The Rolling Stones and The Who – and then both of us, as young students, followed the rise of punk and attended gigs by bands like Slaughter and the Dogs, The Clash, The Buzzcocks, Chelsea and The Jam. We were also making performances from a young age. Paul, as he explains below, was cast as Mister Toad at ten years of age. At exactly the same time, in a different industrial city, I was creating my first original show: the theatre building was my parents' garage and, though I have no memory of what we performed, I do know that the entrance fee was sent to the Aberfan Disaster Fund for the families of the children killed by a collapsing slag heap in a Welsh coal-mining town.

In our teenage years both of us engaged, despite our provincial homes, with cutting edge performance; Paul worked as a 'spear carrier' (acting minor roles) at the Nottingham Playhouse under the direction of Richard Eyre, soon to be artistic director of the National Theatre. In this way he got to see numerous pioneering works by leading radical playwrights such as David Hare. My brushes with modernist performance – watching Billie Whitelaw in 'Not I' while sat next to Samuel Beckett or going to a party with Peter Maxwell Davies after watching his 'Eight Songs For A Mad King' – were rather more random and sporadic, but influenced me to make eccentric performances. These included my reading of 'The Babylonian Epic of Creation' with a backing band of former Hell's Angels. The pillion ride home from rehearsals was exhilarating to say the least...

Our paths crossed at Bristol University Drama Department; the first place in the UK to offer a single honours degree in Drama. We made very little extra-curricular work together – though we attended many of the same classes (and parties) – but by the end of our degrees in 1977 our paths were beginning to arc towards each other; Paul as a director, me as a playwright. Our future ambitions were entangling and we decided to create a new professional company. We craftily – and with the covert help of friendly staff – deployed the facilities of the university to help us set things in motion. The mistakes we made in that first company, Bristol Gate Theatre, (it was far too big) helped us three years later when we started TNT.

Something else happened at university. Crucial to the experiment that would unfold over the next forty years was our exposure to the story of one particular innovative philosophy of theatre-making. At Bristol, we were taught by the scholar Edward (Ted) Braun. Ted had travelled to the Soviet Union in the 1960s in order to mine the archives in Russia for information about the director Vsevolod Meyerhold. Ted's seminal collection and translation of Meyerhold's writings – *Meyerhold On Theatre* – and his lectures on this largely unknown international theatre artist captured our imaginations, which were further fired by conversations over dinner at Ted's house. A brief summary of Meyerhold's work may help to explain why it has had such a profound effect on us and the work of TNT Theatre.

Vsevolod Meyerhold was born in 1874 and was murdered in a Soviet prison in 1940. Even before his father's bankruptcy had given him a taste of privation, the young Meyerhold developed an interest in radical ideas and mixed with working class socialists. As an ignored youngest son, he turned away from his family's business world and pursued a career in acting. In 1898 he joined the most progressive theatre of his day: the Moscow Arts Theatre, under the artistic direction of Konstantin Stanislavski.

Stanislavski was a conflicted innovator. On the one hand he was a modernist, shunning the overblown histrionics of star performers. Reacting against them, Stanislavski developed a restrained and naturalistic style of acting that sought an exact imitation of everyday behaviour. At the same time, however, Stanislavski was a romantic who believed that there was 'something else', something beyond or within appearance necessary for a meaningful theatre. Unable to reconcile his invention of a modern and almost industrial form of acting (later universalised in film and television) with an irrational and romantic search for the 'soul' in theatre, Stanislavski passed the responsibility to a Studio within the Moscow Arts Theatre with the participation of Vsevelod Meyerhold.

The Studio was a place of research and experiment. The results, however, were too radical for Stanislavski and he halted them before they could be shown to the public. This provoked Meyerhold to set out on his own experimental path, working as a director for provincial and independent theatres. He combined his youthful radical beliefs in theatre as a place of community and social unity, with an admiration for the Symbolist movement which sought a ritual art to unite artist and audience around a spiritual essence. A loose alliance of European and Russian painters, composers and writers, the Symbolists sought a mystical and poetic life of wisdom at odds with the conservative ideas and conventions and, as they saw it, the limitations of the material world. At first Meyerhold pursued his aims beyond naturalism in rather static, sculptural productions. He reduced the depth of the stage (famously to just two metres in his production of Maeterlinck's 'Sister Beatrice') to create the effect of a sculpture or tableau. His productions made powerful and immediate visual impressions, but movement tended to detract from the pictures.

In his first revolt against Stanislavski's naturalism, Meyerhold chose to freeze the body. His efforts met with limited success. Yet, his experiment was not without results. In pushing Stanislavski's rejection of exhibitionist melodrama into frieze-like contemplative performances, Meyerhold discovered a new sensibility, but not yet a way of realising it for an audience. To express this new sensibility, he repurposed a sermon by the puritanical priest Savonarola on the Virgin Mary. He turned "do not assume that Mary cried out at the death of her Son.... her appearance would have revealed not so much sheer grief as a combination of grief and joy" into the simpler "tragedy with a smile on its lips".

Meyerhold's next move was to stop looking for his aesthetics in stage design and return to his first passion: the performer's body. This time, rather than freeze the body, he sought to liberate it. He found inspiration and techniques in the traditions of the improvising clown: the histrionic cabotin and the *commedia dell'arte* player performing in the village square. He began to model a vision of a new actor: a highly trained, physically and emotionally flexible performer who could be sculptural as well as light and comic in their movement, while at the same time serious and committed to presenting the play clearly. He sought out performers who could use histrionics, mimetics and gymnastics to explain the action rather than blind the audience to it by their virtuosity. Meyerhold imagined a new kind of 'monk clown' committed to the laughter of the body, but also to the search for the 'something else' that Stanislavski and the Symbolists were also seeking.

In 1905 a failed revolution in Russia affected the Russian Symbolists, the immediacy of the political struggle highlighting the passivity of their mystical mission, and they began to change their art. They shifted their search for communal unity with the audience from a mystical event to a quest for social liberty. Meyerhold directed perhaps the most famous product of this shift – Alexander Blok's play 'The Fairground Booth' – in which mysticism now appears as no less oppressive than other manifestations of Russian hierarchy. However, the return to the world of solid matter is no easy choice: a Harlequin figure – "Hello, world! You are with me again!" – leaps through a window towards the horizon of a lush green landscape only to crash through a painted flat and fall with a bump onto the boards of the theatre. In the production, Meyerhold made full use of his newly devised, animated acting style to subvert Symbolist imagery and generate action around visual contradictions rather than pictorial unity. The effect is "grotesque". When Harlequin is shot, he falls across the footlights almost into the audience, crying out "I'm bleeding cranberry juice!" The moment is amusing and subversive, but it is also tragic. The character is dying; outside the theatre political hopes are being crushed.

"Tragedy with a smile on its lips" was realised. Not just as theatrical technique, but, through Blok's words and Meyerhold's staging. This was a way to examine the world; not mechanistically but still seeking that 'something else' that drives the theatre and the world. A way that, in Meyerhold's words, "does not recognise the purely debased or the purely exalted. The grotesque mixes opposites.... deepens life's outward appearance to the point where it ceases to appear merely natural.... [realising] the artist's constant desire to switch the spectator from the plane he has just reached to another that is totally unforeseen".

From then on, Meyerhold developed his new acting to train new actors. He created a set of exercises that he called Biomechanics. He mixed together high and low art in productions of new plays and in his rethinking of classics. He combined tableaux with vigorous dance and disrupted the 'fourth wall' of the naturalistic theatre with actors moving among the audience or indulging in badinage with spectators. The secret of his new theatre was not 'One New Modern Style' but a judicious mixing of many styles, new and old. Meyerhold had taken Stanislavski's confusions and turned them into virtues.

When revolution came along in 1917, Meyerhold joined the Bolshevik Party and put his theatre and its innovations at the service of the party. Now, he sought a revolutionary communality between the actors and audience, who he had come to regard as the "fourth creator" after writer, director and actor. What had started as a subversion of naturalistic styles now became more extreme. His sets often looked like machines, with pumps and flaps that would move in response to the emotions of the characters. In the first flush of revolution, Meyerhold could get away with crude effects and partisan stories, buoyed up on the enthusiasm of new audiences. However, as the revolution went into retreat with the rise of the party bureaucrats and the ascendency of the dictator Stalin, Meyerhold responded with both subtlety and boldness. In 1926, he restaged Gogol's great absurdist satire on bureaucracy, 'The Government Inspector': a story of small town, early nineteenth-century corruption. No one was fooled. When Gogol wrote the play in 1836 everyone knew that he meant the Tsar and the bureaucrats in St Petersburg and in 1926 everyone knew Meyerhold meant the new Soviet establishment and Stalin.

Yet, somehow, Meyerhold had created a production that proved both withering in its criticism and elusive of the censors. He had marshalled all his evolved techniques: stylised movement, vaudeville grace, poetic and allusive symbolism, detailed tableaux combining closely observed behaviours woven into complex choruses, symbolist mystery figures, extreme grotesquerie, and a chilling finale in which the townsfolk (frozen in horror at their discovery that they have mistaken a poor clerk for the real

Inspector, whose arrival is now imminent) are replaced by wax dummies at the curtain call. In that final moment, strangling the audience's applause (a gesture we would echo with the corpse of Meyerhold at the curtain call of 'Harlequin'), Meyerhold physicalised the hollowing out of the inner life of the revolution and its people. The popular success of the production secured, for a while, its survival and that of its director. Somehow, in a secular, atheist and increasingly murderous state, Meyerhold's return to an almost mystical grotesque had insulated him from any simple accusation of political criticism. However, after 1926 Meyerhold was allowed to do very little meaningful work, and in 1940, like millions of other victims of Stalinism, Meyerhold was tortured and murdered.

While we listened to Ted Braun's account of this remarkable artist and read the director's translated writings, we also 'did' – we acted on the inspiration. We picked up on work that was influenced by the memory of Meyerhold. Paul travelled to Poland to spend time with Grotowski's Laboratorium, while for a year I was a member of 'The Group' – a band of students guided by Grotowski's ideas about 'para-theatre' (actions beyond theatre) – and participated in their many hours-long improvisations both in studios and across outdoor landscapes. We both attended workshops given by Eugenio Barba and by other members of Odin Teatret, whose commitment to physical training and neo-Symbolist dramaturgy owed something to Meyerhold.

In 1980, two years after the collapse of our Bristol Gate Theatre, during which time I had been working as a freelance playwright, I received a phone call from Paul to invite me up to Calverton to help bring the 'Harlequin' production to life. I invented for myself the role of "company dramaturg" (not a common term in British theatre at the time). Paul's work had been enriched by his experiences after Bristol Gate: first directing a community theatre in South Yorkshire and then working for an established physical theatre company (from whose acting company the initial performers in TNT would also come). We were ready to create a mixture of our popular and experimental influences. What the result of all this would be was quite unknown to us.

The actors who had joined Paul – Simon and Mark – brought common experiences with Paul that I did not share, including a new scepticism about the role of the guru-director and the abuses that that kind of privileged power could facilitate. Simon had dance skills and an accelerated command of acting skills learned 'on the job' during the extended first tour. Mark had circus and gymnastics skills and brought new kinds of physical presence and expression. Paul had chosen *commedia dell'arte* as the root popular form for the first production (with other diverse popular elements thrown in); it was a manifesto piece as well as an entertainment, in which our hero Meyerhold (as Harlequin) battled in art with his mentor and opponent Konstantin Stanislavski (as Pierrot) only to discover a far worse nemesis in the dictator Joseph Stalin (as *Il Dottore*).

TNT's first brochure with Paul Stebbings as Rasputin in 'Harlequin'

'Harlequin' is a complex tale – involving theatrical aesthetics, revolutionary and reactionary politics, and modernist poetry – but it had to be accessible. Hence that final rehearsal run of the show to the three young children who had been hanging about the miners' welfare hall. During this run the actors were forbidden to speak any of their lines, having to communicate everything to the children through movement. The fact that the children remained engaged throughout was the first suggestion that there might be more to this experiment than a one-off random test in an obscure location.

The following chapters tell the story that follows from that first show at Calverton Miners' Welfare Hall. It is a story of numerous productions, new relationships, an expanding audience and, with occasional reverses, a growing entanglement with the cultures and political upheavals of many different countries. It runs right up to our most recent productions, at the time of writing in 2020, and probably the most unlikely of all texts for us to produce: a rethinking of George Bernard Shaw's 'Pygmalion' for a #MeToo generation. This show, like that of 'Free Mandela' which quickly followed it, still has the multiplicity of styles of a classic Meyerhold production, with movement sequences, a silent movie chase, cross-dressing, nods to 'My Fair Lady', and a framing that invokes the classical myth of Pygmalion. Its central character, Professor Higgins, is no longer Shaw's irascible bachelor, but a toxic and hollow personality with a vacuous and emotionally detached sidekick. This 'hero' provokes gasps from our audiences with his line "you damned insolent slut, you!" This is no charming 'costume drama'. When Liza says at the end of the play, after her transformation at the hands of Higgins, "I sold flowers. I didn't sell myself. Now you've made a lady of me I'm not fit to sell anything else. I am for sale", this is tragedy, barely able to sustain a smile.

While much has changed since 1980 (we would not in those days have sold 2,000 tickets over three nights in Istanbul for 'Harlequin' as we have for 'Pygmalion') much is the same. We still approach the text as a never-completed construction, one not to be revered but respected-by-questioning. Behind everything, from 'Harlequin' to 'Pygmalion', is always the experiment inspired by our late teacher, Professor Ted Braun. It asks the following research questions, still relevant to our future: is it possible to make experimental theatre while avoiding the obscure modernist path to a niche audience? Is it possible to apply a physical theatre training to performances with intelligent texts on serious themes, without becoming bogged down in gymnastic or abstract theatre? And, if the answers to the first two questions are 'yes', how far and in what ways can such an aesthetic – combining experiment with popular forms – travel, develop and engage with a changing world?

What follows are our findings.

The Visual

By Paul

In writing about directors and direction, words come most easily. But the word is only a part of direction and it is easy to be lost in words. The visual image speaks loudest and clearest. Take an example from Lev Dodin's Maly Theatre of St Petersburg. His 'Gaudeamus' was an astonishing and fully realised piece of work. It follows the (mis)fortunes of a group of young soldiers in the Red Army, part of a 'Punishment Battalion', military slaves. The stage setting is artificial snow and little else. We, the audience, follow the desperate half-lives of the boy soldiers in their frozen Hell. I knew the company from my time in Russia, but I watched this production in London. After ten minutes I ripped out my translation earpiece and enjoyed not just the cadences of the most beautiful of Slav languages but the mastery of imagery on this simple raised platform covered in artificial snow. Midway through the piece one convict-soldier meets a poor local girl as they queue for water and a fragile romance begins between the desperate and the lonely. But lovers can dream and the dream takes place before our eyes. A piano rises from the snow. They lie across it and embrace. The couple shake the boots from their feet and, without seeing the keys, play a duet with their toes. As the music ends the entire piano rises on wires into the sky with the lovers entwined upon it. What could be spoken to rival that image?

Of the great directors, Meyerhold was the one most concerned with the visual vocabulary of theatre. He preferred to collaborate with visual artists rather than designers. His most celebrated partnership was with the radical female sculptor Popova. She built abstract forms rather like small Eiffel towers for his actors to run up and down as if they were performing mice. Meyerhold said the single most useful thing about design for the theatre: "Every theatrical set should be a machine for acting". In other words, far more important than its visual appearance, a set should be physically usable, designed to be animated by the actors; something to climb upon, hang things on, move around and spring from, and easily, safely and quickly transformed in meaning and shape. TNT has been collaborating recently with the German performance artist Jorg Besser; he is also a builder and a welder, teaches anatomical drawing and hails from a small town in eastern Germany where he grew up in the dark days of the DDR. His other persona is 'Egg Man'. Dressed in a body-hugging silver suit and goggles he pushes a giant egg made of mirror glass into spaces and places where no one expects a giant reflective egg on wheels. Many TNT sets are also on wheels, some can be climbed, others reflect light and almost none reflect reality. Sometimes we hardly bother. Our play about Martin Luther King used a few white poles and white chairs against a black curtain. Across the back of the stage was a long metal chain. The actors danced with the chain as King read his letter of rebellion penned in Birmingham Jail. If we question directors, should we also ask stern questions of designers? I think so.

The gallows in TNT's production of 'Oliver Twist'

There is little worse than a beautiful set delivered to a company just before the dress rehearsal. Theatre is the art of the imagination; we cannot compete with cinema but we can beat it by conjuring the imagined. Transformation is far more exciting than illustration. If an actor picks up a broom and rides it into battle, we know it is a horse. In 'Oliver Twist', our most performed production, the entire play is given on the gallows. The entrance to Fagin's den is the trap door through which he will fall to his death.

Our first set, that of 'Harlequin', was an 'A-frame' ladder covered in sticky taped copies of the Soviet newspaper *Pravda*. Stalin burst through the centre, later spraying Meyerhold's blood across the torn newsprint in the shape of a hammer and sickle. Every theatre has an 'A frame' ladder, the ideal machine for acting. All we had to carry were a few hundred copies of *Pravda*, which in those days were not hard to find. Perhaps designers make life too easy for directors. "Where is it set?" is so often the first thing asked about a Shakespeare production. I think this is wrong. A director should ask what does the play mean, what is it about? After that we can find visual imagery to illustrate the answer.

Designers naturally wish to draw attention to their art; lighting designers too. This can skew the work as everyone and everything is pulling in their own directions. In 'Hamlet' the action shifts seamlessly in and around one place: Elsinore Castle. We set the TNT version on a simple half circle of wood just lower than a table. When actors stand on it they are outside on the battlements, when they sit on it they are inside the palace. There are no scene changes and the production proceeds at the pace that Shakespeare envisaged; for we know he intended to have no pauses between scenes. Shakespeare only ever used one set and that was the Globe: stage, balcony, trap door, curtained room to the rear, and an audience you could see. A meta-machine for acting.

I end this discussion of the visual with two living images – one comic, one tragic – which I hope illustrate what we wish to see in the new theatre. The transformation of objects in front of the audience is far more satisfying than the presentation of objects designed in an office. In '1945!' (later called 'An English Tea Party') our music hall comedian-Father wishes to declare a Royal Marriage. He places his kitchen chair on the table, takes an old umbrella as a sceptre and a battered tea pot as an orb. Now enthroned, his bullied son crowns him with a woollen tea cosy.

In the final scene of our 'Death of a Salesman', shadowy salesmen fill the stage with suitcases, which stand in vertical rows. Willy Loman's wife and sons gather round a single upturned case, the one he dragged from hotel to hotel throughout his wasted life. The salesman's suitcase has become his gravestone, his hopeless epitaph in a graveyard of suitcases.

Chapter One: ‘Harlequin’, ‘1945!’, ‘The Mystery’

By Phil

The story of the Russian Revolution can be told in different ways. The most common is that its failure was inevitable: that a Communist social ethic is at odds with the fixed qualities of human nature and a violent enforcement is its only possible outcome. On the other hand, if it had been a workable alternative social system (defeated by circumstances or human failings) to the one that now brings us face to face with our own extinction, then its demise was a dreadful moment of missed opportunity. Either way, the descent of the Revolution into dictatorship and nationalism was probably the defining event of the twentieth century. The rise of Nazism, the drift to global war in 1939 (with the first use of nuclear bombs), and the suppression of democracy in numerous young nations emerging from the yoke of colonialism might all be attributed to its contorting of a shining idea into sordid self-interest and repression. If anything was a mass tragedy, whatever its cause, it was this.

No surprise then that, following Meyerhold’s dictum – “tragedy with a smile on its lips” – we should turn these events into a tragic-comedy in ‘Harlequin’. What is more surprising is that British audiences on the small-scale theatre circuit in 1980 were interested, coming to laugh and identify. Audiences responded with empathy to Harlequin/Meyerhold’s optimism and joy in liberation and then reacted in sympathy as his hope for a better, wilder, more intense art and a freer and more aesthetic life were dashed under the feet of the tyrant Doctor. ‘Harlequin’ was quite explicit in its historical references, but many in the audiences, in Britain’s small non-elitist venues, seemed to find their own equivalent experiences (though not the same consequences); hopes crushed by bureaucrats and villains.

When Communism – or whatever it was by then – finally collapsed in 1989/90 (and we were there), the American political scientist Francis Fukuyama famously declared ‘the end of history’. The great conflict of two systems had, he said, been resolved in favour of the capitalist one. There would be no further systemic conflicts or challenges. Although conflicts and depredations upon the planet have since continued, if not intensified,

Fukuyama had seized on a popular perception that alternatives were finished, that hopes for a better world were at an end and that we had all better make the best of the only one left standing. Fukuyama's intention was to provoke celebration. Others, happy at the demise of dictatorships, were more sanguine.

In Poland in 1989, where 'Harlequin' (re-titled 'Glasnost Harlequin') toured for four weeks visiting 22 cities, the audiences' reactions were, surprisingly, not dissimilar to those of audiences in Britain. Although the vast majority of Polish audiences had experienced the Soviet Union as a wholly malevolent force, the play's conceit – that the outpourings of creativity in 1917 represented for radical artists an idealist hope for better times – was something that could still conjure sympathy and identification. Our Polish audiences were able to 'read across' from that hopeful assumption in 1917 to their own (often dashed) hopes of a triumphant and liberalising Solidarność, of the effects of the ministry of a Polish Pope, of free expression, of the advent of a market economy, and the disappointments (and sometimes repressions) they had experienced. The play also helped them to do this; not only was the title changed, but also the curtain call.

Instead of leaving the corpse of Meyerhold/Harlequin on the stage, the character stands and takes the curtain call alongside Stanislavski/Pierrot only to be interrupted by Russia/Columbine carrying a small baby. The two male clowns accuse each other of being the father, until Columbine hands Harlequin the baby and he shows it to the audience; it bears the characteristic red birth mark of reforming Soviet leader Mikhail Gorbachev. All smile, then Harlequin reacts – the baby has wet himself and the clown sniffs its nappy – all three performers turn to the audience, opening their palms to the audience as if to say "so, now what happens?"

It was simply luck that the historical context of our manifesto performance should return with such contemporary relevance. It was the kind of coincidence that would be repeated many times: with the story of Civil Rights in the USA, of Western interventions in the Middle East, of poverty and crime in Victorian England. What we might have thought were experiences specific to unique situations turned out to have sharp parallels and associations in different countries and across different cultures. We saw, repeatedly, how it was possible for audiences to 'read across' from the experiences of an 'other' (even their enemy's) to their own; to share something, even if it was only loss. In the community of the theatre experience, in building the three-way trialogue between actor and actor and audience, with such materials it was possible to cross barriers of loyalty and identity into empathy, sympathy and even mutual solidarity.

But TNT had never set out with such an end in mind. Indeed, we had no idea when creating 'Harlequin' in 1980, or '1945!' and 'The Mystery' in 1981, that any of them would ever be seen beyond Britain. The aspiration to take this work to other cultures was one we inherited by invitation and then by diverse audiences' responses; once received, however – a positive result from our wider experiment – it became a principle to test and push further; to travel further. To put similar combinations of difficult and divisive materials to audiences in diverse cultures and see what happens.

Such continual testing may partly explain how it is that a theatre company with what is at least a democratic and liberal 'agenda' is so popular in many countries that have recently moved closer to authoritarian governance. We have never adopted a strategy of creating or seeking an audience to 'fit our product'; indeed we were early on castigated by a powerful curator/producer for bringing in the 'wrong' audience to a fashionable venue ("Paul, do we really want those people in our Arts Centre?") Instead, we have retained an interest in performing to audiences who are not like us and are unlikely to share our opinions. Rather than avoiding such meetings, we have learned to welcome them as spaces in which minds may change and common ground may be enlarged.

As the "fourth creator", audiences make the play in their own significances. They sift it through their own experience. So, Martin Luther King's struggles against racism in our 'American Dreams and Nightmares' have been seized upon by all sorts of groups among our European and Asian audiences as 'readable across' to their own experiences. In Israel the critique of nascent fascism in 'The Wave' not only engaged Jewish audiences, but Arab audience members claimed its warnings as having equal or even greater relevance to their own predicament. In China, the very distant (in time and place) concerns of 'Oliver Twist' were 'read across' by the audiences to the effects of the burgeoning Chinese economy.

A portent of this generous space of cross-reading occurred very early on in the TNT story, during a tour of the company's second production, '1945!' (later re-titled 'English Tea Party' and, later again, 'Hitler Killed My Canary'). The plot of the play involves a British soldier who, on the final day of the Second World War, accidentally kills a young German female civilian. He experiences a nightmarish hallucination in which he finds himself suddenly back in his English home, which has been reduced to rubble in an air raid. There, his father can speak only in lines from variety and music hall routines, and his girlfriend Sally has been replaced by the corpse of the woman he inadvertently shot. Through a series of grotesque routines and recitations, and a parody of a marriage ceremony (in which the music hall father plays the priest and the corpse plays an uncooperative bride), the British soldier, Neil Down, seeks to understand the meaning of his dream. All the time, his father and 'girlfriend' conceal the truth. In despair, Neil constructs a courtroom from the rubble, makes his father a judge and his German victim a witness, and demands to be prosecuted for all the war crimes perpetrated by all sides in the Second World War.

The ventriloquist act in '1945' or 'English Tea Party' or 'Hitler Killed My Canary'

It is an unusual scenario, very loosely based on Witold Gombrowicz's play 'The Marriage', a 1975 production of which Paul had appeared in at London's Cockpit Theatre. The text is a collage of combatants' poems and twisted music hall routines. With a story that refuses to apportion blame on a national basis, the production seemed unlikely to appeal to an audience turning up for an evening of nostalgic war time popular songs. It was therefore with some concern that the cast of '1945!' observed that the ushers at the High Wycombe venue were arriving in Second World War period British Army, Land Army and Air Raid Warden uniforms. This intensified when some of the audience appeared in similar attire. A culture clash of a very negative kind seemed in prospect. The opening surreal moments of the play were received in a shocked silence. Once the music hall sequences kicked in, however, the audience began to laugh, and by the end were more moved than outraged by Neil's attempt to take all of the war's sins upon his own narrow and inadequate shoulders. In that provincial English town, there was an empathy later echoed in the responses of young German audiences who seemed relieved to not have to answer for crimes on the grounds of their nationality. Instead, the audience were asked, on the basis of their humanity, to consider the nature of crimes for which they had not been responsible. At the end of the performance, one of the older High Wycombe ushers, a former Second World War soldier like the play's hero, remarked to a member of the cast that the feelings of bewildering absurdity and nightmare in the play were similar to those he had himself experienced in combat.

'1945!' followed 'Harlequin' in deploying a giant 'canvas'. In place of the Russian Revolution was the Second World War. Although the play hinged around a single incident, it embraced the war in general terms, with its central character attempting to redeem his own (possible) war crime by taking on the guilt for all the crimes of the war: nuclear bombing, the Holocaust, the Katyn forest massacre of Polish officers, the fire-bombing of German civilian cities, and so on. It sought not to argue equivalence or even relative value in these crimes, but rather to stage the difficulty for any individual trying to relate their own agency and responsibility to the scale of a global war.

The play did not solve this problem; it staged the human predicament and asked its audiences to respond as a temporary community to its existential dilemma. This might seem rather dry. However, the script mostly consisted of music hall routines and gags, after an opening that used transcripts of actual radio communications between Second World War British tanks during combat. The grim quandaries of the play's central character were mostly considered during gales of laughter. In '1945!' corpses dance and make jokes. The response to an accusation is not an excuse but a tap dance routine, and secrets are betrayed not with a whisper but in the middle of a comic recitation.

While the use of a popular comic form, with a clear cultural-historical connection to the time of the portrayed action, served to provide the smile on the lips of tragedy (that crucial component of 'the grotesque') it also served to bring audiences together in laughter. The communion that Meyerhold and the Symbolists had sought through semi-religious ritual was apparently available in shared paroxysms of hilarity if that collective ecstasy was explicitly framed by the tragedy of the situation. Without trying to pretend that this was very different from the common bonding of any audience enjoying an entertainment, there did seem to be a different edge when set in the context of avoidable killing and calculated genocide. The laughter was not an act of disrespect to the victims, nor insensitivity to the nature of the crimes, and certainly not a vindication of the criminals responsible. For the grotesque to work, the absurdity of the comedy had to be matched by the dreadfulness of the tragedy. Together, an alternative emerged: a communal laughter rather than the violence of one community against another. Instead of repeating the cycle of violence, by seeking blame in one community and victimhood in another, the play displaced guilt and took it – impossibly – onto the shoulders of the individual, represented by the floundering figure of Neil the soldier. '1945!' provided no absolution from the absurd horror of total war; but its bringing together, through laughter, of strangers in the dark of an auditorium, offered another way of being.

It is important here not to attribute to the TNT company conscious intentions for all its outcomes. While the communal aspect of '1945!' chimed with Meyerhold's hope for a similar effect, we had not set out to achieve it. It just happened. It owed more to the company's pursuit of the technical requirements of the grotesque (pushing comic actions to the extreme), and then its reacting encouragingly to the audience's response.

While the qualities of 'Harlequin' and '1945!' were essential for establishing TNT on the British small-scale theatre circuit, other things worked in our favour. Learning from the mistakes we had made in Bristol Gate, we kept the acting company small: two persons in 'Harlequin' and three in both '1945!' and 'The Mystery'. All the props, costumes and sets for the first two productions fitted into a Mini car. The cost of van hire was avoided. At the same time, this kept the focus on stage on the actors' bodies not on the splendour of scenic elements. The 'rough' aesthetic of ordinary materials added to the egalitarian aspects of the performances.

The company 'infrastructure' was almost non-existent. The necessary legalities were observed, but administration was often indistinguishable from rehearsal. Paul would dash out of the rehearsal of a scene to answer the phone in an office to the side of the stage. Disruptive, certainly; but when it came to selling a show it was hard to beat the enthusiasm or information of an actor who has just been working on the production in question.

Rehearsal space was not always accessible. 'The Mystery', the company's third production, was partly devised and rehearsed outdoors in the garden of Paul's parents' house. Rehearsal breaks were often taken up with informal games of cricket. When art centre rooms were available for rehearsal, the nearby pub often served as an idea generator. Socialising has always played and continues to play an important part in the life of the TNT company.

After early evening rehearsals of the first few productions, the company would adjourn to the same pub to play darts. If a problem scene had proved intractable in the rehearsal room, it was rare for a solution not to pop into someone's head during a round of "arrows".

Socialising with audiences on tour was also an invaluable and indispensable part of the company's touring. Apart from the fleeting – and occasionally more enduring – romances, necessary for any touring artist on what could at times be a lonely and unromantic road, socialising also wove crucial connections with networks of supporters, influencers and facilitators. A conversation in a bar after an early performance in Durham led to an invitation to visit the "castle" of two audience members, Maz and Alison. Not quite sure how seriously to take the description, the company set out next morning only to find themselves approaching the towering edifice of Brancepeth Castle. They had not been joking! This led to a sustained connection to the family and the castle, pre-empting the company's later 'castle tours' throughout Europe (described in 'Prisons, Palaces and Fragments', below). It resulted in the company rehearsing in the castle, but also giving performances there when the family turned part of the partially renovated fortress into a small arts venue.

The basic TNT model of "experimental with popular appeal" served as an encouragement to those, like the family at Brancepeth Castle, who wanted to facilitate contemporary performance. We proved to them that such work could attract and entertain wide audiences. Our theatre was not for specialists or enthusiasts.

It was while participating in a mini-festival at Brancepeth Castle in 1983 along with a group of contemporary musicians (far more badly behaved than our company), that we experienced the music of the leading contemporary trombonist and composer John Kenny. To this day John is a crucial member of the TNT 'family' and the composer of much of the company's music.

Socialising – and the hospitality offered – could be very generous and intense. This was particularly true of some of the less fashionable or more geographically isolated venues. Outstanding as social and communal events, transcending simple performance, were the company's visits to the venues of the Highlands and Islands circuit around the north of Scotland. On these tours of 'English Tea Party' and 'Wizard of Jazz' (1987) shows were followed by the company's musicians providing accompaniment for a *ceilidh*. The island audiences expressed their gratitude in generous hospitality to performers who had struggled, often in small boats across choppy seas with unwieldy instruments, to arrive at their remote venues.

However, the small-scale theatre circuit in Britain in the 1980s was not all castles, whisky and warm island hospitality. Although the 1970s and 1980s in Britain saw a multifarious burgeoning of small-scale theatre companies of different kinds – feminist companies like Monstrous Regiment, socialist companies like North West Spanner, radical theatre-in-education companies like Pit Prop, physical theatre companies like DV8, gay companies like Gay Sweatshop, postmodern companies like Impact, visual performance companies like Hesitate and Demonstrate, and so on – the financial and cultural environment was never very friendly to any of them. While some were publicly funded, there were often assaults on this funding. Grants were threatened or removed due to controversies around particular productions. Political and bureaucratic shifts in arts funding policy or public funding in general could hobble a range of disparate companies in one go. So, while in retrospect this may appear to have been a golden age for the emergence of new and innovative companies, it was also a period of precarity. Small-scale theatre makers were vulnerable to reactionary campaigns led by local politicians or national newspapers or to those who simply wished to reduce public spending. Almost none of those many small companies survive to this day.

For a while, however, there was a genuinely viable touring circuit in Britain. It was made up of different kinds of venues, from smart arts centres to converted chapels or former industrial buildings, to poorly resourced village halls, zero-resourced student union bars and fully functioning studio theatres in university drama departments. The social nature of these venues varied as much as their architectures. Some were labours of love run by cultural pioneers who nurtured their large audiences (in York, Penzance and Aldershot, for example). Others were empty shells where the company would find one of their 50 posters pinned up outside the venue and the other 49 in a pile under an office desk (Darlington). In the Universities it was often necessary to stage an excerpt from the show in the students' bar in order to draw an audience.

With all this variety, there were sufficient venues for a small and popular company to just about survive on the fees and box office takings alone. Today that touring circuit no longer exists. It had mostly disappeared by the mid-1990s. Even in the 1980s its origins in progressive cultural changes in 1960s' Britain were mostly forgotten by those attending its venues. But the politicians and members of the cultural elites had not forgotten. They would come for the small venues with their business plans and ultimatums. TNT was fortunate to catch the last few years of the circuit. Without it the company would not have continued beyond a single production. Despite its rough nurturing, however, it would eventually become necessary for TNT to abandon the remains of the circuit altogether, as it shrank beneath the company's wheels. The bureaucratic aggression of the funding bodies increased in inverse proportion to how little they offered.

A small sign of a possible alternative trajectory appeared as early as 1981 when the company were invited to Amsterdam's "Hippy" arts centre: The Melkweg. We made our first German tour in 1982 and in the following year were invited to participate in an Off-Broadway Festival in New York. There was surely an audience for the company's work beyond the UK. While, paradoxically, the generous reviews we received from Berlin to New York helped our profile in Britain.

In many ways TNT's third show, 'The Mystery' appeared to follow the successful process of production of the previous two. A serious content, supported by considerable research, was established. The iniquities of monetarist economics across Europe and North America and the failure of contemporary Keynesianism to provide a viable alternative were addressed. We had a traditional academic economist advise us, so we could describe the economic theories accurately. A familiar popular form with easily available materials was deployed: British pantomime. Britain at the time was riven by the monetarist policies of the new government of Margaret Thatcher, there were riots in big cities and mass unemployment as traditional industries were dismantled. Later, we re-made the show as 'Funny Money' for European audiences and there was no difficulty for us or them 'reading across' from the UK experience to their own.

This apparently smooth process was not the whole of the story. Although 'The Mystery' would turn out to be every bit as popular as the previous two productions, it established a new working method that would prove problematical in future productions, including the next two: 'Don't Look Back!' and 'OOPS!' Rather than, as before, going into rehearsals with an already well worked and rewritten script, 'The Mystery' began with a scenario. The structures of the scenes were developed through improvisation and discussion in the rehearsal room, and then final scripting took place at the end of each day. The resilience of the popular form of 'Panto' helped to resolve some of the stickier impasses that developed during devising in the rehearsal room; covering over cracks that would widen in future productions.

One particularly intractable problem during the devising of 'The Mystery' was how to demonstrate the effects of inflation – too much money chasing too few goods and putting up prices. How to physicalise an economic concept? After many attempts to get some meaningful comedy out of an inflatable plastic globe, we solved the problem with an over the top 'custard pie' fight. The audience were encouraged – in the spirit of Keynesian inward investment – to hurl plates of runny pizza topping at an under-resourced pizza salesman, an updating of the traditional nursery rhyme figure of 'The Pieman' met by 'Simple Simon'. The mixture covered his face and hair in a wall of goo. While the economic analogy might have been a little stretched, the blinding of this character – first left alone, distressed and helpless, on the otherwise empty stage, and then having to be led off by the other two performers – said more about the human costs of macroeconomic policies than an interpretative speech or a symbolic prop.

(At which point, Paul notes that he played The Pieman and subsequently spent several years cleaning custard out of his ears for the cause of art.)

Despite a feeling that sometimes we were only reaching theatrical solutions by the skin of our teeth, the end result was coherent, topical and popular with audiences. It scored a particular success at the Edinburgh Festival, where it raised the national profile of the company. It also benefited from the performance of Mark Heron, the third escapee from the physical theatre company, bringing a new level of high-energy acrobatic physicality to the mix.

'The Mystery' begins with a business presentation. Three men in suits introduce themselves and offer the audience an investment opportunity in the only kind of theatre in Britain that makes a reliable profit: Christmas pantomime. They count out the actual box office takings from that evening and explain that they intend to invest this in their own pantomime production. In order to persuade the audience to part with more of their cash in investing in the businessmen's pantomime, they will perform a 'no frills' version of it. The three men exit and re-enter as pantomime characters acting out the story of 'Simple Simon' who proceeds to run into a series of obstacles on his way to making his fortune. These include an encounter with Griselda the witch, a shipwreck in a storm at sea, two violent policemen in the form of Tweedledum and Tweedledee, and so on... until, finally, the jolly story descends into a murderous fight for the box office takings and the businessmen once again address the audience. They apologise for the failure of their monetarist fairy tale and promise a better second half in which they will introduce compassionate Keynesian reflation, and so fund brighter costumes, bigger props and a funnier script.

The second half begins in far more upbeat fashion. Before long, however, the plot becomes once again tangled in economic contradictions. The beleaguered hero finds himself in a haunted industrial ghost town and experiences various misadventures – including the plastering of the unemployed Pieman with his own pizza mix – until the frictions between the three businessmen, fuelled by their disagreements over economic policy, erupt through the fairy tale action. The stage set is destroyed. The box office takings are thrown into a tin bath and burned before the eyes of a horrified audience.

The production's satire upon particular economic policies and the politics of those enforcing them was clear to anyone. However, the real dynamic of the show was the mismatch between macroeconomic policies and the human beings whose lives were affected by them. The play provided no economic solution but presented the consequences of not having an equitable and compassionate one. The production also undermined theatre itself. Showing how one actor forced another to do all the work and accept all the humiliation for little reward. When that actor rejected his reward and burnt the wages, he was apparently destroying the financial underpinning of the event itself. (In fact, although we did actually burn one real banknote per night, we had switched the rest of the takings for photocopies. But the audience thought we were wild enough to have really burnt their cash).

Although the script of 'The Mystery' consists of almost relentless pantomime jokes, with the running gag of three businessmen in suits acting the parts of witches, vampire bats, pizza sellers, Simple Simon and so on, it exemplified the 'turn of a page' switch from comedy to tragedy. At one point a gymnastic comic sequence ends with one character completely unexpectedly stabbing another in the back – literally. The large and sharp knife was real and the actor playing the victim was covertly wearing a steel corset (with a cork patch) under his jacket. The visceral effect of the blade very obviously puncturing the actor's jacket killed all laughter stone dead.

Later in the show, the chaos of the audience hurling 'custard pies' at a performer was abruptly transformed by the actors (and a lighting change) into a scene of chilly Symbolist visuality. In a cold blue light and under showers of snow (handfuls of flour thrown into the beams of a spotlight) a half-naked, drenched and shivering businessman on his knees pushed a tin bath across the stage attempting to clear up the mess. All the while sharp cracks, like a whip, preceded the shouting out of stock market prices. Suddenly 'out of nowhere' (but from the deep heart of the drama) had come a vision of human servitude and slavery: the abject human form of *homo sacer*, the person who may be killed or exploited by anybody, embodied by an actor who had begun the evening as a smiling, charming and joking businessman in a smart suit. No one – but no one – could be sure that they would be spared by the system.

Once more, as with 'Harlequin' and revolution, this theme of the individual under a theory-driven system had not been premeditated. It arose from the company subjecting a serious subject to the techniques of the grotesque. It became only fully explicit (to actors and audience alike) during the touring of the performance. In 'The Mystery', the company put down a marker of protest against the traducing of an individual's rights and dignity. Just as, some two decades later, it would explore individual responsibility, agency and burden through Shakespeare's heroes – Hamlet, the lovers of 'Midsummer Night's Dream', Kate the 'shrew' – or advocate for the freedom and rights of every individual in 'Fahrenheit 451' and 'American Dreams and Nightmares'. In exploring macroeconomics, we had arrived at its opposite pole: individuality. This evolving of themes to which we return in different performances, finding different resonances with different national and cultural audiences, is evidence suggestive of the effects of Meyerhold's grotesque. That the grotesque is not simply a technical aesthetic combination, but a fusion of opposites with profound ethical and cultural outcomes. A combination that enables the performance of big and important ideas (about freedom, social change, individuality, responsibility) not in long intellectual or literary speeches, but in clowning and fighting and chasing.

The fusion of the grotesque also seems to have a useful element of *con*fusion. For little else would explain the willingness, and even enthusiasm, of the servants of authoritarian regimes – ones with at best an ambiguous or suspicious relation to the concepts at work in our performances – to bring our work to their countries. For us to find that out, however, the company had to begin a different kind of journey far from the small-scale theatre circuit of Britain.

Travel

By Phil

From the beginning, TNT Theatre was determined to travel. It was because it was willing to take its tiny Mini car over 300 miles from Nottinghamshire to Penzance for the second performance of 'Harlequin' that the Guardian 'stringer' saw the show and wrote his glowing review, setting the production on the road to success. It was because the company was willing to travel to many other towns, villages and cities that it did more than survive one production and one tour, securing a loyal audience and a viable circuit, while making just about enough money to feed ourselves and (sometimes) pay the rent.

Travel, however, was never simply about survival. Not even just about the practicalities of getting a show to its audiences. There has always been something of a nomadic principle – a drive, often literally – in our actions. Even when we have been resident for a while in one particular building, as we were for a few years in the 1980s in the Midland Group in Nottingham, the emphasis was always on taking the performances outwards rather than digging foundations in one building.

This has drawn the company into many extra complications that rarely bother a building-based company: visas, changing fuel prices, open and closed borders, customs regulations, rising and falling currency rates, war zones, extreme weather, and so on. Far more importantly it has drawn the company, and its travelling actors and stage managers, into entanglements with multiple cultures. It has given us a direct concern for political, cultural and ecological developments, which we engage with on and off the stage. These have always been at the heart of the company's themes; but they are all the more urgent when the politics, culture and ecology threaten and amplify the practicalities of your work every day. As when, for example, the company embarked from Munich for the beginning of its tour of 'Moby Dick' only for our Queequeg to be turned back at the Austrian border; the officials refusing to recognise the United Nations documents on which, as a political refugee from apartheid South Africa, he was travelling.

While TNT has always been far more concerned with addressing what is happening in the world through its performances – it's a theatre company! – occasionally it has been swept up in historic events. Some in the moment of the journey, others that came looping back in time. In Dresden, a few days after the fall of the Berlin Wall, we found ourselves in a march against the regime, at the time when its leader, Erich Honecker, was proposing a motion to his party's Central Committee that protesters like us should be fired upon. Fortunately, his motion was defeated.

When TNT presented its adaptation of 'The Wave', a play about how an educational experiment in 1967 in one World History class of a US school backfired and triggered the rise of a local fascist movement, we were joined by a special audience member. A pupil who had participated in that original class experiment in 1967 had travelled continents in order to join us for a performance.

In the breakfast room of an Isle of Man hotel, the morning after the premiere of 'American Nightmares', we listened open-mouthed to our producer Grantly Marshall's account of the 1970 Kent State shootings. The Ohio National Guard had killed four unarmed student protestors and injured nine others as they tried to object to the US bombing of Cambodia; Grantly was standing close to the Guard as they fired.

Despite the transitory nature of our business (or maybe because of it) we have occasionally been asked to represent a particular place in performance. So, in 1987, we wrote 'Amerika! Amerika! or The Charlie Chaplin Putsch' in response to a commission from TamS Theater in Munich. We created a dark comedy based around events during Hitler's 1923 Munich Beer Hall Putsch. Some of the events of that failed coup occurred a short walk from the theatre. So, when characters raced into the theatre, from the 'riots' outside, it was as if they were chased in by History.

On the Isle of Man, off the north-west coast of England, we were asked to address the ambiguous life of the Island's 'hero of independence', Illiam Dhone. During our research, we found Illiam to be neither a hero nor a villain, but a hollow man. He was so empty of convictions or of any kind of inner life that he seemed to melt and reform himself into whatever shape was required by the times. Less of an opportunist and more of a needy man, he seemed moulded by whatever was closest to him. At the same time, we discovered a rarely mentioned figure in the events, who was Dhone's opposite, and in some ways his complement: this was the Countess of Derby, whose passion, depth of personality, courage and ruthlessness offered us more dramatic electricity in a tale of complex Civil War politics than we could ever have imagined.

The Countess of Derby confronts the shifty 'hero' of 'The Ghost of Illiam Dhone'

These, however, are only a few of the theatrical 'products' of travel. The journey is a thing in itself, and a theatre tour is reliant on that journey and the qualities of the relationships of those who journey, both to 'the road' and to each other. For some the road is an adventure to be savoured. For others it can be an ordeal to be tolerated in order to take the shows to the audiences. For everyone it is very hard work. Journeys are sometimes long. On any one tour there may be many changes of currency, culture, language and cuisine. While there is no necessary connection between one traveller and another, a certain sensitivity and understanding of both the treasures and tolls of travel can cultivate empathy with other travellers, voluntary and involuntary; from refugees, to commuters, to fugitives, to pilgrims.

To which Paul adds a quotation from the French author Stendhal which sheds some light on what it takes to tour well:

> Take a cheerful view of all the little mishaps that often spoil the jolliest expeditions – passports, quarantine, accidents, etc. Modern transport creates expectations of comfort and convenience, but a traveller who puts his mind to it can avoid ill humour as a kind of madness that eclipses the objects of interest that surround one and amongst which one shall never pass again.

Chapter Two: Germany, the Saving Grace

By Paul

It is a cold November night. Our van is packed with theatre props, costumes, minimal set, a dramaturg and quite a lot of food. We finish our last performance of 'Hitler Killed My Canary' at the sold out Munich Studio theatre at about 11pm. We plan to drive through the night. Geographically we are heading north-east but culturally it is all East from here. Our destination is the city of Lublin in the far corner of Poland. In our way stands a Wall. Or does it? It is November 1989 and no one is sure. Will the Russian tanks roll tonight?

It is still dark when we arrive at the border. This is not Berlin; we know the Wall is open there. This is the southern transit road to Dresden. Through the darkness we make out line after line of yellow headlights, dim as if running off failing batteries. They are heading West and we alone swim against the tide. These are almost all Trabants, the East German people's car, a lawnmower engine inside a fibreglass box. Last night as the curtain fell in Munich the barrier was lifted here, the guards melted away and the word got out. What do they want? To escape? Or more likely to shop. They can't all be leaving.

It's like a disaster movie, except there is no fear on these people's faces. They smile and wave, our number plates mark us out as fellow Germans. We act the part and wave back and indeed we have one German with us, the dancer-actress Inga Kammerer. As dawn breaks we enter Dresden. There are already demonstrators on the streets. One holds high a painted placard with Stalin's face crossed out. An irony as I have my Stalin costume in our van. Here, away from the pierced Wall, there is anger and an edge of fear. Now, as we write in 2020, we know about the happy ending to this great drama, but that Dresden morning no one could be sure. Empires do not usually fall without a crash. Phil suggests that we walk in the middle of the march in case an attack cuts off its tail.

That TNT should be there at the birth of modern Germany was not so much a coincidence as a duty. Germany transformed TNT from a minor British theatre company into a global arts organisation. Germany transformed itself from a defeated, divided and occupied nation into probably the most successful nation on earth; certainly the most cultured. More people go to the theatre in Germany than in any other country in the world. At one point the City of Hamburg had the same Culture budget as the Arts Council of Great Britain. Michelangelo went to Rome, Shakespeare went to London. We went to Germany. So did the Beatles. After the traumas of the Nazi dictatorship the Germans knew there was only one cure: not religion, not politics, but culture. This attitude continues to this day: Germans believe that culture can heal. So, alarmed by a rise in populism and intolerance, in the autumn of 2018 the federal government allocated an extra €350 million to the arts.

1983. TNT arrives in Walled-in-Berlin to perform at the surrealist culture centre Café Einstein. We are given the keys to our rooms on the top floor. The keys are marked "Künstler" or "artist". We are no longer just actors. We are part of German culture and accorded a respect we have not known in our own land. Since then we have hung onto Germany's coat tails as it careers into the twenty-first century. *Danke.*

In 1983 I had a shortlist of small theatres in Germany from an actress I met at a theatre training session in Cardiff. The list was indeed short; nothing more than a few names and phone numbers. I phone a Munich number. No one at TamS theatre picks up the phone. I ring daily in a ritual of hope as it costs nothing to be ignored. Then to my surprise someone does answer, and three months later we are on our way. The mini tour begins at a converted discotheque in Frankfurt and goes via a week in Munich to our own contact: the Café Einstein in big bad Berlin. The play we offer for this experiment is our own: 'An English Tea Party' (later called 'Hitler Killed My Canary'). Of the three performers in this dark comedy of war and guilt one is half German, Maggie Fox. Her language skills have helped to organize the tour (and her comic skills will flourish in her own company: Lip Service). After a low-key performance in Frankfurt we arrive at TamS Theater, which is to become our spiritual home for the next five years. We have no idea that TamS is the most loved small theatre in southern Germany. We land on our feet and soon fall in love ourselves with TamS, with Munich and with several of the staff. Like any self-respecting love affair it will all end in tears of recrimination. But for a few glorious years it places TNT at the heart of Munich's artistic scene and gives us a window to a wider world.

One of the most ignorant clichés about Germany is its lack of humour. And if the Germans have a long tradition of comedy, this is nowhere more true than in Bavaria. Opposite TamS's theatre in the uber-kool quarter of Schwabing is the most famous cabaret club in Germany. TamS itself was the creation of Phillip Arp, the heir to the great surreal clown of pre-War Germany: the Bavarian, Karl Valentin. Valentin was a cross between Charlie Chaplin and a Brecht anti-hero. He would have fitted in well with Monty Python or the Goons. One of his fiercest critics was a certain A. Hitler. The Führer was a man who couldn't take a joke but, to be fair, Adolf was an Austrian vegetarian who hated beer as well as satire.

After the horrors of the War, Philip Arp and his actress wife, the formidable Anette Spola, set up their theatre in an old bathhouse in the Bohemian quarter of Schwabing. One of their first productions was borrowed from Valentin: onstage lessons in Bavarian for Germans. TamS developed into one of the most important alternative stages in the country. Critics piled into the first nights of their shows, which included everything from Athol Fugard's dissections of Apartheid to evenings of Italian Futurism (in Italian). There were 99 seats so that no one had to worry about safety regulations. Funding was difficult but their solution was simple: TamS is an acronym for "Theater am Sozialamt" – theatre on the dole. No wonder TNT felt at home. I would like to take this opportunity to thank the UK's Department of Health and Social Security for its unstinting support during TNT's formative years.

It is easy to write about failure, about adventure and even about success. But how do you write about explosive hedonism without sounding like some second-rate rock star? Berlin in the 1980s was one of the most adrenalin fueled cities in history. There were concrete reasons, and not just the Wall. The Wall did not go through Berlin it went around Berlin. Berlin was an island and the journey off it was tedious and grim. So people in Berlin tended to stay in Berlin. And those people were special. Many were 'refusniks'. In order to keep West Berlin from vanishing, the German Federal government waived military conscription for anyone who went to live in the City. Take your pick: two years in the German army or two years in the funkiest city on earth (sorry, New York). A no-brainer, even if many spent those two years out of their brains. In the mad materialism of the late twentieth century no one had less reason to believe in the value of purchased objects than a West Berliner. The forces of the Warsaw Pact could have waltzed into this urban island any day they chose. The half-city's defences were merely symbolic. So who, apart from draft dodgers, would want to live in this hostage town? Well people like Gunter Grass (the Nobel prize winning author) who wrote that he lived in Berlin because "it is the city closest to the reality of our age" and people like David Bowie who felt more alive here, on the ultimate edge, than anywhere else on earth. TNT was drawn to Walled-in-Berlin like a moth to a candle. And the hot tip of the candle was the Café Einstein.

The Café Einstein began life as the villa of a Jewish film starlet, was confiscated by the Nazis and then, after the war, became a brothel. Sometime in the 1970s it was rescued from decay and became probably the coolest café in the coolest town on earth: a haven of art, experiment and fine dining on the fault line of ideologies. The ground floor was a manicured yet faded 1920s café-restaurant. One room was panelled in walnut from floor to ceiling. The waiters were dressed to kill and frequently featured in magazines for their eccentric style. The first floor was an *avant garde* gallery, the garden possessed a stage. At 3pm each day a gong sounded and a metre of fresh *apfel strudel* was delivered to the main salon. Café Einstein opened for coffee and croissants at 10am and closed when the bar tender lost his patience with the last customers at some time way after midnight. The offices lay in the bomb shelter basement. I recall stepping over a potato peeler who was alarmed to be greeted by an artist (there was a lot of German hierarchy even among the alternative types who ran the Café). Navigating past the vegetable peeler I stumbled into the office to find that any attempt at business was likely to stall as the staff were hunched over mirrors of cocaine. This was, I think, 11 in the morning, so the day was yet young.

TNT were guest artists for two summers at the Einstein. Our deal was the box office (modest) but also the upstairs apartment and anything we could eat or drink from breakfast to nightcap, except lobster and champagne. This included the hallucinogenic mushrooms served up by the chef to favoured artists. One foolish actor, who shall remain nameless, consumed a spiked omelette and headed east through Checkpoint Charlie to experience the wonders of Stalinist Socialism from a fresh perspective. I myself was whisked off to David Bowie's favourite nightclub 'Der Dschungel' after one sweaty open-air performance of 'Harlequin'. For someone brought up in Nottingham, the sheer number of transvestites of both or any gender was an eye opener that I will not forget. At 5am, I and my host (a leather trousered photographer named Heike) retired to a French restaurant for a gourmet dinner and what happened after that is none of your business.

Meanwhile one of the founding actors of TNT, the circus-trained Mark, headed for a day trip to East Berlin with rather more unusual consequences: wedding bells. While admiring the art in the National Gallery he began talking to a young East German; after almost two years of patient bureaucracy and exceptional hospitality from a kind British consular official, Mark returned to London with his bride. But there was no happy ending to this tale. The East German missed the solidarity she had known in the grim high rises of Communist Berlin. She missed her own language and was appalled at the materialism she had once aspired to. She longed to return, but that was impossible. So she moved to West Berlin to, I suppose, stare longingly over the Wall which so many of her former fellow citizens dreamed of crossing.

If anyone went to East Berlin for the day they had to change a certain amount of West Marks for East Marks at a poor exchange rate – so one had a lot of money which could only be spent in the East as the currency was unconvertible (fake). I usually ended up hurriedly trying to find a bar to consume my last Ost Marks in liquid form before the midnight deadline. But bars were few and many booked out in advance. Often the last chance was a small bar by Alexanderplatz which specialised in one of the world's foulest drinks: a Cuban liqueur distilled from communist bananas. It remains for me the taste of the unexotic East. I raise a glass to Mark and his lost wife. They tried.

I was fascinated by East Berlin. I believed, prompted by leather trousered Heike, that to be in Berlin meant you had to be in both halves of Berlin, that you owed it to the City to know it as one despite the efforts of the grim-faced guards on their watch-towered Wall.

I learnt one very clear lesson about theatre in East Berlin. I acquired a ticket to the Berliner Ensemble and crossed the Wall on my usual day visa in order to see a performance of Brecht's masterpiece, 'Drei Groschenoper' ('The Threepenny Opera'). This might be the finest piece of theatre created in the twentieth century or at least the best musical until 'West Side Story' (but less sentimental!). Now I had the chance not only to see it in the original, but in Brecht's own version. Brecht had died thirty years before. The production had died at about the same time. Every move was exactly as laid down by the Master. Every move was stilted and forced. There was no life in this deathly theatrical experience. And what an irony that Brecht, the great inventor and improviser, the fleet-footed magpie of modern theatre, was reduced to this. Except that at one level the production was brilliantly perceptive. Its ossification reflected the society around it: the dead shell of a socialist utopia, a dull imitation of what a Communist state might have been in the imagination of that other fabulous East German, Karl Marx.

The whole of the Democratic German Republic of East Germany was a theatre set. For a while I was privileged to poke around behind the scenes, where I saw that the walls, and indeed The Wall, were a stage set made of cardboard and glue.

TNT straddled the so called *Wende* – the period of unification. And the new provinces of eastern Federal Germany became happy hunting grounds for us in the 1990s. Audiences starved of English, but hungry for culture, packed the great theatres of the east. Stralsund, Schwerin, Eisenach, Gorlitz, Dresden, and above all Leipzig, with its elegant theatre, became our stamping grounds. We even managed to perform for two heady years at the only festival to survive from the old to the new regime: in 1990 we were invited to the Karl Marx Stadt Festival, in 1991 to the Chemnitz festival. But they were in the same town. The letterheads of the 1991 invitation had "Karl Marx Stadt" crossed out in blue crayon and "Chemnitz" typed in on a 1950s' machine that dented the yellowed paper. At Torgau, where we performed 'Wizard of Jazz' in February 1990, we were invited by the mayor to a dinner. He leant across to me and whispered with pride: "All the intellectuals in Torgau are here tonight". Part of me misses that world. It was a world that knew the value of art and ideas. Why else did Mark's lost wife try to return? I would not have wanted to live in that world. The West won. We won. But we lost too.

So what of West Germany? Well this is now my home. I like to think of this country from where I write as the most civilised in the world. How ironic that the country that created the vilest totalitarian regime in all history can have created the most humane, democratic and probably pleasant place on earth. Perhaps it is because the trauma of the past was recognised that the present can be so benign. Countries such as Japan and Britain or even the USA are unable to criticise their own colonial and militaristic history without feeling that their modern identity is threatened. Here in Munich the recently opened museum of the Nazi Regime stands on the cellars of the Gestapo beside Hitler's offices, his Nazi acropolis. The Nazi party headquarters is now a music and theatre school. This combination of memory and transformation is a symbol of what the Germans have done. And it is fascinating to reflect that art, and especially performed art (theatre, orchestral music, opera), has been the cornerstone of this extraordinary change. After the war, all ideologies were suspect, and religion has clearly some problems with the non-interference of God (Hitler survived so many assassination attempts from the Munich Putsch in 1923 to the July Plot of 1944 that surely any mildly interested deity would have tipped the scales and altered the explosive trajectories in the right direction?). Art became the salve to the wounded German psyche. A small town like Ingolstadt, north of Munich, has a full-time opera, theatre and ballet company.

After several years working in Germany, our German work became more important than our British touring. We had an agent in Hamburg (the tough and radical producer Manuela Buske) and we were co-produced in Munich by several small theatres, including that of Gunnar Peterson with whom I was to reconnect decades later. I also bumped into a clown, Rusty

Raynor the first European Ronald McDonald. An early TNT fan, he stepped into the breach when we needed a new Sigmund Freud and went on to play Otto the dead German in 'Hitler Killed My Canary'. A year later he invited me to see him perform Scrooge for one Grantly Marshall, whose company was playing at Munich's Amerika Haus theatre. Like a Catholic Church erected on the ruins of an Inca temple, this fascinating relic of the American occupation was constructed on the bombed foundations of Hitler's SA headquarters: the infamous Braun Haus. Here Rusty was playing in Dickens's 'Christmas Carol' to huge audiences of around one thousand a day. These were astonishing numbers for a play in English and I was intrigued (and greedy) to meet the producer.

It was already refreshing to work in an environment where bums on seats replaced subsidy as a means of artistic survival, given such adventurous and open-minded audiences. There would not be a TNT theatre without the enlightened subsidy that nurtured our early years but by the time we had established an international reputation, subsidy had become a curse, forcing us into a straitjacket of bureaucracy and patterns of touring that were a recipe for both personal poverty and artistic sterility. Secret Arts Council meetings determined our annual fate, our grant applications tried to fulfil criteria set by bureaucrats not artists. These bureaucrats, it seemed, could only justify art as social engineering. So, by the time I met Grantly Marshall, I was ready to move in a more radical direction and abandon the British circuit we had so carefully built up, to reject subsidy, to throw ourselves to the wolves.

Decades later it looks like the best decision we ever made. Grantly had the circuit, he had built up a following in the big theatres of Germany and Scandinavia ever since he founded a semi-professional theatre while studying at Munich University; The American Drama Group Europe. By the time I met him, that company was fully professional but reliant on expatriate actors of variable quality. I choose my words carefully: directors such as Barry Goldman were doing good work but the raw material was not always there to create consistency. TNT was able to offer Grantly Marshall a core of British professional actors, a high reputation in Germany and writers who could produce work for his circuit rather than attempt to shoehorn existing scripts that were not suitable for his audience.

Grantly is famous for his obsessive ambition to take theatre to every corner of the globe, his ten-hour working days, his ability to beg, borrow and (almost) steal finance for his projects and his abrasive manner which reminds one of a 1920s' Hollywood producer. He likes to shout. He likes to browbeat and never surrenders on the smallest point. He drives me and his actors up the wall, but that same drive has taken us to global success. And he takes the risk; he puts his (borrowed) money on the line, he is a natural gambler. I am the opposite; I would rather endure poverty than debt. If theatre is a casino, Grantly plays so many tables that one loss is not important as the other tables will come good. Before Grantly Marshall we just managed to maintain a repertoire and could never afford a failure. After Grantly we played the big time all the time. That might mean a school's show at 9am and more education audiences than ever before, but we stopped living like church mice and moved into a cathedral. It was a marriage made in theatrical heaven: Grantly had the theatres and the touring circuit and we had the productions and the artists. TNT almost vanished for a while, subsumed by the American Drama Group Europe, but reinvented itself and emerged with the new millennium as a united force that would become the world's most popular touring theatre.

None of which would have been possible without Germany. It is the core German theatre audiences that pay the bills. We can tour to Japan for twenty years and take nothing out of Japan beyond the cost of going there and being there. And that is a fine thing. But someone has to pay for the rehearsal and the administration and that is what the Germans have done. *Danke* (again).

And to end on art, the fullest expression of our German TNT was two years ago when I was reunited with Gunnar Peterson after twenty years and directed 'Julius Caesar' with the grand old man in the title role. For decades he had performed a summer show in the astonishing courtyard of the Glyptothek museum in central Munich. The museum is built in the style of a Greek temple and houses the finest collection of classical sculpture outside of the British Museum. The audience sit among statues and columns, while each table is served bread and whole bottles of wine, free with every ticket. On a summer's evening, open to the stars, this must be one of the most magical stage settings in Europe.

We worked with Schlegel's marvellous translation, written some 200 years ago. The German cast, led by Sven Socker as Brutus, grabbed the audience by the throat. I created a plebeian crowd from Roman tomb paintings manipulated by the cast. Helen Beauchamp played cello, French horn and sang soprano and the audiences queued down the street on every dry evening for eight weeks of summer. As the light faded each night the Ghost of Caesar appeared in the tent of Brutus and long cello notes drew the one honourable assassin to his death, while a statue of the emperor Hadrian looked on from beneath a German sky.

Stage Imagery

By Paul

Monty Python made a good point. In one of their sketches an interviewer questions a famous actor on the challenge of playing King Lear and he bemoans the problems of playing the mad king with his "dentures coming out.... what with having to keep the crown on". Spencer Tracy, on the other hand, identified acting's greatest challenge as "not bumping into the furniture". I agree. I believe that furniture is the enemy of theatre.

A seated actor is a contradiction in terms. How can you complete an action from a chair? The greatest crime of all is an actor seated behind a table. What is there left except a floating head? TNT uses as little furniture as possible. Even in the banquet scene in 'Macbeth' we have no table. Banquo's Ghost races through the castle unhindered, the audience become the feasting thanes.

We performed the whole of 'Julius Caesar' without a single chair. But some seats are better than others; stools are good because they leave the body visible, thrones are powerful image-things that need to be *occupied* rather than sat upon. An upturned dustbin in 'Pygmalion' can create an image, informing Alfred Doolittle's rough and ready character.

Visual imagery is more important to German than British theatre-makers, but everywhere theatre suffers from the idea that an image is a painting, a fixed moment of beauty or power rather than a continuous motion made by actors. In TNT's 'Gulliver's Travels' we dramatise the whole book, not just Lilliput, and update the satire. In our Lilliput, the Gulliver actor is on stilts and the Lilliputians use kneepads and long costumes to appear three foot tall. In the lesser known Brobdignag section (the Land of Giants), Gulliver is back on his feet but all the rest of the cast are on stilts. Nothing else changes visually, and because the conceit of the production is that the mad Gulliver has been captured and displayed by a fairground showman on his return from his voyages. There are no lighting changes. This is an eighteenth-century freak show. When the showman wants darkness to enact a scene change from Brobdignag to the flying island of the mad scientists (yes, Swift predicted flying saucers!), the Showman

TNT's 'Gulliver's Travels'

asks the audience to cover their eyes when he shouts "Blackout!" and uncover their eyes when he shouts "Lights up!" This live action replaces the dead hand of the technician on the lighting board. The audience enjoy the conceit. The production retains its rough charm. The imagery is startling and active. And that is before we even talk about the fascist pantomime horses in the land of the Yahoos…

A good example of active visual symbolism in a well-known production was achieved by the magnificent Mark Rylance in the London Globe's version of 'Twelfth Night'. Having a free afternoon in London I rolled up to the Globe and bought a five-pound ticket for their production of Shakespeare's finest comedy. It was an all-male version of this gender bending play of pain, sex and poetry (not necessarily in that order). Rylance played the Countess Olivia, self-centred, self-indulgent and generally adored by all except the man she wants; a man who turns out to be a woman. In a physical *tour de force* Rylance glided around the stage as if on a wheeled trolley. Did he learn this from Japanese Budō dance? The effect was delicate and alarming. Olivia's nature was revealed. This was no pantomime dame. This was high art. And still we laughed (a lot).

Which leads me on to 'Twelfth Night' itself. If I had one caveat about Rylance's deservedly famous production, I would say that the ending made no attempt to stage Shakespeare's favourite song: "The rain it raineth every day." Favourite because it is the only song to appear in two plays, the other being 'King Lear'. At the end of the Globe production the clown Feste simply sang the song before the curtain call.

I wanted to question that. So when I directed the play later, I re-examined the finale. As the couples gather for the traditional happy ending of a Shakespeare comedy, one man spoils the party: Malvolio. Cheated, tricked and humiliated he storms out of the palace. The Duke Orsino tells Feste to go and find him so that the nuptials can commence on a festive note. This is usually the end of the play. But surely we must know if Feste can find Malvolio and whether and how he balms his soul? Since Feste does sing the song and has been told to find Malvolio, why can't he sing it to the man he has humiliated? So we had him do just that. We created the sound of rain and had Feste in his jester's garb find Malvolio, still dressed in the tattered remnants of the laughable yellow stockings with which he has sought to impress his mistress. Feste opens a battered umbrella, sits Malvolio on his knee and starts to sing. The rest of the cast gather in the shadows and harmonise. Finally the glum Malvolio melts and hugs his ex-tormentor like a tiny boy. The red clown, the yellow man-child, the tatty umbrella, the melancholy melody and the rain unite. Finis.

MALVOLIO: I'll be revenged on the whole pack of you!
Exit

OLIVIA: He hath been most notoriously abused.

DUKE ORSINO (To Feste the clown):
Pursue him and entreat him to a peace:
When that is known and golden time convents,
A solemn combination shall be made
Of our dear souls.
Exeunt all, except Clown - who finds Malvolio in the rain.

CLOWN [Sings]
When that I was but a little tiny boy,
With hey, ho, the wind and the rain,
A foolish thing was but a toy,
For the rain it raineth every day.
But when I came to man's estate,
'Gainst knaves and thieves men shut their gate,
But when I came unto my beds,

With hey, ho, the wind and the rain
The toss-pots still had drunken heads,
For the rain, it raineth every day
A great while ago the world begun,
With hey, ho the wind and the rain
But that's all one, our play is done,
And we'll strive to please you every day.
And the rain it raineth every way.
(Spotlight fades to black).

Chapter Three: 'Cabaret Faust', 'Wizard of Jazz', 'Moby Dick'

By Phil

'Cabaret Faust' (1984) – a show about tempted actors in the 1930s, lured by high art and Nazism – was the apotheosis of our publicly funded British touring. Its tour ran from September 1984 to May 1985. If we ever thought that this was some kind of breakthrough we were mistaken. In less than a decade almost the whole touring infrastructure we were riding would have fallen victim to the public funding cuts of the Thatcher government (1979-1990). At the same time, in a pincer movement, additional cuts in education funding meant that schools and colleges could no longer afford to either book our shows or send parties of their pupils to them. School students, searching for cultural markers, were left to the tender mercies of mainstream mass media.

Nevertheless, 'Cabaret Faust' marked a watershed for TNT. The rhythmicality that had always been such a feature of the earliest shows was suddenly lifted onto another level of sublime possibility with the arrival of composer John Kenny and the musicians he was able to recruit to a series of 'music theatre' variations on the TNT experiment. Rather than a subtle underpinning of the action or occasional virtuoso verbal-musical outbursts, the music and these musicians became co-workers in production and delivery. In 'Cabaret Faust', 'Wizard of Jazz' and 'Moby Dick' the music, musicians and their instruments were never simple accompaniments bolstering the action, but were drivers of the action, no different in dramaturgical significance to leading characters or storylines.

The music spoke and the music was not linguistic. The music would be the main agent of the action, and then the music was a material abstraction quite elusive of anything as crude as action or psychological meaning. Music's mutability, rawness, vibrating presence and refusal to be defined made it every bit as complex as Hamlet. For a company with roots in a set of principles partly informed by Symbolism, the arrival of a world class composer and classically trained musicians – with the capacity to switch between playing in symphony orchestras and smaller contemporary music ensembles – abruptly expanded the emotional and sonic range of the work. The possibilities of extreme grotesquerie were cranked up a few notches. For despite (perhaps because of) the sophistications of these artists, there beat hearts of crude humour and an appetite for low 'larking about' among them.

It was our great fortune that these musicians, as much as their acting counterparts, were open to abrupt switches from sublime harmonies to blowing raspberries and farts. This was a music that could raise the tone, and in the space of a bar drag it back into the gutter, from where the view to the stars is often clearer than poetry's. Then they would go the other way and sleazy jazz would unexpectedly lift off into ethereal plainchant.

The plot of 'Cabaret Faust' follows the entangled life paths of two working-class brothers from a Northern English industrial city in the 1930s, both of them talented performers. One, John, stays close to his working-class roots and the trade union movement, while the other, Henry, moves away to smart, rich London to seek his fortune as an actor on the West End stage. The piece is based around Christopher Marlowe's 'Doctor Faustus' (*circa* 1592) and its updating to 1930s' Germany in Klaus Mann's novel *Mephisto* (1936, famously filmed by István Szabó, 1981). Using sections of Marlowe's text and the acts of popular English working-class entertainers of the time, 'Cabaret Faust' dramatises the dilemmas of the two performers. One wants to stay close to his roots, make communal performances for his fellow workers and support the workers' movement; the other convinces himself that he can best serve their shared cause by making his way in 'legitimate' theatre and using his status and position there to benefit his former comrades.

Taking inspiration from the Doctor Faustus story, 'Cabaret Faust' explored personal and grand scale social and ethical quandaries. Starting from tragedy (we always knew our heroes would be doomed) rather than statement or argument, once the writing, composing, rehearsing and performing were in operation, the themes of the final blend emerged as greater than the sum of the parts. In 'Cabaret Faust' we began with individual dilemmas, following how small compromises made with the best of intentions might balloon up into monstrous incorporations in crimes never contemplated by the individual. We explored how individual frustration with slow social and collective methods could lead to acts of isolated and self-destructive extremism.

The Mephistopheles of 'Cabaret Faust' is a shape shifter. He switches identity at the 'turn of a page', able to transform the nature of his temptations in the twinkle of an eye. This Mephistopheles tempts our West End hero, Henry, to join a theatre tour of Europe, which turns out to only include the dictatorships of Nazi Germany and Mussolini's Italy. After his performance in Germany, Henry is enticed by a seductive Mephistopheles into a nightclub with the obvious promise of sex. Exiting through the door into the nightclub, Henry emerges blinking into the middle of a Nuremberg rally, a documentary recording of a ranting Adolf Hitler is played and the set transforms into the face of the German Führer. An apparent sexual temptation turns out to be a political one.

This apparent betrayal of the democratic cause by his brother tips the languishing John into desperate action. He decides to assassinate the leader of the British fascists, Sir Oswald Mosley, at one of his blackshirt rallies. Henry rushes to the rally to dissuade his brother, but in the ensuing struggle the gun goes off, a brother is dead, a brother is a killer, and both are swept off to Hell by Mephistopheles.

In the Elizabethan 'world view', being dragged off to Hell by demons was pretty much universally understood to be a bad thing involving endless suffering. Equally, in 1980s' Britain, Nazi Germany was generally understood to have been a very bad thing, an aggressive foreign power that not only bombed British cities, but committed genocidal atrocities on an industrial scale. Indeed even now it serves in UK education as a useful ethical marker for evil. This would usually have left a 'Cabaret Faust' audience with a fairly easy ride; sitting comfortably in judgement on the compromising Henry who ends up, unwillingly, in the embrace of fascists. Except that the official understanding of Nazism in the 1930s was very different to the one that is presented for school students' consumption today.

In the 1930s, large sections of the British establishment looked either favourably or tolerantly on the rise of Nazism. We first showed Mephistopheles at work drawing members of the establishment into his conspiracies; and then we drew our audience into the same complicity. Staging the visit of the British Prime Minister to Munich, the front rows of the audience were asked to wave bunting consisting of alternate Union Jacks and Nazi swastikas; volunteers from the audience were recruited to don fascist armbands and help Mephistopheles beat up a heckler at a rally of Mosley's blackshirts. Just as Marlowe's 'Doctor Faustus' reflected how Catholicism's theological certainties were being rocked by Puritanism in 1590s' England, so 'Cabaret Faust' seemed to pull the rug of moral certainty from under its British audiences, so that the official moral-political certainty of 1980s-hindsight was exposed as a recent construction. The reality exposed was of individuals in 1930s' Britain having to rely on their own moral compass and their own sectional traditions, not on an establishment or official communal moral certainty (which would only come with the outbreak of war).

As with the emerging themes of the tragedy of revolution, individuality in the world and the abject *homo sacer* of TNT's first three productions, so a theme of individual moral ambiguity in a sea of general ethical uncertainty emerged from 'Cabaret Faust'. It showed the competing forces and complex individual agency at play in the moment of moral decisions. This was something greater than the sum of the intentions of the various parts of writing, music, performance, and so on; those interlocking Union Jacks and swastikas were provided in order to give historical background, yet the grotesque dynamics – for example, of placing what for a British audience at least were presumed symbols of 'good' and 'evil' in proximity and on equal terms – worked its mutating magic on the disparate materials of the production to create a subtler tragedy than any of the creative team had individually envisaged. At such good times, Meyerhold and his ideas were writing, directing and designing for us.

Though we updated 1592 to the 1930s, the set for 'Cabaret Faust' looked back. It was a medieval 'hell mouth', like the open mouth of a dragon-beast as would have been seen on the wagons of the medieval play pageants or at a medieval Mystery Cycle. It was built as a series of platforms, so actors could move around on different levels, and it had small and large doors that facilitated puppet shows and scenes in nightclubs, stadia, theatres and finally it became Hell itself. For the Nuremberg Rally scene, a black rectangle dropped down above the open mouth and a peaked hat was placed over the head and it became a demonic Hitler face; not even something as solid as the wooden set could be trusted, all certainties were fluid and changeable and tiny individuals had to find a right way or burn.

In 'Wizard of Jazz', TNT once more plagiarised itself. In the same year as its devising, 1987, the company had been commissioned by TamS Theater to make a play with them and the result was 'Amerika! Amerika! oder Die Charlie Chaplin Putsch'. This play followed two hapless foreign (English and Irish) comedians in Munich as they first get caught up in the chaos around Hitler's failed 'Beer Hall Putsch' of 1923 and are then sucked into the reassembling of the fascist cause after his defeat. The production sought those parts of the roots of extremist reactionary politics that grow in the loam of sentimentality and the sickly nightmares of popular culture.

Later that year, when a chance arose to make a new music theatre piece to follow 'Cabaret Faust', the same theme of dark and unhealthy drives in the deep subconscious of popular culture gripped our imagination. Part of the attraction to this theme, though it may not have been consciously understood by us at the time, is that in dredging from popular performance's shadows we were hacking at our own foundations, examining our own practices and motives.

'Wizard of Jazz' is about a group of British army musicians who abscond from their base on the eve of the Normandy landings in 1944; their singer is an Al Jolson impersonator and they have heard that this famous American star (a Lithuanian Jew who 'blacked up' and imitated the black minstrel sound) is appearing at a local US Army base. The army musicians are seeking Jolson's blessing. The band (and the whole stage picture is based around the instruments of the actual TNT musicians) are hiding out in the cellar of a local pub, where Richard, the uptight landlord, is far from delighted to discover them. The band win Richard over by converting his tawdry pub into 'Rick's Bar', complete with an Empire State Building made of beer crates and a sink plunger. The Landlord swaps his morose nostalgia for the fading British Empire for a bright new persona as Humphrey Bogart's cynical hero in the movie 'Casablanca'. This messing with Richard's mind backfires on the band as the gullible and now wildly drunk Landlord goes off to find Al Jolson at the nearby army base. He falls into a sheep dip and staggers to the US army base, where he witnesses a sermon given by a racist Southern Baptist preacher, Allen Johnston. He returns to his pub and the expectant band, whipping the soldiers up into a frenzy of race hatred that ends with them lynching their ("blacked up") singer.

It is easy to forget – after three decades of catastrophic Middle Eastern military adventures, waterboarding, Abu Ghraib, Guantanamo Bay, Enron, Lehmann Brothers, the rise of the religious Right, the blunderings of George W. Bush and the extremist populism of Donald Trump – that throughout the 1980s, the United States of America was for many the torchbearer for all that was good in the world. Still associated with the liberal values of leaders like the Kennedy brothers, the US was Hollywood, glamour, relaxed sexuality, general prosperity, freedom of speech, democratic elections in which the defeated gracefully and peacefully handed over the reins of power to their opponents, and the nuclear force keeping small European and Asian nations safe from invasion by aggressive 'Communist' neighbours.

In 'Wizard of Jazz', as in TNT's adaptation of John Steinbeck's 'The Grapes of Wrath', in productions of Arthur Miller's 'Death of A Salesman' and 'The Crucible', in 'The Wave' and in 'The Life and Death of Martin Luther King' we ripped into some of the darkest recesses of the 'American Dream'. We explored racism, poverty and inequality, soulless commerce, witch hunts, and the seeds of fascism inside US culture. Across these productions TNT sounded a long warning about the dangers of having illusions in the rhetoric of 'freedom' coming from the USA: a country that locked up a staggering percentage of its Black population, was dominated in large areas by leaders who believed that the world had been made in six days and that human and dinosaurs co-existed, and ran its fossil-fuel based economy with entire disregard for the future's great-grandchildren.

Eventually, from the 1990 launch of the First Gulf War onwards, America's foreign policy and economic and ecological woes would puncture the Dream. Fewer and fewer people would be attracted by the now compromised politics or economics of the USA; this disillusion with the standard bearer of 'freedom and democracy' may be one reason for the rise of authoritarianism in places where 'US values' were once influential. Where the USA remains dominant, however, is in entertainment and while 'Wizard of Jazz' has not been performed for many years, its performing about the deep contradictions in US mass culture hopefully prepared audiences to continue to remain on their guard in the face of the digital tidal waves of Facebook, Netflix, Instagram, box sets and the latest 'Star Wars'.

'Moby Dick' was a huge contradiction to all this. Rather than dredge the depths, our production celebrated not only the heights of US literature, but also the finest aspirations of US political culture. The Pequod, in which Captain Ahab and the crew sail in pursuit of the elusive white whale, is a symbol of co-operation, independence and common aims celebrated in the face of their own rank, order and authority. The company's staging of the action, with the shape of the boat being rebuilt for each scene, with planks and ropes held in place by actors and musicians, with musicians acting and actors beating rhythms, was itself a model of onstage democracy, industry and cooperation.

Many have tried to attach a symbolism to the great white whale, but the point seems to be that it is a beast that might mean anything, and it is this very inscrutability that drives Captain Ahab to lead the murderous pilgrimage. There is something Promethean and mythic about the Pequod's mission to snuff out not knowing, to pierce through the whale's great white surface of illusion. This is the apotheosis of industrial science up against an organism that cannot or will not explain itself; that refuses to be accountable to the most advanced materialist society on the planet.

When the ship goes down and all but one of the sailors and officers drown or die in the jaws of Moby Dick, TNT's actors and musicians were swallowed by a large white rectangle of cloth. There was no attempt to represent a whale; instead the magnificent hubris of subjecting life and existence to rational and industrial pursuit and examination – at a social scale – was overwhelmed by a shape without colour or explanation. Winston Churchill's description of the Soviet Union's motives in 1939 – "A riddle, wrapped in a mystery, inside an enigma" – could apply just as much to whatever it is that finally drags down the magnificent Pequod. The wedding of visual imagery and physical theatre with music as a new agent in the drama gave a new emotional depth and range to the performances, but it also expanded the popularity of the forms. The muted musicality of the performing body could now be heard, explicit, complex and subtle, in the work of TNT.

Some Thoughts on Music Theatre

By Paul

Greece. A public bus near Volos. The driver is playing music that would challenge a concert audience. A Balkan shifting drone anchors complex chords. TNT is performing at the European Music Theatre Festival in this port city. The success of our production of 'Moby Dick' gifts us a place on the Greek music scene, becoming regular performers and eventually collaborators with the Athens Concert Hall (Megaron). Years before, we had made a breakthrough for the company at the Munich Biennale, hosted by Hans Werner Henze, a giant of contemporary composition. And at the very birth of TNT the musicality of our work was recognised in Britain. We were invited to the Music Theatre symposium of the Royal College of Music where I first met John Kenny, composer and trombonist and began a collaboration that has lasted until this day. Since 'Cabaret Faust' in 1984, every TNT production has been graced with a musical score. The composers have stayed with us, each with their own style: Tom Johnson's sung and live instrumental scores such as 'Oliver Twist' and 'Hamlet', Paul Flush's electronic scores created on keyboards such as 'Don Quijote' and 'Macbeth' and John's own scores, recorded by groups of extraordinary musicians and then edited in rehearsal. Recent examples are 'Free Mandela' and 'The Tempest'.

Even plays that would seem to be unsuited to a composed score, such as 'Death of a Salesman' or 'Pygmalion', have been 'unlocked' with original music. And here Shakespeare is our ally. The music for a modern Shakespeare production is often little more than a fanfare, or is relegated in case it undermines the text. I recall the great Japanese drummer Joji Hirota being hidden behind a giant bamboo screen in one production of 'Macbeth' at Stratford. Why bother? We know Shakespeare had no sets, no theatre lights, improvised costumes and no amplification. In the sixteenth century, every Shakespeare play would have been accompanied by music. In 'Romeo and Juliet' he writes text for the musicians (who grumble a lot). These lines are nearly always cut. What a shame! Classical Greek theatre had music, its chorus danced. Oriental theatre has music as its backbone. Sometime in the nineteenth century, just when naturalistic realism raised its ugly head, European theatre plunged the audience into the dark and fired the musicians. But some modern theatre poets rebel against this. Arthur Miller begins 'Death of a Salesman' with a trumpet note and talks of the musicality of the play. Tom Johnson helped TNT realise 'A Streetcar Named Desire' with aching live jazz, often played with the text. I will never forget the Georgian actress Amy Clark's haunting blues ballad; Amy played a stellar Stella.

Back in Greece we are turning a 1930s' electricity generating station into a performance space for 'Moby Dick'. We will use the galleries and open concrete ledges to suggest the ship. 'Moby Dick' remains TNT's most ambitious production, our most complete synthesis of theatre, dance and music. Confronted by an 800-page novel of huge textual complexity we chose to represent the prose-poetry and profundity with a mere 30 pages of dialogue and allow the combined performing arts to conjure the essence of this epic tragedy – perhaps the only one to equal the genius of Shakespeare.

We began rehearsal with an open mind and the following:

- Four actors who could sing.
- Two dancers who could act (and sing), one a choreographer.
- Three musicians who could act (in varying degrees).
- Trombone, percussion, sound sculpture, recorders, electric piano, Alpine horn.
- Four wooden barrels. Four two-metre wooden planks. Eight wooden boxes. Rope of variable length. Six harpoons. Sail cloth of various sizes. No whale.

The audience have no idea who is an actor, singer, dancer or musician. The cast are all crew. The ship too manifests itself in many ways: we are able to build two decks or an enclosed cabin, a crow's nest, we even make the swinging bowels of the ship with ropes and planks. The White Whale is never seen but is conjured from the deep by working the sound sculpture with a violin bow. Whales are chased by dancers, harpoons fly through the air, gales crack the firmament. Pip sings an upbeat spiritual before madness overtakes him. Captain Ahab commands the storm but cannot shake off the obsession that will lead them all to a watery grave. The cast drown as shadows behind a giant sinking sail and only Ishmael floats free. I am still haunted by a melody with these lyrics:

Some men die on the ebb tide
Some men die at low water
Some ships sail and are never seen again

Some men die in a cold sea
And no man knows their grave

The performance at the Palli Electriki in Volos is one of those moments where we achieved our vision of total theatre. I recall one breathtaking moment when the unusual configuration of the audience almost brought us to disaster but created magic: we have rather sharp harpoons in 'Moby Dick'. One is launched through the air and the dancer Tom Ward catches the harpoon mid-flight and pirouettes, landing as if skewering a whale. Tonight the actor throwing the harpoon fails to notice that there are audience sitting at the side of the playing area and the harpoon sails towards them, all gasp. But Tom is there leaping through space to intercept the harpoon. It was as if we as a company did the same, launching ourselves into mid-air to land exactly in the bullseye of the audience.

The following day the Mayor of Volos take us on a boat trip in the gulf. A whale surfaces, rolls over in our wake and follows our ship.

The artist Chrysia Apostolatou is in the audience that day. She invites me and Tom Ward to collaborate on a project at the Athens Concert Hall. She is keen to stage a music theatre piece inspired by Italo Calvino's *Invisible Cities*, which happens to be one of my favourite books. Chrysia has assembled seven composers, a choir, a jazz quartet and a small orchestra plus funding from the Concert Hall (Megaron). What she needs is a script, a director, a choreographer and actors to play Kublai Khan and Marco Polo. We quickly reach agreement and I and Tom are on board. Tom Ward is a phenomenon: he has danced the Prince in the all-male 'Swan Lake' on Broadway and sang as Frank Sinatra in the 'Rat Pack'. He is from Glasgow and takes no prisoners. He will choreograph and play Marco Polo and I will write and direct and play Kublai Khan. The structure of the book is a series of dialogues between Marco Polo and Chinese Emperor Kublai Khan. The Great Khan is as inquisitive as he is vain, as vulnerable as he is powerful, a hypochondriac despot struggling to understand the wider world. He needs Marco Polo, who is none of these things. The Khan asks him to tell him stories of his travels. The stories are chapters of fantasy, the cities Polo conjures have airports and dripping taps, are full of wonder and banality and are neither medieval nor Chinese. The Cities are ways of seeing.

The seven composers each choose an invisible city. So far so good. But when I present the linking dialogue between Marco Polo and the Khan to the group, an issue is raised. They do not want any English onstage. I pause, then agree. My solution: Marco Polo need not speak, a dancer as eloquent as Tom creates his own words and worlds without dialogue. But the verbose emperor needs sound. So, I will improvise a language, somewhere between cod Kabuki and 'Transylvanian Vampire'. I add surprise sounds like a sudden "Ping!" I know what I am saying in English, the servants and guards of the Emperor speak Greek, I must guess what they are saying in the original play. I have seldom enjoyed performing as much as this. I am able to explore sound without text but with meaning. I can concentrate on the musicality of my speech. I can create a character who is truly exotic, and I surrender my own language to do so. The choir and musicians surround me, overwhelm me and lift me, like an operatic tenor, to heights I cannot achieve by myself. The choir are always onstage, they are my subjects and they sing like angels who have only a vain and fragile God on which to attend. It's all Greek to me. The production works surprisingly well, it is funny and accessible as well as a profound retelling of an iconic novel.

Politics prevented the production (titled 'Marcopolis') from having the long run it deserved, but it was filmed and selected by the International Theatre Institute to be shown at festivals. This was a just recognition of a project where I and TNT needed to be the opposite of the emperor I portrayed: humble, responsive and flexible. Enablers. The final line of the novel is one of the most profound I know:

> And the end of all our striving will be to know Babylon and to be not of it.

Chapter Four: Poland

By Paul

I am on a night train from the Hook of Holland to Moscow. I plan to get off in Poznan in Poland. On the platform should be Małgorzata, a young assistant of the world famous theatre director, Jerzy Grotowski. I tend to feel vaguely fraudulent as a witness to the work of the great man, because my relationship with Magosia was anything but professional. I know a lot of the theory of Grotowski; I knew in passing many of the great actors in his company; but often I knew them better as people than artists. I queued for their carrots in black market stalls that stood in the snow. I drank vodka with then, I listened to others who had trained with them, and I participated in projects and workshops at a minor level. Grotowski's book, *Towards A Poor Theatre* is essential reading, but a little dull. Grotowski was a serious man and when I (sort of) knew him he was well on the way to becoming a guru who had decided that having established the primacy of the actor and deliberately impoverished his staging, he would abolish the actor and direct not them but the audience. All of which was fascinating but not what I, at that age, wanted to hear.

So I hung around Wrocław in the tower block apartment of my fragile-fierce lover, drank rough vodka and smoked her Bulgarian cigarettes while listening to our favourite chansons by the "Russian Bob Dylan", the gravel-voiced Bulat Okudzhava. I had met Magosia on a collaboration project with Grotowski's Laboratorium. I think it is worth describing that process, because whatever my (and many of his ensemble's) reservations about destroying theatre to make theatre, Grotowski's understanding of the essence of acting is unrivalled. I have written of the 'Great Tradition' of European theatre theory, how it runs from Stanislavski to Peter Brook. It is quite possible that Grotowski actually achieved a balance between what he said and what he did better than any of the other Titans. Grotowski achieved what he set out to do and his theories and his performances were circular in the sense that it was impossible to judge which came first.

Mansfield, north Nottinghamshire, is a mining town not far from where I was born. I was engaged there by the only English company to seriously explore Grotowski-influenced physical theatre in the 1970s. I had passed a rigorous audition, aided by my theoretical knowledge of Grotowski's work. Now we got to work with some of his minions, including Małgorzata and an eccentric actor who had recently left the passionately anti-Soviet Polish army. For some weeks we had been training in a style of abstract physical improvisation. This meant improvising without formal language and using the body as an instrument of physical communication. We learnt to create stories and situations with fellow actors that worked beyond language.

One autumn day we meet in the late afternoon and go for a walk around a lake on the edge of Sherwood Forest. Language is already banned. We will not speak recognisable words for the next twelve hours. At about 5pm we go back to the theatre and begin a strenuous two hours of abstract improvisation, controlled by drumming. We are told to be separate, each actor (men and women) both in our own world but together. The insistent drumming pushes us to the very limit of our endurance. But as with all intense physical exercise, reaching the edge of that limit creates a type of ecstasy.

Małgorzata is watching, hawk-like. One by one she removes us from the studio and blindfolds us. I am led by a careful hand along a corridor and up steps. I guess I am in the centre's small cinema. I am laid on the floor and told not to remove my blindfold nor to sleep. I hear the door close and I am alone in the utter silence of a darkened cinema. Thoughts, images and ideas spin through my mind. I try to block out language and concentrate on pictures, places and the memory of faces. Gradually the emptiness of my mind calms me like cool water on a summer's day. Many hours later I hear the door open and I am led, still blindfold, back to the theatre. Once there I can open my eyes. The seats have been removed and in the almost empty space is a tree, a real tree with candles on its branches. At the base of the tree are a few simple props: a wooden sword, a paper crown, a few sticks, an empty bottle, a bell.

We now have the night before us to create a story using these objects and our own bodies. Hour after hour we make kings and kingdoms, betray lovers, drink water as if it were wine, laugh, cry, fart and spout gobbledegook in imaginary languages. The tree has to come down. The candles must be snuffed out, but carefully, because when the last flame dies this world will end. And it did. Just as the last candle went out at the very last performance of Grotowski's own theatre, in his play about the end of the world: 'Apocalypsis Cum Figuris'.

There was still one more act in this night of what was a type of theatre: we were taken in silence back to the forest to watch the sun rise. It was over. Were we performers? Who had we performed to? It was a deeply satisfying event. Whatever we had created was lost forever and may have meant nothing to anyone except ourselves. But the impulse, the interior journey, of Grotowski's art left an important mark upon me, even if the work of TNT was to be more open and inclusive. And Małgorzata? She loved to sing; once we buried a vodka bottle (again at dawn) in the Bishop of Southwell's rose garden. It was a sung service. We drifted apart not least because she wanted a child and I wanted a theatre company. She married and had the child. A few years later, I stood beside her grave watching her young son drop a rose onto her coffin. The saddest act of all.

Ten years later the TNT van enters Poland again, it is November 1989 and as the Berlin Wall falls the Soviet empire shudders. Some months earlier, I had met a Polish director at a festival in Bonn. As we sat in the bar, I talked to him about our Stalin and Meyerhold play and his eyes lit up. He made a surprising offer: that his company based in Lublin could set up a guerrilla theatre tour of Poland, passing us along the informal network of anti-establishment groups and even church organisations. The tour could cover most of the country and last four weeks. Any box office receipts would be eaten up by the cost of organising the tour, so of course we would receive no pay, just a few soft currency Zlotys if we had big audiences. I agreed straight away. I knew the other two actors, the dancer actress Inga Kammerer and the *commedia dell'arte* maestro Enzo Scala would jump at the opportunity to take Stalin to the East. TNT dramaturg Phil Smith would also join us in this grand adventure.

So now we are setting off for Lublin in a hired van paid for by the British Council who award us the princely sum of £400 to bring down the Soviet Empire. Our van is stocked as if for a military campaign: everything from German beer to a large case of tinned tuna. Poland is on the edge. The shops are empty. We halt for the night in Wrocław where the Lublin Company has arranged for us to stay in a student hall of residence. There is no toilet paper, just strips of old newspapers stabbed through metal coat hangers. More importantly there is no petrol, but this would be solved by our hosts who had arranged for a theatre company in every town to hoard drums of petrol for us. These we tip into the van via makeshift funnels. A cold task standing in the snow. Early winter 1989 is unusually cold, even for Poland. 15 below freezing. We arrive in Lublin after another long drive east. We pass cracked concrete tower blocks and enter the walled city. Lublin exudes an old-world charm that borders on time travel. The Communists despised these feudal relics and lavished resources on the new suburbs. So Lublin and other old town centres remain preserved as if in aspic or ice. The fantastic architecture remains: witness to the great days of Poland during its astonishing Renaissance. This is where Copernicus invented the modern world view. But it is not just the Renaissance that is there for all to see, it is also this century as no one painted out the pre-war adverts, some in German, or is it Yiddish?

Using Lublin as our base, we tour Poland, performing to audiences that pack into studio theatres and community halls. Once I recall a front row made up entirely of priests and nuns. Our performance releases the energy of the audience; in our story of revolutionary betrayal and murderous Stalinism they see their own political and cultural struggle. When, as Stalin, I spray a hammer and sickle in dripping blood on a wall of *Pravda* newspapers, the audience gasp. This they thought was not allowed. Perhaps it isn't. But times have changed and our very presence is a symbol of that.

As we drive through the frozen countryside we often see queues of Poles waiting outside churches. Pope John Paul is on the Papal throne, God has spoken and the Russian atheist devils will be expelled. We hear this again and again. The sense of religious and nationalist belief is overwhelming. I remember one new church, vast as a hangar, and yet unpainted, just bare brick and concrete. It was minus ten outside the van. Nothing but snow, ice and the unbearable flatness of central Poland. The huge church doors were open because most of the congregation were forced to stand outside and peer into the church to witness the Mass booming out from loudspeakers.

How could Gorbachev's idea of a revivified Communism compete? Well it didn't. But the tanks might have come. No one knew. It had happened before. Gorbachev might be toppled, the Red Army did not need to cross the border. They were already here. Fear and hope fought and, for most, the solution was prayer. And maybe a little theatre. Theatre matters to the Poles. Poland's great poets wrote poetic dramas. If Poland has a soul it is expressive, wild, angry and free; but never was a country more abused by its shark-like neighbours. Yet, Poland never gave up; at times it almost relishes its identity as holy victim. An example: I am walking towards a theatre through the icy streets of some town I forget and my liaison asks if we can stop at a church en route. Ever the curious traveller, I agree. We enter the baroque building and my host hurls himself to the floor and genuflects before the Virgin Mary. He calls to her as if she were his mother, which I suppose she is. Stands, brushes the dust and grit from his coat, smiles as if he had just performed well and leads me out of the church.

In Bialystok, by the Soviet border, we perform in a discotheque. The sound is turned down but the music videos continue as the white clown declares his undying love for Nina, in the moving words of Chekhov. That night we stay in a motel in the forest, which sounds grand except that this motel is a summer retreat. The bedrooms are so cold that Enzo sleeps in his Harlequin mask. Through the goodness of his heart, the motel manager had opened his doors to the street drunks who sleep on the stairs outside our rooms instead of freezing to death in the road. We hear wolves howling in the forest.

In gorgeous Cracow we perform in a rock venue. The stage is sticky with spilt beer. The audience are wonderful. Sadly, we cannot celebrate this as our German beer cans have frozen solid in the van. But we can participate in Revolution. It is December 1989. Cracow is by the Czech border. Across that border the Velvet Revolution is in full swing, but no one knows for sure if it will stay soft as Velvet. We attend a meeting of theatre workers. We sign the declaration of support which we send to Prague. Before the reader mocks us for believing this had the slightest impact on the fall of Communism, it is worth remembering that the Velvet Revolution was led by a playwright, and a good one too, Václav Havel. One of the demonstrators on the streets of Prague that day will become our East Europe producer and take TNT back to Poland every year.

In Warsaw we perform in a real theatre: the vast wedding cake skyscraper given to the people of Poland by Stalin himself: The Palace of Culture. It is rare to enter a capital city and see your venue dominating the skyline. I had set up the performance as I knew a remarkable woman from a chance meeting at a Greek theatre festival: Anna Chodakowska. She is a leading actress at the National Theatre of Poland (housed in the same building). Anna is also a singer. She became known as the Voice of Solidarity; her soaring soprano is the leading vocal on a crucial LP, a political and national mass. We took tea at her house, surrounded by her small dogs. Anna later became an animal rights activist which was more than her yappy pets deserved.

We almost get rumbled after the show in the Palace of Culture. The British Ambassador decides to attend. Of the three performers only I am British, even though Inga lives in London. Enzo Scala has never set foot on the Scepter'd Isle. We debate whether he should anglicise his name to "Vincent Staircase". That night the theatre intelligentsia of Warsaw pack into the first-floor studio theatre. Once again the performance seems to release a pent-up energy in the audience. An energy magnified by seeing, in this building, donated to the conquered people of Poland by Stalin, that same dictator portrayed as a terrifying clown, a doctor who murders his patients. In circumstances such as these we never rush off to the privacy of a dressing room, but meet and greet our audience, field questions and enjoy the buzz. I am chatting with the singer Anna, when I note with horror that the British Ambassador has cornered Enzo. There goes our £400.

I hastily join them to find that the Diplomat could not be more diplomatic. He and his wife are praising our work and the astonishing irony of its location. Then the ambassador asks Enzo where he lives and he replies confidently: "London". Now the killer question: "Really, whereabouts?" I hold my breath. Enzo smiles his winning smile and gives the only London address he knows: "Trafalgar Square". We all freeze before the Ambassador's wife rescues us by turning to me and asking: "And you, Paul, are from Nottingham?"

Then we crash the van. En route to a performance in the steel town of Stalowa Wola, Inga was unable to control the vehicle on black ice. We slide sideways down the busy road, through a gap in the traffic, miraculously, and crunch into a snow-filled ditch. Phil, giving comments on the previous night's performance, tears his notes in half. As we come to rest, Enzo declares, astonished, "we are... alive!" The van door is lying yards away. A passing tractor pulls us out of the ditch. The theatre sends a car to collect us. Our insurance sends the wrecked vehicle back to Germany by truck. From then on we were on our own on public transport. And worse than that, we have no way of storing food or other supplies (no beer!). If the shops were sparse when we entered Poland, three weeks later the entire Eastern block is in melt down. We once stopped at a café and were served with their only available dish: spaghetti in salted milk. You may imagine our Italian actor's response to that culinary disaster!

We stagger through the final weeks of the tour on unheated trains, twice bumping into the same group of Romanian gypsies who happily take over whole carriages and defy the conductor to ask them for tickets. We feel a gypsy like solidarity.

The tour ends in Wrocław, where the ghosts of my past flit by. The performance is on the top floor of the Gothic University building. The lift broke long ago. Enzo and Inga set up while I go with the organiser to collect lights from a cellar disco. The organiser tells me that he will happily take photographs during our play for the knock down price of $100. He might as well have asked for a million. I say "no" and try to smile. It's still cold.

We arrive at the cellar and collect antique lights that look as if they should be searching for enemy bombers in the night sky. If the lights are heavy that is nothing compared to the dimmer packs that control them. We stash our haul in his battered Fiat Polski. Drive across town; heave the lights and dimmer packs up five double flights of stairs. We perform the play. The organiser is running the lights. He misses most of the cues as he is popping up and down taking photographs. At the end of the performance he offers us the film for a knock down $80. This time I do not smile.

We drag the lights back down the stairs, drive them across the frozen city, take them out of the Fiat, down more stairs to the cellar. I even manage to sweat. Now, I say, where can we eat in this city of half a million souls? The photographer looks worried. He consults with a friend and suggests a club, the best club. They will have food. The four of us set off, packed into the tiny Fiat. The club exists. We are welcomed rather too enthusiastically. No, we do not want to dance. Do they have anything to eat? We are ushered to a table. The top hits of Russian disco boom across the dance floor. It is difficult to speak let alone be heard. A waitress arrives. "Vodka?" she asks with a smile. "Food?" we reply. She laughs. "Of course we have no food. This is a club. This is Poland". We take the vodka. I reach in my pocket. I have one tin of tuna left. I have a pen knife. I cut open the tin, catch my thumb on the sharp rim and bleed into the cold fish. This is possibly the lowest point of my touring life.

Fifteen years later we are back in Poland. Our producer is based in Prague, another of the oddballs and eccentrics who defend our barricades against normality. Svata had been an accountant for Ernst & Young, his wife teaches English; he became involved in promoting our first hesitant steps in the Czech Republic. For obscure reasons, such as the need to drive a van from Prague to Edinburgh, Svata started to help us. He then realised that he would rather promote theatre, or more specifically TNT and ADGE theatre, than spend his life looking after rich people's money. Since that happy day he has not only booked regular month-long tours of the Czech Republic, Slovakia and Poland but has driven the van, set the lights and presented us with fastidiously precise accounts.

In 2018 I was back in Łódź, a city where, in 1989, we were hosted by the radical Teatr 77. They had given us beds on the top floor of the city museum amongst the stuffed animals. I recall waking to be greeted by a stuffed bear in a glass cabinet. In 2018 we open our 'Pygmalion' in Łódź. Five hundred teenage students are packed into a barn like theatre. There are another five hundred due in the afternoon. Phil Smith writes elsewhere about this production and how we applied the TNT style to what might otherwise have been a wordy, even dusty, museum piece. I am still concerned; will an audience of young Poles connect? I need not worry. The audience lap it up, seeing in the mistreatment of Eliza a mirror of their own lives in our own time. Before the performance, Svata introduces me to a teacher who has faithfully supported the company for many years. During the interval that same teacher sprints to a local shop, buys a large bouquet of flowers and returns for the second half. At the applause, she presents me with the flowers and her students gather round for selfies with the cast. It is a reminder of the many bouquets we received all those years ago at the end of the Cold War.

We now perform in Wrocław twice a year.

Actors on our current production of 'Tom Sawyer' posted photos on Facebook of the Grotowski Research Centre. I did not comment on their post or parade my connections to the only genuine theatre genius I ever met.

And Magosia? In the words of Leonard Cohen:

"I remember her well in a Polish hotel, I don't think of her that often..."

Letter to Katie

(In 1995, at some time between the productions of 'David Copperfield' and 'Moby Dick', Phil Smith wrote a letter to the designer Katie Sykes describing some of the basic principles of the company. Here are some excerpts.)

"The shows should be full of ideas, but not subservient to a concept, they do not animate a concept – the show should be a material and theatrical event not an intellectual one: what does that mean? In 'The Mystery' ('Funny Money') we had a 'message', an analysis of two economic models – monetarism and Keynesianism. Yet, the play became something other than a satire on those economic philosophies. At the end of the play one of the three businessmen presenting the play revolts, seizes the box office takings and burns them in the tin bath.... it did not symbolise anything (it was not revolution, for example), but rather the tragedy of people suffering under the yoke of any wrong idea.... We always aspire to move not to a statement, but to music. Not to a mobile manifesto, but to the rhythm of unfolding ideas, images, actions and abstract un-explainable sounds and motions."

"The rehearsal process should be kept open in its treatment of material, text and performance – so that profound changes can be introduced late on in rehearsals and during a run of performances: for example, when we rehearsed 'Wizard of Jazz' Paul played the Landlord as a large, barrel-like, booming man, with a padded shirt, but just before the opening performance we turned that around and made him a tight, thin, highly strung, incredibly tense man with vertical lines, his energy being pulled into the ground – most evidently in an over-long and thin tie that reached down to his groin..."

"...the set should be like a motor or an engine, a vehicle that can be ridden, a shelter to hide in and behind, its illustrative force always secondary to its practical use to the actors as springboard, door, etc. ... Illustrative, decorative touches are not irrelevant. ... a set or prop is like a walking stick – first of all there to solve a problem, but secondarily maybe it will be painted white to illustrate the problem..."

"....the set must be deconstructible, capable of an unexpected metamorphosis by the most simple means. In 'Oliver Twist' a coffin lid opens as a front door. In 'The Mystery' a plank between two stepladders served as a backdrop, a bed, then the whole lot was pushed over in rage. ... there is no absolute, religious, mystical value, the audience must make value for themselves and we hope to provoke them to do that in some ways rather than others."

"TNT is essentially Rough Theatre as defined by Peter Brook in *The Empty Space*. To borrow a phrase from the Russian 'Eccentric Theatre', "we prefer Charlie's arse to Duse's hands" (referring to film comic Charlie Chaplin and the classical actress Eleanor Duse). Rough Theatre is the 'democratic' form of people making heaven from profane, rough, raw elements. In that sense it is a very optimistic form even when presenting catastrophic events – the actual making of the performance is an affirmation of the positive resources of people. Hence the importance of the manner in which the actors can change their stage world – so the acting machine must be deconstructible and reformable – an over-arching metaphor of people changing their own worlds, from their own resources, without an intervening god, author/god, director/god."

"....the actors.... must have open, dilated bodies and an emotional warmth as the audience's very positive reflections.... from whatever tradition it does not matter.... as long as those trainings apply principles of movement springing from the lower trunk, that open the body, and are expressed in terms of oppositions within the body...."

"....a man called Alexei Levinski.... is carrying the true spirit of Meyerhold's Biomechanics.... a shambling, stooped man, who plays with a stick in his exercises. Shifting weight, opening the body, moving like a vaudeville artist who has transcended their material out of the jokes and into a purely theatrical world.... He seems to have been crushed by the world, but when he moves he seems to shake huge weights from his shoulders and dances with feather-like lightness. I asked Levinski how influenced Biomechanics was by vaudeville or music hall and he responded by saying 'yes, in some of the movements.... for vaudeville is the language of urban Europe'."

"...our poetics are those of 'the grotesque'. We make connections on stage that do not usually occur in daily life: businessmen in suits play pantomime characters.... But there is something more to the grotesque.... the individual elements of these strange compositions should in themselves be pushed to the limits. For example, in 'The Government Inspector' a young officer in unrequited love commits suicide: Meyerhold stages this by multiplying the person of the young officer into a chorus of officers, strumming invisible guitars; as his beloved is wooed by another, a single officer fires a gun, and the whole chorus of officers stagger and fall. Romance and death are interwoven, but each is pushed to the extreme – the extreme romance of the chorus of invisible guitars, the extreme death of collective suicide."

"....'from comedy to tragedy at the turn of a page' – is an important constituent of the grotesque – the speed, the instantaneous switch from comedy to tragedy. This creates, we hope, a kind of (what Brecht called) binocular vision in the spectators – the ability to simultaneously consider different, clashing visions of the world...."

"....we should always be prepared to ignore all this and do something new. Our pieces are not formulas.... In the chapter John Rudlin wrote on TNT in his recent *Commedia dell'Arte – An Actor's Handbook* he criticises TNT: 'In the escape from the authority of authorship, they willingly sacrifice anything (even the form on which they claim to be basing their performance) to immediacy of theatrical effect'. Exactly! Theatricality is all that we rely upon...."

"TNT is physical theatre in which words are very important.... we use degraded words, like old jokes, gags and propaganda.... and we make them into a heightened language. An unsentimental poetry made up of rough elements. We often quote: taking acts, words, phrases from different sources.... 'Moby Dick' is a collectively acted story told in a pub."

"....we are against the bureaucracy of the stage. By that I mean scene changes or any utilitarian action that is not a part of the performance's theatrical world. All necessary movements must be integrated into the theatrical world.... anti-bureaucracy politics is very significant to the twentieth century given that the bureaucratic mode has been so murderous in Stalinist gulags and Nazi concentration camps. Bureaucracy is life-destroying in small and extreme ways and has no place in our theatre of liveliness...."

The Body

By Phil

In the face of the increasing technologising and digitisation of performance and the advance of mass and ever-more distributed and hand-held media, we have been 'old fashioned' in our commitment to the body rather than the screen. The body, for us, is first and foremost in performance: expressive, erotic, open, generous, present, excessive, athletic.

The corrosive power of digital technology and screens is increasingly recognised. Among cultural critics, and psychologists like Joshua Cohen and Christopher Bollas, there is a questioning of the culture of constant confession, exposure and performance. It renders us increasingly likely to develop 'normotic' personalities, devoid of inner life, in which we know how to act feelings but not how to feel them. TNT's resistance to the blandishments of media may appear new and radical. But it is part of a long-standing commitment to the unmediated body and the rights and

Hamlet and a Budo-inspired Ghost in TNT's 'Hamlet'

importance of bodies; partly taken from the traditions of clowning and physical-symbolist theatre on which we have drawn, but also from the particular beginnings of TNT.

The body is mortal; it does not last forever. Yet, without it there is neither thought nor feeling, neither action nor reaction. When the body dies it becomes something else; this is true of plants and white whales and miners and professors. It is not just in death that there is such change; change is as much present in life. The body is always changing and always in movement; even when standing still or sitting down, the body is only able to stop from falling to the ground by minuscule and mostly unconscious shifting of our limbs to maintain balance. In the theatre, everything is based on that very shifting; everything on stage is about change and adaptation. Every walk across the stage begins with a fall that is caught up and held at every moment by a shifting of balance. When all the members of TNT have finally departed the stage of this life, what will be left will not only be the texts and the photos and the memories of the surviving spectators, but also all the gestures and the trace of the responses those gestures conjured in the bodies of the audience members. We work in *physical* theatre, not just because it is more eye-catching or a better way to get a performance across in a popular way than literary theatre, but because the body is so important. Both as the test of our respect for each other's rights and as the means of our connection with the fragile planet beneath our theatre buildings.

Paul adds: It is January 2020; we have rehearsed a complex scene in 'Frankenstein' without words. It was a huge relief. It clarified the frantic actions of the scene in Victor's laboratory where his fiancée, Elizabeth, enters and with horror realises he is building a creature. He cages her and Igor throws the switch and brings the Creature (and with it the robotic future of the world) to life. The theatre, the truth of the scene, was all in the body of the performers. They needed to find a melodramatic and grotesque style to tell that story. The words are mere decoration, a stimulant to action. This is our body of work.

Chapter Five: 'Video & Juliet', 'Don Quijote' and 'Le Petit Prince' – a multi-lingual English theatre, how does that work?

By Phil

Following the success of 'Amerika! Amerika!' at TamS Theater in Munich, we were offered a new commission and set about creating a Faustian play in which we considered the 'judgement of Europe' through a trio of its cultural giants – Michelangelo, Shakespeare and Freud – and one of their creations: Juliet from 'Romeo and Juliet'. Threatened with an eternity in hell for their cultural complicity in the horrors of the twentieth century, the threesome mount a romantic theatrical defence. Shakespeare re-casts himself as Ron, an American Romeo (a rodeo rider), as the threesome struggle to absolve themselves from any blame for the works of art, poetry and psychology that ended at the gates of concentration camps. How could Europe stumble into such violence and abominations given the shining examples of imagination and truth-seeking in Renaissance sculpture, Shakespearean poeticising and modern psychoanalysis?

The plot of the 1988 'Video & Juliet' was a conceit. We were not putting the trio of artist-philosophers on trial, nor their works. We were asking how those who had access in Europe to the very highest achievements of art and poetic science could eschew, or misappropriate, or find things to twist within, the works of our three heroes, to justify or generate indifference to the crimes of genocide and total war. We struggled.

Unlike 'Amerika! Amerika!', with the solid historical events of the Munich Putsch to secure its surreal situations and 'plays within a play', the fantasy framework of Dantesque judgement was a little too flimsy for 'Video & Juliet'. A little too 'rich'; too much sauce and not enough vegetables. First, disagreements about the script (quite justified ones, as it turned out) and, then, cast changes disrupted the work of rehearsal; yet, eventually a play emerged and it was well received. Well enough, at least, for us to revive it as 'Europa Eureka' in 1991 in England, in an equally troubled attempt to resolve its problems.

Despite these hiccups, 'Video & Juliet' signalled an important new strand in TNT's work: multi-lingual performance. 'Amerika! Amerika!' had introduced English and Irish characters who spoke in English, while the rest spoke in German, confident that the Munich audience would understand both equally well. In 'Video & Juliet', however, Freud spoke in German, Michelangelo in Italian and Shakespeare and Juliet (Julia) in English, with them all conversing together, slithering across all the languages. The different vocabularies were more tightly and dynamically intertwined; the connections became a message in themselves; a kind of Euro-Theatre. We had performers working in languages and speaking dialogue which, at the time at least, we did not understand; yet, somehow, this seemed to present no barrier to theatrical comprehension or working coherently in the rehearsal room; the problems with 'Video & Juliet' were structural and dramaturgical, not linguistic.

This experience led us to the idea that "theatre is a language". It provided us with a logic which brought Paul often and me, once, to direct in languages neither of us knew well, or at all. Paul directed a Russian version of 'The Charlie Chaplin Putsch' in what was, by then, St Petersburg. We produced a new version of the script, Paul working on re-writes of a play about a 1920s' coup at the same time as a contemporary one, the "August Putsch", was launched on the streets of the Russian capital against the leadership of Mikhail Gorbachev. This 1991 insurrection was led by hard-line Communist Party members of the government and the head of the KGB, who were opposed to Gorbachev's reforms. As he wrote a new draft of our 'Putsch' play, Paul was unsure whether the outcome of the coup would end any chance of our theatrical uprising being staged. In the event, the putschists were defeated by a campaign of civil resistance; the Communist Party of the Soviet Union and the Soviet Union imploded and 'The Charlie Chaplin Putsch' went on.

We delivered an English script of the play to the now 'St Petersburg State Comedy Theatre' and it was translated, rather literally, into Russian. In rehearsal, the Russian actors took the literal translation and worked it into vernacular Russian. But one phrase had completely defeated the translator first and then the actors: "hanky panky" – an English synonym for unspecified sexual activity. Apparently, lacking any Russian equivalent, the actors decided to retain the original English, and so it was that TNT, presumably rather temporarily, introduced the term "hanky panky" into the Russian vocabulary. Or it may be the only thing that survives us... who knows?

When Paul directed 'The Murder of Sherlock Holmes' in 2016 in Shanghai, performed in Cantonese, rather than the Victorian English music hall conventions of the original production, the actors brought to the rehearsal room the conventions of a certain kind of popular Cantonese farce. Although, as far as we know, there is no direct link between this farce style and English music hall (but who knows, the pre-mass media worlds were far more connected than we generally acknowledge, trade and travel did not start with Thomas Cook), the two were sufficiently equivalent to generate similar and complementary effects. The music hall gags were enthusiastically enjoyed by the Shanghai audience. Similarly, in 1990, on TNT's first visit to Russia, although we had been warned that our music hall-based comedy 'English Tea Party' (at that time entitled '1945!'), riddled with old English jokes, would be beyond the comprehension of most Russians, we played two sold-out performances to Leningrad audiences who were tossed in gales of laughter at the old gags.

The Shanghai Dramatic Arts Centre Mandarin production of TNT's 'Murder of Sherlock Holmes', directed by Paul Stebbings. Shun Le as Holmes.

When I came to direct our adaptation of Antoine de Saint-Exupéry's 'Le Petit Prince', I explained to the French actors that the rehearsal room language would have to be English as I speak nothing else; a victim and a perpetrator of the English complacency about other languages. I explained that if the actors wished to discuss issues first in French then I was happy for them to do that, but would appreciate if they would share their decisions and reflections with me afterwards. While discussions in French occurred many times, no translation was ever necessary; a combination of dramatic context, body language, intuition and an occasional glimmer from school French lessons was enough for them to always make sense to me.

We do not fool ourselves into thinking, just because 'theatre is a language', that English might be universal. English – the dominant language of most of our shows – is not neutral; for many places in the world it is the language of the coloniser, the invader and the cultural appropriator. Significantly, most of our work is done in countries where this is not the case. In those places colonised or captured for empire by English speakers – India, Australia, USA and Canada – we play far less often. We are also fully aware that there is a mercantile interest in inviting, allowing and supporting our English language theatre. English is the global business language. While our audience may encounter ideas critical of that 'global business', the language is a message in itself and is – as the world stands today – entwined with an English-based and negotiated trade in financial, material and intellectual commodities.

This is nothing new; this entangling of trade and art. If you visit the ancient sites in England – the Uffington White Horse or the Avebury henge, for example – you will find that alongside them runs an ancient trade route, trodden into chalk or paved with limestone pebbles. Trade and meaning-making have long been interwoven; from those ancient blacksmiths whose transformation of metals made them and their products suspiciously magical, all the way to Bollywood. Our theatre is no different; we may have things to say about the mercantile world, about the way that 'money speaks', about how the use of finite resources threatens the planet, but we are part of that unjust world. Our art of theatre does not rise above it; it wrestles with its painful contradictions, no more so than in the paradoxes of language.

Paul adds: Our long-standing and increasing work in Spanish is an attempt to break down this dependency on the dominance of English. Teatro Espressivo de Costa Rica is becoming a second pillar of TNT theatre, one that exports our productions to other Latin American countries (notably Peru) and also within Costa Rica to remote communities and schools. Some local actors and artists in Costa Rica have now been working with TNT for over ten years.

Theatre Fetishes: technical rehearsals and press nights

By Paul

Nicholas Hytner is a director I admire. He revolutionised the (UK) National Theatre's audience, always a good place to start. In his account of his years as Artistic Director he bemoans the effects of 'Technical Rehearsals'. Just as a cast are about to take wing they are forced to stop and hang around for up to two days whilst lights and set are arranged and cues laboriously plotted. Too often it seems a plot against live theatre. Why accept this?

TNT holds public dress rehearsals without lights. Sets must be in place on day one of rehearsals. They can be painted or improved upon but they do not arrive just in time for some arbitrary technical rehearsal. The technical rehearsal encompasses all that is wrong with standard theatre. The marginalised actors hang around for hours on end just as they need to grab the production by the scruff of the neck and…act. Shortly afterwards comes the 'Press Night'. A double whammy. No matter how long the run, for the survival hopes of the commercial production, the 'Press Night' is the one that really counts. But how absurd is this?

My most frequent note to actors in tough roles as they approach a premiere is: first, perform the play ten times. This is especially true of an actor in a small multi-role cast. For example, the actor who plays Puck in our frequently remounted production of 'A Midsummer Night's Dream' must also play Lysander and Snug. That is a Fairy, a lover and a workman; almost twenty costume changes in two and a half hours. First, the actor must master the practicalities of the role and then their performance can blossom. And here I should salute Dominic Brewer who played our Puck and went on to work with Mark Rylance when that marvellous all male 'Twelfth Night' transferred to Broadway.

Ahah, smiles the realist, ditching technical rehearsals is all very well for touring theatre but in-house work requires it. To a degree, yes, but in Shanghai where I work in-house with the main city theatre, we have ways of breaking down the process; members of the 'theatre club' are invited into the rehearsal room for an early run of the production. Afterwards we and the management talk to them and make changes.

For example, I radically cut back the Sly 'framing' of 'Taming of the Shrew' after just such a bare bones performance. Meanwhile, the lighting designer spends far longer than usual in our rehearsals so that little time is wasted on plotting lights. Even at that large theatre, I insist on the set being in place from day one of rehearsal. On the day of the technical rehearsal I send the actors home at 5 o'clock and work with stand ins to set lights well into the night.

As to the press, there was a time when we were very dependent on critics. The mostly loyal support of the *Guardian* newspaper (and its regional critics) in the UK was essential to our early success, as were our early reviews in Germany's *Suddeutsche Zeitung*. I am not one of those who loathe critics for the sake of it, even though a couple of critics have loathed me (or TNT). We soon worked out that a good review in one country could be trumpeted in another while a poor review could be buried without much fuss. No one reads *La Nacion* in China. While theatre criticism is necessary, important even, I do consider shameful the practice of giving stars to productions, something that is unknown in continental Europe. What on earth is the difference between a three star and a four star production? If Ian McKellen is fabulous as King Lear but the production is flawed, what star rating does it deserve? Complexity is reduced to commodity. Even a local German newspaper will give many columns of newsprint to a theatre production and you will have to read to the end to discover the judgement of the critic.

The only honest commodity in theatre is the ticket. To stand and watch a play in Shakespeare's day you dropped a penny into a box (which was then taken to an office – hence 'the box office'). The thousand or so students who pile into Guangzhou (Canton) University to watch TNT perform Shakespeare, four hundred years after the original premieres, pay just $2 a ticket.

A thought: theatre critics emerged just as the theatre audience was plunged into darkness. Before that the actors looked their audience in the eye. They did not need someone else to tell them how well or poorly they had performed. Turn the house lights on.

Chapter Six: Japan

By Paul

Tokyo, May the 20th. My birthday as usual (I must have spent ten birthdays in Japan). My present to myself is an all-day ticket to the Kabuki theatre. It is rather like watching a cricket test match at the Oval: there are three plays with exciting titles such as 'The Samurai Murder in the Bath House'. Actors in mask-like make-up parade through the audience, boys or young willowy men play the female roles, regular audience members are allowed to shout their appreciation after a particularly good move or speech. There are breaks for beer and bento boxes of exquisite food which are eaten at the seats; there is always music, much of it challenging to the Western ear. Between plays a boy from one of the Kabuki families is inaugurated into the troupe. On stage dynasties fall, lovers pine and die, heroes combat evil, monks offer solace, and no play is complete without at least one sword fight.

Am I describing Shakespeare's Globe or the Kabuki theatre in Tokyo? Is this the last place on earth where we might experience something that William might recognise, however 'alien'? The vibrant theatricality is universal and obscure at the very same time. And I confess that almost nothing I have seen has been more valuable to me than this popular yet deeply stylised theatre. There is physical control combined with sheer exuberance, deep emotion woven with stark stylisation, music and drumming integrated with poetic text, extraordinary vocal technique that explores every resonant point of the body.

Comedy and tragedy, violence and tenderness and all washed down with beer, green tea and sushi. What is there not to like? I am not only inspired I also frankly steal ideas: there is never any stage blood in Kabuki, blood is represented by red cloth. When I direct 'Julius Caesar' (first in German then in English) I will murder Caesar without daggers. Each assassin will stab Caesar with a hand in which is clasped a red ribbon, pulling the cloth out as they withdraw to create a star shape of spurting blood. This killing will be accompanied by harshly plucked cello, which like a Japanese koto, can balance a string somewhere between percussion and melody.

Usually I leave the theatre after a fine performance and feel that I am returning to a dull place. But Japan is one giant theatre where Kabuki blends seamlessly into the giant screens displaying Manga images, the kimonos worn on the subway, the food presented as works of art, and the very wrapping of almost everything in layers of neatly folded paper, plastic and ribbon. Is Shinto itself religion or performance? Is the most complete expression of Japanese Buddhism embodied in Noh theatre? Bustling industrial Osaka is famous for its puppet theatre not just Toyotas. I once stumbled into a performance in Hiroshima of a type of dance drama where the puppets have eaten the actors – giant dragons swirl across the stage until there is literally no stage left. The Samurai who gets the girl has to hack his way through mounds of writhing dragons. In the all-night convenience store the counter staff shout "hello" to every customer. Schoolboys are uniformed like Prussian officers, schoolgirls are alarmingly costumed as Barbie dolls. Taxi drivers wear white gloves and peaked caps worthy of an admiral. Like performers across the world, the people of Japan are always bowing. I want to break out in applause.

Japan was where TNT began our Asian Odyssey. Twenty-eight years and forty-nine tours later we are still there.

I only know it is that many tours because I joined our cast in Japan last year for 'Romeo and Juliet'.

We arrive at a rural Honshu college which regularly hosts the company. We are formally greeted by a female professor and taken to the refectory where students have cooked an array of local delicacies. Each actor and I are allotted a table and joined by students who watch us eat and shoot carefully prepared questions in accents that make answering a challenge. Some of the food is equally bewildering and the students are amazed we can use chopsticks, as if we had mastered a hidden art. There are a lot of selfies (with chopsticks). Around the dining tables display boards trace the history of TNT in Japan. Photographs and posters of long-gone productions and long retired actors jog my memory. And there it is, on the final board: "TNT celebrates their forty eighth tour of Japan". The actors retire to the auditorium while I give a short talk on Shakespeare. Our version of the greatest love story ever told (I know that is true because it is written on the posters) is scheduled to start soon.

The President of the College welcomes the cast. I receive an extravagant bouquet of flowers, my third that week. The play begins with Death, Cupid and live Renaissance music. Do they like it? Japanese audiences are famous for giving little away. Women are traditionally not supposed to laugh as it may reveal less than white teeth, and even today a young woman will cover her mouth when laughing. This reserve rather dents our comic scenes (and 'Romeo and Juliet' is a very funny play). The audience is so quiet that we actually wonder if they have vanished in the darkness of the auditorium. At last the lovers' suicides bring the audience back to life. It may be a cliché' but it is also a truth: suicide is big in Japan. (And if you don't believe me read Murakami's breakthrough novel, *Norwegian Wood.* Indeed, if you want to understand anything about modern Japan you should read Murakami). At the final lines...

Never was there a story of more woe
Than this of Juliet and her Romeo.

...the audience erupts into applause and many grab paper handkerchiefs to dry their eyes. The get-out is interrupted by endless requests for selfies. Potpan the clown is inundated, which is weird because for once he failed to raise a single laugh. Perhaps the Japanese have two lives, the internal one that laughs silently and reflects deeply, and the external life which is a perfect performance of conformity to the rituals and rules of this most structured society. So, theatre, especially non-realist theatre, whether it be Shakespeare or Kabuki, liberates the Japanese because it shows actors in control of their roles. Whereas in their everyday lives, the roles control the human.

We have parked the hired van in the underground car park of the college. When we have finished the get-out most of the audience accompany us, lining up against the back wall of the concrete car park (spotless as is all Japan). We honk the horn and wave as we drive slowly away and the assembled audience bow to us.

We first toured Japan with 'The Wizard of Jazz', which was invited to the Tokyo International Theatre Festival. A rather eccentric Hawaiian American producer then took us on a shoestring tour of the country. The Japanese have a passion for jazz; nowhere clearer than in the writings of Murakami. The production (described in detail elsewhere) featured two actors and a jazz quintet of some standing, notably trombonist John Kenny and guitarist Gary Boyle. Gary made his name in rock music, playing for Dusty Springfield and befriending Jimi Hendrix. His jazz albums sold better in Japan than the West and he regaled us with astonishing stories of record label sponsored tours of Japan in the 1980s where naked hostesses swam across warm pools towards surprised musicians. Gary is as modest as he is talented, and it takes a lot of work to winkle out his anecdotes of the heyday of the rock'n'roll whose vinyl you may own. He tells me that Japan saved his musical career, allowing him to branch out from Rock to Jazz, and that the Japanese market for Jazz albums has long surpassed that of the USA.

Drinking coffee in Japan is synonymous with listening to laid back jazz. The coffee is often served with a strange dish known as *hotto toasto*; very white toast served with melted butter and a little jam. The Japanese make everything their own, even hot toast.

On that same tour of 'Wizard' we stay in temple guest rooms above Kyoto. It might be to save money which is tight. Our temple is deep in the forest that surrounds this most exquisite of Asian cities. There were two actors in 'Wizard'; myself and Carlton, as talented, intense and charismatic as he is tortured. One night drinking alone, he forgets his way back into the forest. He hails a taxi but the driver speaks no English and there are five hundred temples in Kyoto. Eventually the kindly taxi driver deposits the well soused actor at a Police Station. The police give Carlton a cell for the night, taking care to keep the door unlocked. In the morning they serve their guest green tea and present him with a ceramic bowl in memory of his stay. Now able to phone the festival, they deliver him to the theatre in a large police car.

Japan alone among Asian countries has not fallen back on its ancient culture but developed new forms. Manga of course has swept the globe, reinventing the cartoon, rescuing the art from the cloying brush of Disney. In performance, the equivalent is Budō, a style of dance theatre which owes a great deal to Noh but is more personal and abstract. Its whitened figures arise from the ash of Hiroshima and Nagasaki. I spend a liberating week working with a Budō dancer, the title of whose one-man show is 'A Stone In Deep Water'. Budō, like much Japanese art, is about contrast and control, moving from very swift to very still movement, freezing in impossible postures, creating imagery that confronts the viewer rather than flatters itself. White is the colour of the actor's skin (they are semi-naked). White is the Japanese colour of death, which is the purest state of the soul, as it seeks release from the endless cycle of rebirth.

The ability of Japan to confront death in life is very particular. At funerals, families hand pieces of cremated bones to each other with chopsticks. In Gifu I meet a kamikaze pilot. He is the father of our producer in this city of anonymous high rises in central Honshu. In 1945 he was scheduled to fly to his death in a suicide attack on an American battleship. He made his farewells, drank ritual sake with his fellow pilots and was stopped by the commander on the way to his aircraft. He was running a fever. By the summer of 1945 aircraft were scarce and fuel scarcer. He was sent back to barracks and a friend took his place, never to return. Days later

Japan surrendered and he was never called to the runway again. Instead, he walked home to Gifu passing through what was left of Hiroshima. His mother had already arranged his funeral. She screamed when she saw him; for he was clearly a ghost. He carried on walking to the monastery above the town and became a monk, devoting his life to peace and bringing up his only daughter to be open to the world. She rose in the municipal administration of Gifu to heights not normally allowed to women in this male orientated society. She took the risk of inviting a British theatre company to her city. So here I am talking to her father, whose wrinkled face cracks into a smile as he offers me sake.

If Hiroshima is the defining moment of twentieth-century Japan, another epic human folly defines the twenty-first century: Fukoshima. The doomed atomic power station at Fukoshima lies close to the port city of Sendai, a few hours' drive north of Tokyo. The Sendai Shakespeare company is one of a kind in Japan, the only company dedicated entirely to the performance of Shakespeare, and a long-time host of TNT theatre. We have a booking in Sendai nine weeks after the earthquake and tsunami strikes the power plant leading to explosions and overheating in three of the six reactors and in the spent fuel pool. I recall sitting in Beijing by the Forbidden City lakes and asking the cast if they are prepared to proceed with the planned tour of 'Much Ado About Nothing'. They voted to go. We perform in a community hall that has, until recently, been used to house the victims of the Tsunami. I hesitate to say that we were the first entertainment from outside the area to arrive so close to Fukoshima, but we were certainly the first foreigners to offer something other than practical aid. But then we hope that art is practical, that art has a function that somehow lifts us above our animal needs.

'Much Ado About Nothing' is a curiously apt play for this audience: a comedy but almost a tragedy. An abused woman, named Hero, is given a false burial by her father. Claudio, her foolish fiancé, realises too late that he has been tricked into doubting her fidelity. He accepts penance before her tomb, only to find Hero is not dead but alive and forgiving. There is a great deal else in this most perfectly constructed of Shakespeare's comedies, and most of it is very funny. But in the shadow of Fukoshima, it is the story of Hero and Claudio that resonates.

Our 'Much Ado' is not the first Shakespeare play to attempt to heal the scars of this man-made disaster (why build a nuclear power station on a fault line by the open sea?). As they gather for beers after the performance, the cast are told of our hosts' own production of 'King Lear' that has been touring the area for several weeks. This seems to us a rather brutal play with which to heal the wounds of catastrophe. But we are wrong. The director, Kazumi Shimodate, changed the end of the play so that Cordelia and Lear survive the catastrophes that threaten to extinguish their fragile lives.

TNT's production of 'Much Ado About Nothing' onstage in Japan

Not far from Sendai in the mountains of northern Honshu lies a curious village named 'British Hills'. I am here to give workshops. When I step out of the hire car I am greeted by an extraordinary sight: a series of buildings ranging from the Elizabethan to the Victorian, all lovingly created by Welsh craftsmen. I am taken to my quarters in a faux Georgian house, where Laura Ashley wallpaper complements the soft furnishings and a free-standing bath lacks only an aproned maid with a scrubbing brush. When I descend to dinner, my way is barred until someone finds me a tie. Formality calms the Japanese; they assume the British are the same because we too have a monarch and live on an ancient island. I appear to be the only British person in British Hills. The food is relentlessly Japanese, a line has to be drawn somewhere.

I give my workshops the next day to three groups of teenagers who have been sent to this slice of 'Britain' to broaden their education. I know there is a similar fake Dutch town far away in southern Japan. I also know that many Japanese have little interest in travel, that this faux experience is quite enough. I once hitch-hiked with a successful doctor who had never left Japan and had no desire to do so.

The workshops go well enough, they usually do because Japanese students seldom have the opportunity to play at anything other than sport. My theatre games release their repressed sense of joy. School starts early in Japan, but many students go to a second cram school after their normal lessons end. Japanese kids are so exhausted it is expected that many will fall asleep in class. I once gave a lecture on 'Macbeth' in Osaka and perhaps half the audience were snoozing.

That evening I retire to the Falstaff pub. This could almost be a British pub except its toilets are too clean and its beer is too cold. Toilets in Japan are not only clean but often computerised, with heated seats, buttons for various hygienic squirts of water and even a volume dial to allow the sound of calling birds to drown out the shameful noise that human bodies emit. The Japanese are never free from their role, even in this most private place.

I am sitting at the bar eating wasabi crisps and downing an excellent 'nutty' draft Sapporo beer when I am joined by another foreigner; this being British Hills he hails from Northampton. I am further amazed to find that he is a type of actor. Possibly I am being kind, because he is also a type of conman, a fraud. But his fraud is willingly shared by his audience; for this man is a fake Christian priest of a denomination that does not exist. 'Brian', we will call him, used to be a teacher of English in Tokyo until someone suggested that his tall good looks would be better employed pretending to be an Anglican bishop and holding fake wedding ceremonies in chapels built expressly for that purpose. British Hills has a marvellous chapel and weddings and receptions are its bread and butter. Even swish hotels in Tokyo have fake churches where the Japanese bride can wear a Parisian wedding gown and be strewn with confetti after 'Brian' declaims a few words of union. The weddings are deadly earnest; but the couples have already been married by a Shinto priest. The Japanese have Shinto weddings and Buddhist funerals as one promises pagan fertility and the latter an afterlife. So why not add a Christian wedding? The costumes are more romantic than the wrapped Geisha look of the traditional Japanese bride. Organ music is popular too, and 'Brian' has a CD on sale.

I admire 'Brian'. In a land of endless theatricality, he has found a truly Japanese niche. Like many foreigners in Japan he speaks little of the language, his acting career is unthinkable outside the islands he has made his home. He can hardly cope with the demand for his performances; new fake chapels are shooting up across the country. This actor's career stretches comfortably into the future. But is the Japanese future comfortable? Their population is in decline, their modernity already looks a little jaded, Shanghai smells of the future not Osaka. Our own circuit is under pressure as universities close. Unlike the jolly Germans, the Japanese cannot say sorry to their neighbours, so Korea and China will have few of their goods. Immigrants are unwelcome; my dear friend Chris, who has lived and married in Japan for twenty years, can never be a Japanese citizen. It is as if the Japanese are trapped in a role and would rather expire than shed their costume.

I feel I should end these reflections on Japan with something positive. After all, Japan led TNT into Asia and I have never known anything but kindness there. I met Chris Summerville on a freezing train in deepest China, the first year that vast country opened to foreign tourists. He was teaching in a grim industrial city. He soon moved to Japan and married there, as many Westerners do. Intelligent Japanese women often look for a Western partner to escape the stifling role that their society imposes upon them. The Japanese word for wife can be translated as "One who walks behind". Chris lectures in environmental sciences, sorely needed in Japan where the fight to protect their gorgeous islands is often a losing battle with developers. At one point he and his wife moved to a depopulated village in the dense forests south of the ancient capital of Nara. There they were invited, after much local scrutiny, to be temple caretakers. The temple of Hozo Ji is a simple but beautiful wood and thatched building looking out over forests and paddy fields. I spent many happy weeks there during tours to Japan. Living in the temple was rather like camping in a wooden tent.

Heating was provided by a wood stove, the toilet was a drop into a hole. But at night I would roll out a futon on the tatami of the shrine room looked down on by smiling Buddhas and drift asleep to the piping of the bullfrogs in the flooded rice fields below.

One time the four-man cast of TNT's 'Murder of Sherlock Holmes' accompany me to Hozo Ji. We spend a rain-drenched day sliding heavy planks down muddy paths to a Zen archery temple on the opposite mountain. The master bow maker needs the wood. Then after a hot spring bath at a nearby Onsen, we gather at the temple with our fellow labourers. There we perform excerpts and music from the play to a local crowd. To describe the evening as magical does no justice to its spell. We had arrived in deepest Japan and been accepted into its depths by people who are as different from us as any on earth. We could not speak to them, but in this most theatrical of nations we could speak the language of drama and music to our hosts. And they did that most active of things – they witnessed. Arigato.

Chapter Seven: Company Politics

By Phil

Let's be very frank and 'up front' about something. While the acting companies that represent and that, for the purpose of performances, *are* TNT on stages around the world, are increasingly diverse, increasingly female, increasingly multi-ethnic in racialised identity, the core of the company is nothing like that. It rests on the friendship of two white men, formed well over forty years ago. That bond is as strong, if not stronger now, as it was then. We can't change that – our – identity; not in ourselves, but who knows what might happen when we, Paul and I, finally have to accept that there is an end to us, and maybe still a future for TNT?

There was one attempt to turn everything upside down and spread things every which way in TNT; after the tour of 'Cabaret Faust' in 1984 there was a rank and file uprising against the core... one of the performers called a meeting and won a majority of the acting company to reform the organisation as a co-operative. I was not informed of these events by those initiating them. Paul, as he describes below, accepted the majority verdict, but when the co-operative, or at least its main activist, declared the intention to revive an earlier and not very successful TNT production – 'Don't Look Back', based on the Russell Hoban novel *Kleinzeit* – Paul asked permission to mount another production, and that both companies be able to use the TNT name. He was given that permission. Left alone to develop their own company, the co-operative TNT never got as far as mounting anything.

Not because co-operatives are ineffective or impractical (there are many successful examples); but because they need some kind of human continuity and rooting. While the attempt to democratise TNT was done with the best of intentions, it didn't come with any practical commitment to, or resources for, co-operatively putting in the effort required to organise rehearsals and tour schedules, make collaborations and recruit new artists. In the austere and soulless world of what's 'out there', in order to put on generous, radical, liberal, body-centred, thoughtful and, occasionally, just plain odd theatre, it is necessary to have some kind of secure core that can just 'do the business', get things done. Not purposefully oppressive and malign, but centralised enough to book hotels for actors and secure fees and percentages of box office takes from theatres.

We may aspire to a far more liberal, egalitarian and supportive world, but we do not fool ourselves into believing that we are already living in it. Nor are we willing to give up the opportunity for others (actors, designers, musicians, composers) to express similar hopes for the sake of a structural change – a way of our doing things – that would threaten doing anything. To get performances that manifest generous ideas into difficult parts of the world without endangering performers is hard work. In the multiple contexts of a variously divided and conflicted world, it requires very committed individuals to take on an obsessive care, or at least have a drive to, to make it all happen safely. A good structure alone will not get you through; what is required is exceptional individual endeavour and the good fortune to find other exceptionally endeavouring artists who can work with each other, despite, or because of, the challenges and frictions.

TNT evolved from a walkout from another theatre company, with an oblique history in a previous attempt (Bristol Gate) to establish a company. There was never any coherent plan for how to structure the evolving TNT company. What eventually emerged was a flexible and inconsistent shape that places the control of complex ideas in the hands of one or two people, wedded to a porous rehearsal process which Paul was first wholly immersed in but which has since evolved to the point where the actors are expected to create the production with guidance rather than 'be directed into an interpretation'. Rehearsals are more like experimental works of discovery than efficient translations of texts into actions.

Administration still spills into the rehearsal room, just as in the early days. Even now rehearsals are interrupted by phone calls; 'Free Mandela' was plagued by the difficulty of obtaining Korean work permits.

The imperfect structure of TNT is partly historical; it reflects the company's struggle to survive in the Thatcherite neo-liberal period. It reflects our need for resilience; but also, as part of the same imperative, it requires a flexibility that allows a stage manager to go on as Mercutio – and do it well – when an actor is unable to travel because a visa office somewhere has unexpectedly confiscated both of their passports...

Not to speak of the crucial nature of the company's relationship with Grantly Marshall and the American Drama Group Europe. There is a clear division of labour between the two organisations; one in which there is zero interference from Grantly with the artistic work of TNT, except his demand that every production be successful, profound and popular... which is pretty much the same set of criteria we hold ourselves to.

What is Acting?

By Paul

> "Actors should display their brilliant skills to the public."
> Meyerhold.

> "Actors should not just act, they should observe themselves acting." Brecht.

I hesitate to quote myself in the above illustrious company but I sometimes tease actors or drama students with the opinion:

> "Acting is not about pretending to be somebody else."

In this chapter, I will talk about the basics of acting. I will ask what characters are and how we can make them; and I will consider what part a modern understanding of psychology should or should not play in their creation. I will describe what I think of the dominant Western approach to character-making – 'method acting' – and I will emphasise the importance of 'flow' for performance.

So, what is acting? We might begin to answer that with another question: where does acting start? In the brilliant BBC series 'How Art Made the World' it is pointed out that the first cave paintings were long thought to be illustrations of daily life in the Stone Age. But careful analysis has shown that these magnificent scenes are stories that contain magical creatures as well as the observed world. In other words, fiction is there at work within the very first recorded activity of humanity. We live inside both a concrete (I dislike the word 'real' but it cannot always be escaped this easily) and an imagined world. Most of our conversations are with ourselves inside our heads, we dream as we sleep, we invent as we observe, we imagine as we plan.

So the actor is a professional articulator of our shared and even common imagination. In the great square at Marrakesh it is still possible to watch the professional storytellers surrounded by an avid audience. These are clearly

'Ur' actors, living bridges between that cave art and the modern Netflix star. But as film and digital media pull us towards the pale imitation of the real, so the stage actor and especially the TNT performer should gravitate towards the Moroccan storyteller. We are operating in the same space that the storyteller occupies between the concrete and the imagined. Theatre is very concrete, it happens in real time. But what happens in real time, with real people and real props and costumes is there to stimulate the imagined. I remove a red balloon filled with water from the chest of the dying Harlequin and it is better than removing an imitation heart; the Alpine horn blowing deep notes is better than broadcasting a recording of a whale for the final scenes in 'Moby Dick'. I once performed a play about Vikings to primary school children, "Look, Look," I cried from the top of my schoolroom table turned ship, "there, there, the copper roofs of Byzantium gleaming in the sunset!" One hundred faces turned to look at the classroom wall behind them, saw Byzantium, and returned to gaze at me with wide eyes. Not one reacted angrily to a deception: the kids had seen the copper roofs.

We need to recover a child's sense of play, which is quite different from a PlayStation's sense of play. The digital world fills in our imagination while theatre must always expand the gaps in our fantasy, allowing our true self, oppressed as it is by the 'all too real' world, to create.

Why is the word 'play' used to define a stage text? Why were Shakespeare's performers 'players' not 'actors'? Why do the Germans call a theatre a 'Schauspielhaus' – that is a 'show play house'?

Let us return to the word 'player'. It helps us understand what acting is. To act is to do, but to play is to create another world and show it and be in it. My mother understands. She tells me that as a child of eight or so I would take a dustbin lid, a stick and a hat and march up and down in front of the reflecting windows of our house. Was I playing or was I performing? Who was the audience? If we can answer these questions we can come close to defining a performer, a 'player', and allow ourselves to be suspicious of the actor who acts a character so well we believe them to be real. Suspicious of those who encourage us to surrender the communal experience of theatre to individualised admiration and identification. The final destination of that process is Reality TV, where the passive viewer does not need actors because the amateur individual is better at pretending to be themselves than the professional actor.

What does this mean *practically*? Is this not just abstract theory that might help a director but leaves an actor all at sea? I happily admit that characterisation is a useful tool, but it should always be a stepping stone, a starting point that allows a performer to reach *another* level where the best acting takes place.

Very few writers or creators of drama are able to create poetry out of psychology. Maybe Chekhov. Most writers, including Shakespeare, have different aims and skills. Shakespeare is so brilliant at characterisation that he manipulates it at will and abandons it when it suits him; for example, any actor looking to find consistency in Lady Macbeth's history of motherhood, or in Iago's motivations for what he does, will stumble. Let us take as an example the famous scene between Hamlet and Gertrude. The apparent (or psychological) purpose of the scene is for Hamlet to successfully persuade (perhaps, force) his mother to take his side against her new husband, to refrain from sex with her husband and to admit to her shame. But the next time we see Gertrude she defends that same husband against Laertes, and hints strongly that it was Hamlet who was to blame for Polonius's death. So what does a performer do with this unexplained turnaround? Pursuing realism and characterisation, the actor stumbles; there is nothing there in the text, the change just happens. But seeing the scene between Hamlet and his mother as a poetic and imaginative exploration of some of the central themes of this greatest of plays will allow the performer to express the contradictions within Hamlet's mind that are exposed by a scene which lays bare that most troubled of souls. Sex, death, grief, loyalty, guilt, conscience, indecision and the battle of the generations are all revealed with shocking emotional violence and each of us in the audience and on the stage is pulled into a vortex of our own fears and lusts; passions and desires that a non-psychological performance can bring us to experience as simultaneously personal and collective.

Once Polonius is killed, the 'real' situation in Elsinore is hardly changed by this fabulous piece of poetic drama; it was never there to serve any other function – psychological or narrative – except to be simply what it is, in the moment of the shared encounters of these things by characters and audience together. It is in the now that the scene happens; that means that everything can change without following any rules for change. Perhaps something will break in Hamlet himself and his anger will subside just as the raging Laertes arrives to take his place. Yet, having pacified his troubled psyche, Hamlet is not released from chaos, for he now has to confront the deeper wound to Ophelia that will drag him to the edge of the grave (literally and poetically).

The performer playing Gertrude needs to do the difficult thing and stand back and see this whole, to be part of the head of Hamlet, to feed her own character into the wider context of this unrealistic (and yet deeply 'true') drama. She must observe her effect on Hamlet as Brecht would suggest. Eventually she will describe in detail the watery death of Ophelia, an impossible task for a naturalistic or psychological actor who will rightly wonder why Gertrude has such detailed information and why, indeed, either she or her source failed to dive into the stream to save the slowly drowning girl. But Gertrude is not a lifeguard, she is us and we are her; poetic and faulted and witnessing.

I don't believe that these problems are errors of Shakespeare. I think Shakespeare would loathe the endless Netflix and HBO series where plot is sacrificed to characterisation. The soap opera star gradually morphs into the reality TV celebrity. Banality replaces imagination. Acting vanishes.

No one understood this better than Arthur Miller, who is often rightly held up as a master of characterisation. But, like Shakespeare he subordinates this skill to a wider imaginative project. In his extraordinary autobiography, *Timebends* (1987), he more or less accuses Lee Strasberg and his realist school of acting of the break-up of his marriage and the death of Marilyn Monroe. Marilyn was a consummate performer, reaching out to her audience by exposing her vulnerability. She is unblocked. She plays against and with the image of herself. She can be manipulative and weak and shift between these contradictions in an instant. This self-knowledge allows her to see what she is doing as she does it. She can play gawky naivety with razor-like precision. Her tragedy was that she felt inadequate in the thing she did best: stylised acting. Lee Strasberg tried to turn her into a psychological performer that the world would take seriously. Miller accuses Strasberg of feeding off this and driving her away from her true abilities, her true self and her true love. Confused in life and art she stumbled into death. A modern Ophelia.

There is pretend and play, but sometimes the stakes are very high. Grotowski said to me that acting is about unblocking, allowing a flow of feeling and thought to manifest itself. He also said that acting is like sculpture, a stripping away. It is not how we usually think of painting, as a layering up, but like when the painter scrapes away top layers to reveal colours and textures that already lie beneath. The best actors I have worked with have a quality of natural 'flow'; they sweep over blocks like a river in flood. They get on a roll. I would like to think in my acting days I experienced that on stage myself. To enable this, the actor must focus absolutely on their movement and text, engaging their whole body and mind. This is why physical theatre is ideal; a sweating actor who throws themselves around the stage is far more likely to engage their energy and imagination than a seated figure in a drawing room. Get off the chair, get out from behind that table; dive into the gaps in the action and don't hug the scenery! Perspiration is inspiration.

One of the things an actor has to do is learn to let go. In training sessions with Grotowski's Laboratorium or Barba's Odin Teatret, I was taught or encouraged to develop this flow, to work on repeated exact movement patterns interspersed with extreme physical activity. This is also the root of Japanese Budō dance training: explosions of energy followed by periods of extreme control are very exciting to watch and perform. We can see this in film actors we admire: Brando in 'On The Waterfront' or Robert De Niro in 'Taxi Driver' seem to have an almost jazz-like quality, as if they are syncopating a rhythm in their movement and speech. And, of course, Brando and De Niro hardly bother with characterisation, they are clearly Brando and De Niro in a role. The role comes second, they bring the Brando or the De Niro quality to their fictional character, hold a space between the two, and observe the role from their own unchanging self.

Every actor should study Charlie Chaplin, perhaps the most complete actor of all. Watch his complex performance in 'City Lights' and remember that he is directing and acting in front of you, the ultimate observer of the self, at once absolutely in the moment and observing the moment. An artist unblocked. Not so famous – though she starred in a number of films of the 1920s and 1930s – but equally alive in her body was Nellie Wallace, a music hall and variety performer who was part inspiration for the role of Sally in 'An English Tea Party'; trained as a clog dancer, she was known as 'The Essence of Eccentricity', animating her face in waves of contortion, while snaking about the stage on her back in a savagely tight skirt. Such was her display of joyous artificiality and ecstatic contrivance that she was able to play pantomime dames – a role usually reserved for male comedians.

Such models from theatre and live performance, as opposed to film, are much harder to describe and discuss because there is less shared experience of live performance. How do we prove the pudding? But I can try: I was fortunate to work with Jonathan Pryce when I was a child actor at the Nottingham Playhouse in its heyday, where Richard Eyre directed and David Hare, Trevor Griffiths and Howard Brenton were the 'in-house' writers. Perhaps the best performance I ever saw on the British stage was the original production of Griffiths' 'Comedians'. The play is based around a comedy class at a northern adult education centre led by a fading comedian (played by an actual fading music hall star: Jimmy Jewel.) Pryce's character challenges the old comedian to make his work more aggressive and radical; others in the class object. The second act moves on to the class's graduation performance at a local club. Contrasting acts are presented to the audience, the brilliant but conventional comedian (played by the great Stephen Rea) seems to be coming home with the prize. Then Jonathan Pryce's character takes the stage dressed as a skinhead clown. His act is brilliant and violent, radical and confrontational. The old comedian's heart breaks as he recognises the truth upon the stage is an echo of his younger self. In the final act the old comedian, now alone with his skinhead student, confesses to his sexual arousal while liberating Belsen concentration camp and the dark heart of laughter – with no simple liberation from horrors and anxieties – is brilliantly analysed. Pryce's performance was all that I am trying to define here: physical and subtle, direct yet complex, aggressive but caring, profound and hilarious. And these opposites were exposed to us in a rhythmic performance of great skill, at once flowing and easy yet controlled and precise. A great artist in command of a great artistry, by which the very difficult and usually repressed contents of Griffiths' text are made possible.

Years later Pryce discovered a skill for tap dancing that he brought to West End musicals. I too used to tap dance in the early TNT success '1945!' or 'An English Tea Party'. I think this dancing is simply a manifestation of the rhythmic underpinning of any true performance, superficially 'realistic' or otherwise. TNT was once awarded a prize at a Music Festival for a performance of 'An English Tea Party' during which the only instruments played were spoons and tea cups. Rhythmic underpinning and spoken verse have always been part of the work. And if we need other examples then we look to Asia, where Kathakali, Kabuki and Kechak theatre are all performed to the insistent beat of the drum. The profusion of K's in these genres rather proves the point!

If rhythm is the essence and core of this idea, then how much more important is the shared rhythm upon a stage that makes great acting possible. When I tease actors about disliking character, I am also trying to drive them towards seeing that the group is greater than the individual. Soccer players with brilliant individual skills will endure relegation if their team cannot play as a unit. Actors who shine at the expense of their colleagues create dead theatre. Naming no names, I know from actors who have worked at one of Britain's best companies that one star performer had a dressing tent set up at the side of the stage so that he might avoid his fellow artists; memorably screaming at a young actor during a production of 'Macbeth' "I am the King, never walk towards me!"

Within TNT we have had actors who the audience enjoyed, but we knew were acting only with the audience, ignoring eye contact or inter-reaction with their fellow artists and who 'downstaged' their fellow performers.

Downstaging defined: to over-act in the vicinity of the audience while ignoring your fellow performers.

TNT works with choreographers on almost every production, not to integrate dance but to work on shared patterns and rhythms and, for example, to turn scene changes into performance pieces whose beat will extend beyond the task of moving set pieces into the surrounding scenes. Actors are all aware of the importance of breath, but we also need to attend to the heartbeat by which we all are able to breathe and whose rhythm underpins our very life.

A story about Meyerhold and Stanislavski

(This may or may not be fiction, but either way it reveals a truth.)

Stanislavski is directing Meyerhold in the premier of Chekhov's 'Three Sisters'. It is a very long rehearsal period; months and months are spent investigating every aspect of the play, the psychology and characterisation. Stanislavski seeks an almost photographic realism. One day, Meyerhold is trying to capture the frustration of his character. He is failing. Stanislavski pushes him to be more real, more truthful. Stanislavski suggests that Meyerhold tries opening a bottle of wine to express this moment. Meyerhold agrees to try. But instead of allowing this simplest of domestic acts to inform his frustration, Meyerhold exaggerates the physical action and times his speech to end as the cork pops from the bottle. "No, no!" cries Stanislavski, "that is not real!"

"Yes, yes!" replies Meyerhold, "this action expresses perfectly the frustration of the character, and I have involved my whole body!"

Soon afterwards, the two great artists split and never worked together again. TNT would always pop the cork with Meyerhold.

A true story about Paul Stebbings

In the early years of TNT we were invited to perform 'An English Tea Party' (sometimes '1945!') Off-Broadway in New York. In the play I performed the role of a broken down music hall artist in this Vaudeville nightmare, set on the last day of the Second World War. I tap danced in my untutored way. My mix of skill and clumsiness seemed to me to capture my character and serve the nightmare. A famous African American dancer came to the performance and came to speak to me after the curtain call.

"Great left foot!" he smiled. "Shame about the right!"

I would always remain half a dancer. My Broadway dancing dream rose and died in a heartbeat.

Writing for TNT

By Phil

What could be more individual and subjective than writing?

Well, if writing for TNT were the norm for writing for the theatre... many things! For writing scripts for TNT is not about the unique and individual vision of the solo playwright. To begin with, there are almost always at least two of us writing. More importantly, the writing is always something more like assembling a jigsaw puzzle from many pieces than conjuring a unique vision from scratch. Though any originality we might have lies in just such a choice of convivial assemblage over inspired vision. Plus, of course, it all has to 'flow'.

So let's talk about 'assemblage'. This may be anathema to most people's idea of what writers should do: a lone genius drawing on their own recollections or subconscious fantasies to craft something in words. In TNT it has always been different. From the very beginning we have shared, written and refined convivially. I remember how in 1981, Paul and I found time between workshop sessions with Eugenio Barba of Odin Teatret (Barba, like Robert Wilson, Hesitate and Demonstrate and a handful of others, might be seen as inheritors of the symbolist strand in Meyerhold's art of theatre) at Cardiff Laboratory Theatre to work on the script for our second show, '1945!' It would be dishonest of us to pretend we were not informed in our choices and additions to that first draft by the dramaturgy we were witnessing dissected in workshops by day and illuminated by performances at night. We were not 'lifting' or plagiarising speeches or actions but were inspired by the principles we saw applied.

We have *been* plagiarised. In 1983, a New York cable TV company came and filmed our '1945!' performed Off-Broadway. Although nothing came of the promised tape, a few years later an American audience member in Germany excitedly told Paul that he seen the same play in New York the year before.... and, years later, someone niftily lifted our staging idea for one of our shows and drafted it into a very successful touring production of the same play. But, hey, we are artists not lawyers. In the arts, stealing often happens without the thief even knowing. There's a name for that; 'culture'. In fact, the biggest plagiarisers of our work are ourselves.

In 1975, I saw Paul perform a piece of agit-prop theatre in support of students occupying an elite building in our university to demand the provision of a nursery for the young children of students. Paul was portraying the Vice Chancellor of the university as a red-nosed clown and the fake red nose on his nose fell off. He picked it up, looked at it and quipped "it's no skin off my nose". Big laugh. Years later, the same gag was used by Paul in his role of Stalin/*Il Dottore* in our 'Harlequin'; a signal to the audience that this is 'rough' theatre, this is not the 'clean' appearance of an authoritarian art; this could be being performed (and was) in the street; this is an art where things go wrong, where you are openly tricked, where you should distrust us just as much as those we satirise; where you need to think for yourself not just follow the action.

Many of our early scripts were built around existing non-theatre texts – popular songs, patriotic slogans, jokes, comic routines, snatches of poems – and drew on a range of contrasting theatre conventions and genres of performance. These genres are usually blended together in the same performance. In the absence of an identifiable authorial voice and with our sudden disruptions of narrative by gigantic switches of genre – from music hall to melodrama to holy theatre – it might seem surprising that we were not immediately identified as a 'postmodern theatre' and hived off into an artistic backwater for critical praise. We, however, lacked a key qualification for that kind of preferential treatment: our shows were popular and accessible. No matter how many frames we collapsed, or forms we switched across (from documentary to inner soliloquy to tap dance to choral recitation) we always tried to ensure that everyone in the audience was following what was going on. It was (and is) not always easy for our audiences, but we have never intentionally neglected to include them in. If the form is difficult then the content is simple and clear, if the content is complex then the form is simple and clear. And they get to laugh.

We consider our audience as co-writers. At the time when we began writing this book, in 2019, I was working with Paul on an adaptation of the novel *Crooked Letter, Crooked Letter* by Tom Franklin; a story of family, racism, friendship and betrayal in a small Mississippi town. Paul wrote the first draft and then we bounced rewrites – big and small – back and forth between us. This is our usual way; punctuated by occasional long phone calls. This time, however, we actually wrote the final version (or at least what we thought would be) sat side by side in Munich. But no play script is ever finished, it is only ever in the 'latest version'; the acid test of the rehearsal room (not to speak of the first audiences) can bring down a favourite idea or exalt a wild guess or an old gag into a key moment of change, a hinge for the action to swing around.

On this occasion, however, we did not even get to the rehearsal room; I had a phone call from Paul with a few extra questions about the 'final' draft. So I worked through the whole thing one 'last' time. As I tweaked the final lines of the play, a moment of very difficult recognition between two characters and something like the beginnings of reconciliation and mutual forgiveness, I was weeping tears onto my lap as I typed. Not in relief at finishing the writing, but in anticipation of the feelings that I felt the audience would be going through as the words were turned by the actors into actions. This is a feeling I have had many times; a sign I have never known to be deceptive. I get it because as I write I am imagining the actors' bodies inhabiting the lines and actions, and feeling in my body the back and forward of responses, from actors to audience, from audience to actors. So although the subsequent audience may not even have heard of the title of the play at the time of its writing, they are already working as co-writers on it.

We may not bow down at the altar of the 'great author', but we are not ashamed of subjectivity; neither our own nor that of others. We celebrate and admire many individual writers and artists and activists – Cervantes, Melville and Rosa Parks. Our own contributions have always been inflected by our own preferences for the sounds and ordering of words. Our first production, 'Harlequin', was hung around the structures of Italian *commedia dell'arte,* but no performance in that style would ever before have looked like or sounded like ours. Even though we were often stitching and mashing and pasting from multiple sources, there was still choice and love in our decisions. In those earliest scripts – for which Paul set the tone – there were snippets of text from poems by Mayakovsky and Anna Akhmatova, excerpts from a Chekhov play, soliloquies from English music hall stars and Stalin was re-imagined as *Il Dottore* which was another plagiarism of ourselves! We were stealing the character of The Doctor, who revives the fallen knight, from Bristol Gate Theatre's staging of a Mummer's Play in around 1978. Except that in 'Harlequin', rather than a reviving medicine (representing the coming of spring and summer and the warding off of the cold and stasis of winter) our Doctor's practice (gulags, torture and silencing) was of the most frigid and murderous kind.

We have always been thieves of style and unique creators; poets and rascals. This is not a publicity pose, it is our way of working. The activity on the stage is the 'thing' of writing, the rough and ready racing of bodies, the yelling of exclamations – in many of our scripts the percentage of lines that end in exclamation marks is very high. We do not write polite conversations!!! We are scooping up epithets from the gutter. The author – you might believe from our method – is dead. But the collective art of theatre is not. Our work as co-writers is to create a playground on which the actors can swing; just as our set designer must make an acting machine on which the actors can balance and tense their bodies dynamically. The work of the watchers in the auditorium is to make sense of all this, intuiting the dynamic of bodies and drama and draw some meaning from the direct impression and the subsequent reflection on the actors in character, based on the evidence of story, props, dance, poetry and all the rest. The writers' work is making sure that 'all the rest' – the texture and timbre – is working for the whole.

Assemblage is, again, the key. It is the dynamic between our two dominating modes as writers – creativity and *bricolage* – mixing and matching, cobbling and contriving, until in the rehearsal space our dead text is conjured by the actors into what passes, in theatre, for life. Chance plays a major part in all this. But there is also craft. Each piece of the text, each line, each stage direction, must be of precisely the correct shape for the whole picture to hang together; that's tricky given that we have no record of the picture before we start assembling.

A writer sitting at a desk writing does not look much, but unless there is a whole tactile love affair going on inside that sedentary skin, the connections between all the parts of the script are not going to fit together. And – let us be frank – we do not get it right every time. We are only ever a keystroke away from boredom and confusion.

This can be tough. Get things wrong and you sink a show. In Hong Kong in 1996, with a brilliant conceit, we nearly sank one of our longest running productions, 'A Christmas Carol', almost before it was launched. (Don't worry. It is still going, 23 years later!) It was my mistake! I had the idea that all the dead characters in the novel, the many ghosts who feature so prominently in Dickens's tale, should become the narrators of the drama. Yet, ghosts could have no part in Scrooge's change from miser to joyful benefactor; they were always on the wrong side of the line between change and being stuck. Yes, they could enhance the horror of the tale, but they could not bring it to fruition. As in 'Hamlet', the ghosts were not very good at getting things done.

All artists, writers included, should have the right to fail. Without experiment – including wild and irresponsible chance-taking – there is no advance, no growth, no development. However, in TNT we have chosen, and been, at least partly, forced into self-sufficient financing. There is little in the way of a safety net for us any more. Even a small dip in box office success and the money basis of the operation that has taken our work to so many disparate peoples, will crumble. So, somehow, every time we write we must combine the invention of an unfettered improvisation with the creation of a cast-iron text that will be accessible, producible, repeatedly unveiling itself to actors, and a riveting drama for spectators.

At the same time, every time, we must provide something that we have not provided before. Given the necessary blend of intuitive creation and solid technique, there is little room for panic measures or copying. Fall back on what you know, and you may find yourself falling on your back. Favour craft over intuition and you are likely to wander off into flabby repetition. Favour your intuition over your technique and you may go swanning off into self-indulgence. But get the balance right and that may not help you either! Because it's not about the blueprint, it's about the 'building'. Every commission is unique and you had better treat it with the respect that uniqueness deserves.

So, how have we succeeded, at least in keeping the operation afloat on a sea of ticket sales for all these years?

Firstly, we found a producer in Grantly Marshall who shared many of our ideals and has a vision of theatre that is more important to him than his bank balance.

It has also been our good fortune not only to have had the right teachers but also the right combinations of skilled collaborators with whom we have had the privilege to work. It is so much easier to write when you have confidence in those who come after you in the process to take your dead letters and fill them with something like the aspirations you had for them. Artists like Eric Tessier Lavigne, who has been choreographer, dancer, actor and organiser for TNT for twenty years.

The multitude of influences that have cascaded down to us – thanks to teachers who were friends, thanks to friends who were teachers – may have occasionally blended into a brown muddy soup, but, thankfully, more often the combinations have created kaleidoscopes, many colours in weaves and webs of lines and patterns, pigments and iridescences.

Our backgrounds in practical theatre-making have been keys to our lives as writers. Paul and I were both rooted in popular theatre, then at university we studied the modernists, but also the medieval and Elizabethan canon, and never saw any reason not to regard them all as modern – right here, right now – like all good performance.

Paul is a classicist, I am a romantic. Paul likes Bach, I prefer Beethoven. We are always creatively at war; but there has never been a cross word between us. We are masculine and feminine. We are radical and conservative. But we are never quite sure which one of us is which. We have written together for forty years and yet we have never argued, only discussed. If one of us questions the other, we usually assume that the criticism warrants a rewrite. We take each other very seriously. And we laugh together and at each other. We know we are fools trying to understand serious – often life and death – things, and we are no better than the 'worst' member of our audience. We just happen to know a little about how to write; like the electrician knows how to rewire the house or the nurse knows how to administer the anaesthetic.

But that is so much sentiment; nice words. What of hard technique? What are the nuts and bolts that have got us through? What do we do that offers something to anyone else writing their own plays? Well, nothing is simple. So, yes, there are some tricks, strategies, craft, craftiness, sleight of hand, and make believe. But it always has to be done anew every time – rest on your laurels and you will find yourself rolling backwards over the cliff's edge. Then you *really* need something to grab onto. Let us talk about frames. The narrative device that tops and tails the show, sets up the story and then, at best, reappears near the climax of the show and abolishes itself in order to lift the action to a new level. Get a frame right and you will empower your story (you should give it at least two levels all the time). The in-the-moment performance is made dynamic by never being straightforward, but always the content of the frame. Put in an unnecessary frame (as I did in 'A Christmas Carol') and you can drag the whole thing down.

'The Murder of Sherlock Holmes' (1993) is an example of a successful frame. The proposal for its production was rejected for support by the Arts Council England; yet it went on to give more than a thousand performances worldwide. In 2016 Paul redirected the play in Mandarin at the Shanghai Dramatic Arts Theatre; booked to play for eighteen nights it ran for sixty and then transferred to the National Theatre in Beijing. Arts bureaucrats, they can always spot a winner....

So, what worked there? As always with successes there was good fortune, but there were also repeatable technical things. To start with, 'Sherlock Holmes' was 'rough'. Although many of the elements of the narrative performance would be familiar to anyone even slightly aware of Arthur Conan Doyle's detective stories, they had been twisted and re-configured and hurled into the gutter from which they were forced to raise themselves up by their own dirty bodice laces. What was already a popular milieu – a nineteenth-century London detective story – was forced to reclaim itself from our traducing; as the audience watched the machine of the Conan Doyle phenomenon crank itself back into life, its mechanics were exposed to our audience and we could use them for our own – rather than Conan Doyle's – purposes.

We could uncover some of the secrets of the original texts: for example, that Holmes's redoubtable sidekick Doctor Watson was based on a real military doctor who had been one of the few survivors of a terrifying retreat from Afghanistan, which echoed Britain's current disaster in that shattered country. This discovery allowed us to write a soliloquy for Watson, as he boats along the Thames and discovers, to his horror, "an Afghanistan in the heart of London". The affects and effects of colonialism are ever present traumas for all who live in Britain and – perhaps because there has been no attempt to get over it – there has, as yet, been no getting over it. The cautionary tale of 'The Murder of Sherlock Holmes' continues to apply.

The frame and setting of the play (which is described in more detail in Chapter Eight) was a Victorian London brothel (a common institution in the supposedly puritan landscape of a hypocritical and paedophile society). The male managers of this institution are joined by a cross-dressing playwright to put on a performance to prove to themselves and their clientele – (the audience!) – that they are all innocent of the murder of the prostitutes in the brothel. Here it is. At the most basic level – life and death – the modus operandi of a society is stripped bare; power is shown exacted on the bodies of women by a company of men. Yet this is a comedy – for the men in control (among whom there is not just the actual murderer, but in which they are a collective murderer) will eventually expose their own crimes, blurting out their own self-immolating truth the more they seek to disguise it. And there it is; if writing is about anything for us, it is about our academically unreliable and critically unrespectable loyalty to a kind of truth-telling that is energised by what we know is the nervousness of the powers-that-be to certain histories, stories and presences. Histories and stories and presences in which we, as white, privileged, male artists are complicit. This is not the holy part of theatre, this is us trying to tell some truth from the dirt in which we stand.

So, we are not going to pretend we do not contradict ourselves. While our greatest (declared) enemy is the naturalistic performance of everyday life – the kind of acting and action you will see in TV soap operas – we are not above momentarily and partially making our characters out of the same recognisable materials. Then we pull them apart and expose the repetitions involved in their doing so much and changing so little.

Is there a philosophy that underpins all this soul-searching? No. Or only in the very minor sense that the same frisson that makes a character interesting to an audience is the same dynamic that drives us to keep looking for solutions in apparently impossible situations: freedom in the face of oppression, justice in the face of cheating, healing in the face of violence. Never showing solutions, even if we think we have found one; instead, make that looking – rather than dictating – the heartbeat of our theatrical body.

The Writing Process

By Paul

Phil and I have shared the creation of scripts since working on 'Harlequin' in 1980. There are no rules, as befits our efforts to break new ground. We discuss a project, then one of us writes a first draft. In his role as TNT's dramaturg, Phil will tend to stand back and analyse meaning while I work at the 'coal face' of rehearsal and change the text again and again. This can frustrate actors who ask for a fixed script, but we are merciless and even change dialogue after a premier. To us "All text is pre-text". Words on paper allow us to approach the production which is hidden inside a large stone. The words are tools, not an end in themselves. This is true not just of our own work such as the recent 'Free Mandela', but of Shakespeare and hallowed texts by more recent authors we dare not name in case our approach offends the staid guardians of copyright, estate and the dictatorship of the text. Surely theatre does not exist only to stage the works of writers (who are supposed to emerge from their attics with a fully-fledged play ready for a humble production company)? The result can only be realism and endless rewrites of 'Look Back in Anger'.

A standard TNT text will go through many drafts, ping-ponged between me and Phil. Writing and rewriting will be done after or during rehearsal. The script on day one of 'Free Mandela' was 75 pages long. By the premier it had shrunk to 40, much of it different. Same intentions, better realisations.

The play script we begin rehearsals with is similar to the pencil drawings beneath an oil painting. Phil and I have always approached theatre from different angles. Phil has an academic frame of mind. He is also a performance artist and a prolific writer. I am an actor, director and manager. I have a strong relationship with music and dance; Phil is attuned to imagery and symbol. He explores ideas and the borders of performance; I am an amateur historian. We both seek physical expression, he through walking as performance, I through long-distance cycling. We both need to contact the earth and see walking and cycling as parallel activities to theatre. Since a cyclist has the pace of a horse rider, the way we choose to travel links us to the natural rhythm of the human, just as live performance is the most natural of art forms. In this way, through our bodies, our New Theatre is also Old, as old as the hills.

Chapter Eight: 'The Murder of Sherlock Holmes', 'Frankenstein', and 'Dracula and the Eco-Warrior'

By Phil

The success of 'The Murder of Sherlock Holmes' lifted the company onto a new level of popularity. It changed everything for the company. Not simply on account of its own effects, but because of how it allowed new things to happen and new people to engage with us. Crucially, it began a relationship with Grantly Marshall and the American Drama Group Europe. There would be no company, nor this book, without Grotowski, but the same is equally true of Grantly Marshall and the American Drama Group Europe. Without them, it is hard to believe that TNT would not by now have hit an immovable financial obstacle and the whole cultural and artistic experiment have ended with a trashing of theatrical 'test tubes'.

At the same time, it was the artistic qualities of 'Murder' that were crucial. It was the *kind* of theatre that we were making – and are still developing – that drew us together with others and took us forward. While that adventure would take us along unexpected avenues – pioneering Shakespeare to Chinese provinces, repurposing verbose Shavian comedy for the #MeToo generation – we have produced a string of 'rough theatre' productions, with affinities with 'Murder', all drawing iconic characters from crime and horror fiction into earthy original dramas of ideas and morals.

'The Murder of Sherlock Holmes' takes the complacent illusion of Arthur Conan Doyle's fiction – that one could investigate crime in 1880s' London and somehow avoid the realities of murderous poverty, ubiquitous prostitution and widespread child sex abuse behind the Victorian facade of respectability – and then rubs it in the faces of his iconic characters: Sherlock Holmes and Doctor Watson. Though, in one sense, neither of these characters appear in 'Murder'.

The setting for the play is a large room in a London brothel, scene of the murders of a number of its young female prostitutes. The actual theatre auditorium is treated by the actors as part of this room. The four characters of the play are Sweller the brothel owner, Jack Claw the bouncer and enforcer, Pip Pratt the young musician and general dogsbody, and Nathan, a transvestite poet who has been recruited to write an entertainment. Given the inability of anyone – police or brothel staff – to identify the murderer and thereby clear the name of the brothel and its staff, Sweller hits on the idea of staging a play, a crime drama. Written by Nathan and acted by the four men, based around Conan Doyle's famous characters, this play-within-the-play is to argue that, rather than any single perpetrator being responsible for the killings, "society is to blame, and therefore everyone is innocent".

(from left to right) Paul Stebbings, Greg Banks and Joe Hall, Tom Johnson (back) in TNT's 'The Murder of Sherlock Holmes'

There are already some key elements here for our 'rough' strand of drama that will reappear elsewhere in our work:

Dodgy characters; 'rough theatre' is peopled by fools and sinners. There are no saintly intellectuals to speak the message of the play. Mostly the characters do not understand their situation. Instead, the truth is shown accidentally. Lies and tricks and disguises inadvertently reveal the truth that they are intended to hide. Comic incompetence rather than virtue is the flame that lights up the murk. Truths are blurted out of the mouths of stupid charlatans, who in trying to conceal things with too much artfulness only succeed in 'giving the whole game away'.

Framed performance: whether a play-within-a-play, a lecture interrupted ('Frankenstein') or a visualisation of the digital world of Second

Life ('Dracula'), these framed sequences in 'rough theatre' are not showing real people, but *showing the showing* of real people. Strangely, this apparently complicated frame frees up performance itself. The actors can act directly to the audience, sit in their laps, haul them up on stage to become part of the action for a while. The actors do not have to copy real people, but can use the *tricks, jokes, gymnastics, excesses and energy of performance itself* to open up the heart of the play. This frees actors from imitation and at times these sequences take on the feel of free jazz improvisation, when the plot almost disappears and the actors communicate in 'pure' uproarious emotional communication unhindered by logical meaning.

The action of 'Murder' switches back and forth between Nathan's play – presented, the audience are told, to an audience of the brothel's well-heeled clients (i.e. the real audience itself) – and a side room where the characters gather between their 'Holmes and Watson' scenes. The action of Nathan's play – a murder mystery like that in the real world of the brothel – backfires on its performers, as the fictional detection of a crime begins to close in too closely upon the real crimes in the brothel. All the characters fall under suspicion. At the end, the murderer is revealed, but the message of TNT's play, different from that of the characters, is that while 'society is to blame' no one is innocent. As in some of our other original dramas and adaptations – 'Cabaret Faust', 'Moby Dick', 'Wizard of Jazz', for example – all the characters are effectively destroyed, at the curtain either their bodies are destroyed or their lives are effectively at an end. For all the smiles these shows conjure, these are tragedies where we ask the audience to face the reality of sufferings and of injustices that do not end.

The script of 'Frankenstein: The Monster and the Myth' (2005) is as stitched together as the monster at the centre of its action. We began from the assumption that members of the audience were more likely to know this tale from its various movie versions than from Mary Shelley's gothic novel. So, while staying true to the themes of Shelley's story – particularly its monster's philosophical quest to discover the meaning of its existence – we drew on Classic Hollywood movies to draw the audience onto familiar ground, and then to put some shocks through the tale.

We began with an easy target: overbearing and materialist science seduced by the arrogant conviction that if a thing is possible it must be done. We soon moved the action onto far less certain ethical ground. In a snowy waste we showed the monster and its maker arguing about the resilience of a desire to exist even at the cost of deep suffering, and the responsibility of a creator, once begun, to continue his work. Even on that frigid tundra came the drive of life to continue and reproduce. The monster demands a bride for himself, but Dr Frankenstein refuses. At the climax of the show, in a sharp, posthuman twist, when Frankenstein's fiancée is murdered by the monster, the scientist reanimates her. However, faced with choosing either a reanimator or a monster for a husband, the resurrected Elizabeth chooses a future with monsters and her abandoned scientist-husband is killed by an angry populist mob.

Deploying a full gamut of gory effects and the emotional excesses of melodramatic acting, 'Frankenstein' exemplifies a particular quality of our 'rough' theatre: the staging of high ideals and noble content in the most unrespectable and abject of guises. To watch this play is to see buckets of stage blood and dismembered human organs hauled around the stage, to watch electrocution and grave robbery; but it is also to hear complex philosophical ideas. There are ideas here about cloning and the morals and consequences of advanced research, such as that into the uses of stem cells. But there are also ideas that do not come out of books, but out of the hard and dirty processes of existing: from feeling bitter cold, from scavenging food, from desperate feelings of loneliness and unsatisfied desire.

Where 'Murder' and 'Frankenstein' are roughly true to the original settings of Conan Doyle's and Shelley's fictions, 'Dracula and the Eco-Warrior' (2016) wrenches Bram Stoker's 1897 horror out of its late Victorian backdrop and hurls it into the contemporary debate on climate change. It satirises climate change denial and asks what, if the vast majority of scientists are broadly correct, to do about climate change and how to do it. The latter part is perhaps most crucial. After all, we might think if climate change is an illusion, then there is no problem; and if it is a reality, that there is probably no time left for arguing with sceptics when we should be rapidly making plans and calmly implementing them.

TNT's 'Dracula' challenges both scenarios by exploring a more painful truth that any successful solution to the approaching ecological catastrophe has to be found somewhere among the same malicious mechanics that have produced the ecological problems and global threats in the first place.

The detection melodrama of the Sherlock Holmes stories helped to peel away the hypocrisy and misogynistic violence at the heart of Sweller's representative establishment. The gothic thrills and inversions of the Promethean tale of 'Frankenstein' are swift and popular ways to big ideas about existence and bioscience. In 'Dracula and the Eco-Warrior', it is the popular myth of vampiric annihilation (from Vlad the Impaler to 'Twilight') that brings us quickly to global ecological mass extinction. The basic vampire idea poses an existential threat, because it can spread its predation indiscriminately from biter to bitten who in turn are transformed into biters. However, the horror of TNT's 'Dracula' is less this vision of cumulative infection stemming from Count Dracula the vampire (updated in the play to a rust-belt industrialist trying to shift to e-commerce), but rather how his *modus vivendi* (or, perhaps, that should be *modus destruendi*) prevails even among those who are seeking to find solutions to the problems his industries have caused. Then Dracula presents his own solution; at first, by promising to invest in an exemplary town transitioning to sustainable living. But then, when he seems to betray this cause, Dracula reveals a deeper affinity with the ecologists: they both hate humans. The Vampire-Demon and the Earth Goddess Gaia, he suggests, are two sides of the same anti-human coin.

'The Murder of Sherlock Holmes', 'Frankenstein' and 'Dracula and the Eco-Warrior' have been among our most popular shows. At the time of writing (2020), 'Frankenstein' was on tour again (until Covid-19 halted all our tours). For audiences these shows contain some of the most emotionally and intellectually challenging materials of any production we have made. It is a testimony to the capability of large and popular audiences to engage with hard, tragic materials when presented the Meyerhold way. While these shows may not have the stylistic integrity and obvious seriousness of productions like 'American Dreams and Nightmares' or 'My Sister Syria', all three are tragedies disguised as romps that leave their characters in tatters. From under the smiles, the gross melodramas and the broad knockabout routines, all three ask their audiences to stare the tragedy of the world – hatred of women, the burdens of just being, the rush to global self-destruction – right in the face. Because these shows are so serious, and yet are rooted in genres of popular performance and literature – crime adventure, gothic horror, melodrama – they can unexpectedly enthuse even the least interested audience member into engagements with hard things. These productions are TNT's 'gateway drugs'; if the company can hook you on these it can lead you to Shakespeare and far beyond.

Chapter Nine: La Belle France

By Paul

I climb the stairs in Plaisance, Paris. The scene is one from a Zola novel: a wrought iron balustrade around a deep stairwell. On each landing a common toilet. We enter actor Enzo Scala's modest rooms, which overlook a courtyard. He has left me his apartment while he stays with his girlfriend. Each day we rehearse in a dusty warehouse loaned to us by a supermarket chain. There is no money for anything as banal as wages. I live on baguette and goats cheese washed down by litre bottles of vin de table. Each evening the cast of our new version of 'Harlequin' go for a long walk around the romance that is Paris and end up at some cheap bar where we stand against the counter to drink a small beer before walking back to Plaisance to mount the iron stairs.

Our dress rehearsal is performed to a motley group of friends in a warehouse which is due for demolition; rather like the Soviet system we are about to undermine. It is the summer of 1989 and our plan is to head east. At the time we had no idea how far east. We are booked in Germany and Poland, but we will end up in the great cities of the flailing Russian Empire. That dress rehearsal was TNT's first performance in France. Decades later we will be the most popular foreign theatre company in the country, touring each year to almost every significant town in the land. And we will branch into theatre not just in France but in French, collaborating with the director Gaspard Legendre for whom we will write stage versions of the two most popular works of French literature: *Le Petit Prince* and *Notre-Dame De Paris*. As I look up at the gargoyles on one of our evening walks I little think that we shall bring these stone figures to life across the globe; for they will form the grotesque chorus to our 'Notre-Dame' which will tour from Shanghai to Lisbon.

The company's expansion in France owed a great deal to Camilla Barnes, who pioneered a touring circuit for theatre in English with the help of her extrovert husband, a sometime director at the French National Theatre at the Palais by the Eiffel tower. (His puppet-based 'Gulliver's Travels' was a revelation). Early tours were hampered by a devil's bargain between

President Mitterrand and Chancellor Kohl to promote each other's language at the expense of English. When this unpopular policy collapsed senior students suddenly started attending our performances and we created a real momentum throughout the country. A town like Lille can fill its huge Sebastopol Theatre four times in two days for performances of 'Oliver Twist' or 'Martin Luther King'. Curiously our greatest hit in France has been a grotesque version of 'Frankenstein – the Monster and the Myth'. The production combines themes and imagery from the classic films with those of Mary Shelley's brilliant original. It must touch a Gallic nerve because the same production is shunned in Germany. I wonder if it is the ghost of Quasimodo? Both monsters yearn for beauty and a love they can never earn.

Which thought returns us to the gargoyles of Notre-Dame, whose distorted humanity sits atop the fragile beauty of the great cathedral. Fragile even more so since the fire of 2018. TNT has an unerring scent for the actual. Our 'Notre-Dame' was invited to perform at the old theatre in Versailles in the very week the cathedral burned. The cast read aloud the graphic scene from Hugo's novel where the same cathedral burns. Then we presented the play. I was at a performance of the play to a packed-out theatre in Nantes a few days ago (as I write now, almost in 2020). There have been many moments that have moved me while watching theatre over the years. But there was something very special about sitting with so many French adults experiencing their own literature in their own language through the prism of a TNT performance. Here again was the essence of our work: the classic is analysed and the main themes and ideas explored through a selective narrative that strips away minor characters and aims to be true to the original without copying it. Since the title of Hugo's book is not 'The Hunchback of Notre-Dame' but 'Notre-Dame de Paris', we take that as the key. The *building* is the central character and therefore the building must speak, and it speaks through its most famous face: the gargoyles.

Our building can have an attitude, but also push the narrative forward – a distorted Greek chorus: gleeful, mischievous and moral. Puck in stone. The set is a classic Meyerholdian Machine for Acting, the work of the German designer Jorg Besser. Wheeled scaffolding towers are draped with monochrome prints of the actual cathedral that open and overlap and allow the aerialist actor who plays Quasimodo to swing, climb and suspend himself in a virtuoso display of physical acting. But the play also insists that Quasimodo is not the centre of the work. As Hugo intends, this lies elsewhere. If the gargoyles dramatise the essence of the building as a secular work of man, so Frollo represents the corruption of all that is good in us and is manifested by the beauty of that building. Frollo, the celibate priest, yearns for Esmeralda as deeply as Quasimodo, but he wishes to possess her, to own her, both body and soul. Time and again the gypsy rejects him, even when faced with death. When Frollo seems to have saved her from the mob he begs once again for her - what? Body or love? Once again she rejects him, and he bursts from the tunnels beneath the cathedral and cries: "the witch is here! The sorcerer is among us!" The gypsy is dragged to the scaffold. But in Frollo's face tragedy is etched as deep as the gargoyle's grin. He has squandered and betrayed everything; without the possibility of Esmeralda he has nothing to live for and his death at the hands of a vengeful Quasimodo is a mere detail.

Poitiers, the elegant Château de La Roche. Each year we present a Shakespeare play in the gardens of the castle to an invited audience of the De Juniac family (who trace their line to one of Napoleon's Marshalls); continuing a strange connection between the company and castles that began at Brancepeth in the early 1980s. After the final applause, the entire audience and cast walk into the courtyard of the chateau where candle-lit tables are waiting for us, set with the finest foods and wines of the region. Poitiers is famous for chèvre cheese. Each farm has its own label. The French wheel has come full circle: from the dusty warehouse and supermarket goats' cheese of the year of revolutions in 1989 to this bastion of haute culture et haute cuisine. *Quelle surprise!*

The Welsh critic and theorist Raymond Williams proposed the idea of 'residual culture'; that the dominant ideas and places and symbols of outworn dominant powers become affordances for more progressive futures. While we should not be complacent, it is a pleasant thought that our recent access to so many old castle venues might signal just such a generous and long running unfolding.

Young Audiences

By Phil

It is a cold Monday morning in Munich, and winter mornings in Munich can be very cold. Inside the theatre on Leopoldstrasse a packed audience of 17-year-old school students are watching intently. These are the final moments of 'American Dreams and Nightmares: The Life and Death of Martin Luther King'. Bathed in red light, the Civil Rights leader lies dead in the arms of his closest comrades. A freedom song rings out from King's widow and then the words 'Free at last! Free at last!" The play is over and the students rise from their seats to give the actors a standing ovation.

This does not happen at every daytime TNT performance to audiences of school students. Fifteen to eighteen-year-olds in any place in the world have plenty else going on in their lives, rather than giving attention to what's going on in a theatre; partly because much of that 'going on' may be going on with other members of the audience. Which is exactly why this sometimes distracted and occasionally bumptious audience is so dear and so important to us.

Theatre is all about possibilities. A good actor moves with possibilities; if they set off in one direction, they always move just a little in the opposite direction before pushing off the way they want to go. Even when resting on stage, the good actor's body is in an energised state; even if the actor knows exactly what they are about to do in ten seconds, still their body is poised for those ten seconds as though ready to do any number of other things. The same with the action on stage; many people watching our 'Romeo and Juliet' understand from the start that the rebellious lovers will die, but they will often forget that, because the actors play characters for whom, in that moment, there are all sorts of possibilities: escape, contentment, obedience...

So an audience of possibilities and a theatre of possibilities should be a dream team. Sometimes, however, it is those we are most like that make us most angry; our brothers and sisters, for example. There is another fact: the power ratio is not an equal one. An audience of any age rarely exercises the power to direct a performance in the way that its performers do. On the other hand, fifteen to eighteen-year-olds are not freshly born chicks waiting to have their brains programmed by the movements of an adult hen. These are young adult individuals, many of whom will have already experienced many of the joys, woes, opportunities and responsibilities of a grown-up world. They may be carers for parents or for siblings with disabilities, they may be fathers or mothers, they may be published poets or on the point of signing papers for a professional sports club; more likely they are wondering what they can achieve in and with the world and what the world might do with them. In other words, they are like so many of the characters in our plays from Prince Hamlet to the mixed-up lovers in the forest of 'Midsummer Night's Dream' to that young woman, Rosa Parks, boarding a bus to make the first gesture of the Civil Rights Movement in the USA. They have choices to make – little different from the ones approaching our audience – and some of them, for both characters and audiences, are not going to be easy ones. The great thing is – for the plays, for life and for theatre – that very few members of our young audiences have yet to make their minds up about everything.

An audience which is as poised to move in as many different directions as a good actor is a great audience for such an actor to play to. With them, the performers can feel the swinging of emotions from the audience and within the audience; just as, we hope, the audience is feeling the same volatility in the character. We have to believe in that possibility for movement, for the changing of minds and the embrace of new feelings and attitudes, in order to broach the subjects we do: struggle, desire, justice, fairness, individuality, loss, failure, love and death. If we thought that the only outcome would be the repetition of the emotional mistakes of older generations (including those of our own) or the excavation of ancient prejudices, we would give up right now. It is the good audience that saves each and every performance from losing heart and conceding defeat; and young audiences make up a healthy proportion of our saviours.

Many of our actors come from the UK, a group of countries where we are often prey to two dominant attitudes. One is an attitude towards children and young people in general, the other towards theatre for children and young adults in particular. While writing this part of the book I was struck, on visiting part of my own city, by a cage put around a basketball court in a side street strewn with dog faeces. No doubt erected to protect the windows of parked cars from the basketballs, the effect was to cage and separate the young who played there. I contrasted this with a memory of my young son, about five years old at the time, immediately welcomed into a riotous game of football in the square of a small town in Northern Spain, the ball whizzing unremarked past the ears of elderly women and crashing against the window of the butcher's shop with no word of reprimand.

In TNT we try to break from the British tendency to see children as problems to be contained or suffered rather than joys right now and hopes for the future. Equally unlike dominant attitudes in the UK – where there is scandalously little theatre made specifically for young people, and a prejudice against it as the kind of employment that actors take when they cannot find 'serious' work – we embrace performing to young audiences in Germany, Italy, France and beyond as the bedrock and heart of our work.

This is not a sentimental attitude; we depend for our survival on these audiences. Many of the stories in this book are about adventures in Kuwait, China, Russia or South America, but very few of them would ever have happened, let alone be told, were it not for our touring to the often young audiences in large theatres in Europe, and in particular in Germany, France and Austria. The relative affluence of these societies and their enthusiasm for live theatre allow us to charge ticket prices and gather sufficient revenue to keep TNT alive and send its many productions out on the road, sometimes on very long and obscure paths.

Paul adds a memory: *Siena, Italy, 'Romeo and Juliet', 2019.* TNT is performing a play about Italian Renaissance teenagers to an audience of Italian teenagers in a Renaissance theatre.

Popular Theatre

By Phil

Why would we want to draw on previous and existing traditions of popular theatre? Well, there is a clue in the title. We like 'popular' because it means we reach a lot of people, and we don't subscribe to the modernist prejudice that art with integrity can only be performed to a minority or elite audience. Indeed, the opposite; we think it can *only* be performed to a broad-based and diverse audience, able to subject our work to their scrutiny. A lively and provocative audience may pose an existential threat to the performance itself, demanding a militant response from the performers to reclaim their space of expression. Well, better that than the unthinking passivity of consumers soaking up the formalities of the event and none of its meaning. Mind you, it's far easier to write that in a book, than performing to six hundred students at 9am in eastern Slovakia.

For us, the drift towards the popular came, strangely, from the modernist. The structure of '1945!'/'English Tea Party'/'Hitler Killed My Canary' was taken from Witold Gombrowicz's play 'The Marriage' and realised in scenes of variety and music hall. In subsequent shows, we drew on British pantomime, Italian *commedia dell'arte*, silent movie comedy, fairy tales, horror, Pythonesque 'surrealism', and so on. Not simply because these forms grip and entertain audiences, touching on deep and recognisable archetypes, but because they often contain seams of dark comedy and grotesque which fitted our experimental and anti-naturalistic approach.

Our embrace of popular and unrespectable genres comes from a belief that art is not for artists, it is for all people who wish to engage with it. Hence we have steered away from the high-modernism of our contemporaries, which we have personally enjoyed as spectators, but which seems only able to attract a niche-arts audience. In itself, there is no great harm in that; innovations in popular art often come from just such enclaves. Indeed, we have drawn inspiration from just such marginal innovations. Until Meyerhold found a popular audience after the Russian Revolution, he was the ultimate marginal artist, creating symbolist visions for, often unconvinced, provincial audiences. But our commitment to the popular is based on the idea that, rather than seeking a necessarily small audience, who we know agree with us, we turn outwards to people who do not believe the same as we do.

Teatro Espressivo de Costa Rica's 'Lord of the Flies', directed by Paul Stebbings with music by TNT composer Paul Flush. The production also toured to Peru.

We have never performed so much as at present (2018-20) throughout Eastern Europe, in the face of the rise there of authoritarian populism. Not a mindset that you would expect would respond favourably to our work. And, indeed, there have been occasional demonstrations against us: students holding up placards denying climate change in protest against our 'Dracula and the Eco-Warrior', the actor playing Fagin having to bring a performance of 'Oliver Twist' to a halt to call out a small group of Marseilles school students shouting "kill the Jew!"; his intervention provoking applause from the great majority of the young audience. Such disruptions are remarkably few and far between, given the nature of our material and the supposed dominant attitudes of the societies in which we play. Yet they embody the reason for our presence there; our desire to place the most extreme and 'out there' physicality and thinking onto the popular platform, mediated by technical skill and popular form and story, and see what happens.

Chapter Ten: 'Oliver Twist', 'Lord of the Flies' and 'Gulliver's Travels'

By Phil

In 1994, at the request of Grantly Marshall, we set to work on an adaptation of Charles Dickens's *Oliver Twist*. We rehearsed at the Bristol Old Vic in the West of England. For the first time, we created an adaptation of a complete novel direct to performance, and under the same title. Up until then such sources had been sampled, as with Klaus Mann's *Mephisto* for 'Cabaret Faust', or merely nodded to without much content taken. This new development might, in other hands, have signalled a retreat from experiment and physicality into literary theatre. In fact the opposite was the case. For, in some ways 'Oliver Twist' is the quintessential TNT show. Rather than us becoming bogged down in a disembodied literariness, the grotesquerie of Dickens's imagination and his rampaging socialised awareness of Victorian reality's surreal parody of human life provided a moral and narrative costume in which to dress our Meyerholdian actor-clowns.

The set consisted of little more than a scaffold and a coffin. The latter doubled for a doorway, a coach, a table, and, among other things, a coffin. The play began with the organiser of a gang of young pickpockets, Fagin, being hauled to the execution scaffold. He demands his right to make a defence. Fighting to be heard, he argues for his own innocence on the grounds that far greater crimes than his are every day being perpetrated by the entirety of wealthy and respectable society. This 'society' is represented for Fagin and for the play, in the figure of Lord (we elevated him to the peerage) Brownlow; Oliver Twist's grandfather.

The play that follows is Fagin's defence. It includes our outing of Dickens's own anti-semitic demonisation of the character of the criminal organiser. By the conclusion of the dramatic action, despite his callous ways and murderous crimes, Fagin is vindicated, but dead. For this, our play, is a comic-tragedy and Fagin sums up his case for the defence by dancing at the end of a rope.

'Oliver Twist' has been performed well over 500 times. Rather than as a historical curiosity, the play is often viewed as a disturbingly contemporary and apposite account of the operations of people-smugglers and modern slavers in the darker recesses of the world's leading economies, and of the prevailing excesses of deregulation and exploitation in the developing ones. We were surprised when Chinese audiences recognised their own modern society in the Victorian mirror, and were even able to identify their own equivalents for the characters of Fagin, Oliver and Brownlow.

'Oliver Twist', in its TNT version, somehow pulls in two directions. On the one hand, it is an adaptation that takes serious liberties with the original text. It repurposes the novel for a social critique that refuses to wrap things up neatly in the 'happy ending' of the Dickens original. It openly displays an awareness of the original's failings. It pushes some of Dickens's caricatures and grotesques to greater extremes (which is where grotesque should be). On the other hand, Dickens's masterpiece pushes back. Rather than creaking under the assault, it seems to become even more itself, throwing off the shallow sentimentality of many modern adaptations (the 'Oliver!' musical version, for example, dodges some of its more profound issues). No matter how hard we worked the material, the genius of the original responded with equal force. The significance of this for the future of the company would be hard to exaggerate.

'Oliver Twist' demonstrated that TNT could adapt a classic text with the requisite degree of extravagant content, lose nothing of the company's characteristic style, while the performance remained recognisably an offering of the original, in texture and story as well as in spirit. 'Oliver Twist' began a whole string of adaptations that are still continuing almost a quarter of a century later. As a result we have accessed large audiences seeking an engagement with an existing work of literature, but who are willing to be delighted by an unexpected encounter with an adaptation that is not a faint copy of the original, but something vividly itself. The picaresque grotesqueries of Dickens were also present in texts like Cervantes's *Don Quijote* , Paul Auster's *Moon Palace* and Oscar Wilde's *The Canterville Ghost*, but we were also able to find a purchase on realist novels of extreme events such as John Steinbeck's *The Grapes of Wrath*, William Golding's *Lord of the Flies* and Ken Kesey's *One Flew Over The Cuckoo's Nest* (although in the latter there is a seam of paranoid absurdism in the novel that is unexplored in the more well-known movie). The extreme and absurd illogicality of these stories – poverty, barbarism, brutality and imprisonment – lent themselves to an approach that could shift between serious, surreal, comic and poetic.

In adapting William Golding's novel *Lord of the Flies*, we faced a difficult and very particular challenge from the realistic content. For the book concerns the ferocious adventures of a group of young boys of around ten years of age stranded on a deserted island as a result of a plane crash. While the events are extreme and, even in prose form theatrical and ritualistic, the grotesque behaviour of the children – including the beating to death of their weakest member and setting the island on fire – is effective and meaningful because it arises directly from their everyday behaviour as English public school boys. (In England, 'public school' means a private school, where very high fees are paid to attend, and are thus largely the preserve of the rich and the powerful).

Concerned that the incongruity of adult males playing the roles of preadolescent boys would appear physically, and perhaps emotionally and psychologically, distracting, Paul chose to cast female performers in the roles of the boys. Their expert portrayals of the manners of young boys, and their generation of a vortex of emotion, was both convincing and overtly performed; held up for examination and critical viewing, while also involving and horrific.

William Golding's novel is itself strange and disturbing, set in an exceptional context, and depicting outrageous responses, but we were able to intensify the dynamic between mannered public school routines and violence by deploying the crashed aeroplane as the play's set. The damaged fuselage served both to represent the alien terrain of the island, but also the brokenness of a civilisation which had brought the world to the brink of nuclear destruction. This is implicit in the novel, which takes place during an unspecified war.

Toys and other objects rescued from the plane, which in the context of ordinary school life were apparently innocent, took on a sinister quality. A portrait of the Queen became an omniscient and otherworldly witness, remote and helpless. A set of cricket stumps became dangerous weapons. Both the dramatic effectiveness and the thematic bite were increased by the emergence of savagery from the accoutrements, costumes, routines and recreations of English upper-class, public school life, rather than some regression to 'primitive behaviour'. The circumstances of hardship and precarity did not create the violence; rather, they stripped the mask of respectability from the aggressive entitlement that lay beneath. Thus the conventional and conservative interpretation of Golding's novel, as a pessimistic indictment of core human brutality, was upended, by our close focus on the material details and social siting of Golding's story.

In our adaptation of Jonathan Swift's *Gulliver's Travels* (1996) there were no such concerns about realism – given the story's floating islands and telescoping of scale, its vulgarity, exaggerations and free-ranging satire on bureaucratic, servile, credulous and various other absurdities. The challenge had nothing to do with finding any kind of realistic basis for the action. Indeed, as part of our research we watched a TV adaptation of the book which foundered on exactly such an attempt. Instead, our performance took the form of a travelling show. A showman's cart is hauled on. Its owner announces an extravaganza of nonsensical "yarns" and "sweet fantasies", while an incarcerated Gulliver, presumed insane, shouts from within the cart: "It is all true!"

The Gulliver of our adaptation is trapped in an unbreakable cycle; the harder he tries to tell his "true story", the less likely he is to be believed. Worse still, the more our Gulliver – like Swift – exposes the absurdity of what is taken for the 'real world', the more he feeds the showman's pessimistic message that this is the only world and we all have to put up with it. While 'Gulliver's Travels' and 'Lord of the Flies' were miles apart in style, they shared in their cores this tension; between a world-weary cynicism about 'human nature' and a passionate ranting against the distortion of human behaviour by social inequities, constraints, exploitation, oppressive order and pandering to ignorance.

The Horsey Houyhnhnms offer Gulliver the skin of a slaughtered humanoid Yahoo to clothe himself in TNT's 'Gulliver's Travels'

At the end of our 'Gulliver's Travels', Gulliver is rescued from the performance by his fellow performers. For a mixture of reasons, they rise against the showman, and lead Gulliver to freedom. The showman is left alone on the stage. For a moment the act of theatre itself is stripped bare. There is only the business of theatre and a lone human. Just as at the climax of 'The Mystery', back in 1981, the pantomime collapsed, the set destroyed and the apparently real ticket money burned in a tin bath. In desperation, the 'Gulliver's Travels' showman first threatens his fleeing actors. Then turns to the audience, begging their indulgence: "you laughed, you cried, there was no satire, no offence. It all meant nothing, it's just a children's story. It was not about your governments, your scientists, the money in your pocket". Of course, the audience know he is lying. After all, this is theatre and theatre is about making things up, pretending to be things that it is not.

In order to make our final moment of theatre, we had turned theatre against itself, destroyed its dignity, pulled down its trousers and showed its ragged underwear. We had reduced the play's most powerful character to acting like a beggar. Unable to withstand the trauma, the showman physically collapses, he can no longer perform. There is no play left. With his last effort, he pulls himself up. To himself, this time, he speaks: "I'm finished, ruined, go home. The end."

This is not Gulliver speaking. This is not the hero. This is 'the villain', the insensitive master. Yet, now, through this least sympathetic of characters, we ask for sympathy. For he, like us all, after all the niceties of social rights and wrongs, our navigating of human foibles and directing animal passions as best we can, must face the last moment of our drama, our 'doing': "The end". Not because this is any kind of holy moment – everyone will face this time in their own way, flavoured by their own circumstances – but because it is grotesque, absurd. Only when the whole frame is thrown open, only when the passage of the play has passed by, can the lone actor leave the stage and take the theatre with him. This moment of material and existential emptiness, a look into the abyss, is achieved by a conjuring with conventions. By juggling with the frames of character and fiction, we had arrived, actor and audience together, in the warm theatre, in the darkness, at a moment just before the actors return and the applause begins: for a guest appearance by Nothing.

Actor Training

By Paul

Is there such a thing as the innate ability to act? Peter Brook noted that many actors had come to him offering total commitment and enthusiasm but that that had never been enough. At the age of ten I starred in my school play as Toad in 'Toad of Toad Hall'. I received one of my best reviews to date in our provincial school magazine. So why did I feel comfortable on stage at that age? Or even: why was I cast? We invite actors to our castings in London (from a huge number of applicants, often four to five hundred per role). When auditioning I never look at the biographies until after we have seen them perform, solo and in a group. It is surprising how often the well trained and experienced fail to impress compared with the 'talented'. It may not be popular to believe that nature rather than nurture has a major role to play in actors' excellence, but I cannot deny the evidence of decades of casting.

So assuming that a performer has the innate ability, and that with that ability comes a sense of calling, of the necessity for them to act, where next?

If TNT means The New Theatre then we must seek the new actor. But since we do not have the resources to start our own academy, we have to deal with the reality of a theatrical training system that is increasingly focused on styles of performance that are certainly not new. Or if there is novelty there, then it is directed to the digital world where acting is merely a measure of confidence and ability to communicate, rather than an art. (In my own younger days, Telephone Sales companies were always keen to recruit actors; I lasted 3 hours and walked out of the Sales office at lunchtime to take up a more satisfying job as a window cleaner.)

Drama schools, most of them now offering degree courses, have blossomed in Britain and elsewhere since Phil and I received our degrees (First Class Honours, since you're asking) in Drama from Bristol University in 1977. There are so many drama schools they have created a new audience for theatre. But if I mention the names Grotowski or Brecht, let alone Meyerhold, at a casting session I am usually met with blank stares.

I think the 'new actor' needs innate ability and then a rigour. This rigour is about developing a specific type of skill. Too many actors come to us and say "I can or will do anything: musicals, short films, TV, pantomime, modern drama, Shakespeare, etc, etc". What we are interested in, however, is the actor who can do at least one thing outstandingly well; someone who has a biography that shows choice, adventure, ideas and personal development.

TNT was founded by three actors and a dramaturg: myself, Mark Heron, Simon Clewes and Phil Smith. Mark trained at Jacques LeCoq's physical theatre school in Paris and was a master of circus skills; Simon was an art student and fluent dancer. I had trained academically in drama and then just worked: first in community theatre and then in the Grotowski method in a professional company. I think this wide exposure helped us. As the company has expanded it has not always been possible to fill our productions with artists from such diverse and yet specialist backgrounds. So, what we have done is develop veteran performers who have learned our style on the road and who develop the skills TNT needs in performance by performing.

Training in Meyerhold's biomechanics or Grotowski's physical theatre is demanding and at times rather dry. TNT does not advocate this as the sole root of fine acting. Personally, my development would have been impossible without a year as director and actor at South Yorkshire Community Theatre in the late 1970s. There I learnt what it was to perform day in and day out to tough kids on summer playschemes, to the disturbed in psychiatric hospitals and to the elderly in their care homes and lunch clubs. The latter being one of the finest audiences on the planet.

So my advice is to get out and perform, perform outside your comfort zone and to people not at all like you. At the same time, train and develop skills. An actor's body is her instrument. Care for it and improve it. Don't smoke. An actor who can cycle 100 kms in a day or run a marathon is always going to be better for that. Take dance classes even if you think you cannot dance. Take singing lessons even if you think of yourself as not being able to sing. Sword fighting skills and pole vaulting are a plus. Balance is interesting. How many actors act mainly from the neck upwards? How few use the floor in an audition, or lower their heads beneath their waist to express anything? Watch Chaplin.

Beware of symmetry. It is your enemy. *Commedia dell'arte* is the greatest Western physical theatre tradition. Explore it. It teaches the asymmetrical. An actor who gestures with both arms and hands towards the audience or another actor is making a mistake, their energy is dissipated (which is why Asian theatre bans the move). The most common TNT acting exercise is the 'Harlequin Jump'. It teaches dynamic asymmetry. (That and some other useful exercises are outlined below.)

Do not make the mistake of thinking that all this athleticism, bodily presence and musicality is somehow the mark of just the marginal performer. Sir Laurence Olivier in his prime was the master of the alert physical performance. Unfortunately, the best recorded example of this skill is his Othello, tainted by his 'blacked up' Moor. Olivier also brings us back to the point about rhythm and acting; for this great classical actor reveals a surprising aptitude for tap dancing in the film of 'The Entertainer'. We should perhaps end these notes on acting and training by referring to Max Wall, the gangly legged (and often drunk) music hall acrobat. Samuel Becket adored Max and insisted he was the best actor to ever grace his plays. At eighty years of age, a tipsy Max Wall fell to his death down the stairs of a pub. His fall a brilliant physical finale, a tragedy at which one has to smile.

Or as Meyerhold might note: "Tragedy with a smile on its lips".

Theatre exercises

Taking our lead from the Polish director Grotowski, his collaborator Barba and their actors, this is classic physical theatre training. First practice and perfect three or four simple physical performances:

1) The Harlequin Jump

A leap that lands with one hand on hip, the other outstretched and bent at the elbow with the fingers pointing upward. Meanwhile one foot is turned at the end of an extended leg and the other foot planted firmly on the ground at a right angle (almost third ballet position but with one foot up). Then a second leap reverses the hands and legs to face the opposite direction. The head of course follows with the eyes focused on the upturned finger of the outstretched hand. (It's not as tricky as it sounds, young kids love doing this jump in workshops). This pleasing exercise offers an iconic stage presence: an actor can work on this, allowing the concept of the asymmetrical to enliven their performance. Action should always have a reaction, and indeed a pre-action. The goalkeeper bounces the ball, leans back and kicks the ball high over the pitch. This is Meyerhold's "triple action" – that is pre-action, action, reaction. (See 'Directing Theatre' chapter below for an explanation of pre-action.)

2) The Archer

The classic exercise for developing the above skill is the Archer. The actor starts with feet planted apart in a strong position facing out. Lift the right arm, as if holding a bow. Bend back with feet now in third position (at right angles to each other), mime the taking of an arrow from the quiver on your back with your left hand. Lean forward to thread the arrow on the imaginary bow string. Regain central balanced position and pull the bowstring and arrow across your chest, breathing in as you do so. Finally, release the arrow with a sharp exhale of breath.

3) The Bullwhip

Place the feet firmly on the ground, wide apart. Raise the left hand at a right angle to the body with a bent elbow. Raise the right arm as if holding a powerful whip. The pre-action is a backwards lean with the whip arm as the left arm moves forward. Then comes the whip – a flick with the whole body where the arm itself cracks the whip. The left arm will automatically compensate by moving in an opposite direction. Then the arms return to their initial position; the reaction to the act of whipping.

4) The Lion

This is a physical exercise that allows breath to take centre stage. Lower yourself to the floor so that knees, toes and the palms of your hands are on the ground. Your thighs and arms should be at right angles to the floor. Take a deep breath and as you do so sit back on your heels without moving your hands, this will create a 45-degree angle with your arms; keep your head low. The deep breath should be held. Exhale as you return to your initial position but keep going forward until the arms are at a forward diagonal and raise your head and make a rasping sound with the final push out of the single breath you are exhaling. Sticking your tongue out for this final sound helps. Repeat three times. This is an excellent way to begin warming the vocal chords. You can add more sound on the second and third exhale.

5) The Flow

The Flow is fast walking or running between these exercises. The group starts by walking around the room, dodging and weaving and avoiding group patterns. At a signal, a clap or whistle, the actor chooses one of the above exercises and completes it three times. Then the group runs around the space, again dodging and weaving. A clap. Another exercise. Then a very slow Budō-inspired walk. That is with the foot that is not upon the floor being held and moved a constant two inches above the ground until it is impossible to balance. The foot then hits the ground and the back foot travel forward is done in the same manner. The effect is quite similar to a Michael Jackson 'Moon Walk' and equally satisfying. Alternating these exercises with running, walking and Budō movement and taking special care with breath is a classical 'Flow' exercise. No words should be spoken throughout, and the whole Flow can take anything from twenty minutes to an hour. Some flows can be accompanied by live drumming. Other exercises can be integrated (the Harlequin Jump, for example, is a TNT addition). Such training can inform performance, not only in terms of physical control but in liberating the actor from the constraints of realism and connecting them with their work in the same way as a musician or dancer might find a key to their art.

Intensity, focus, rhythm, pre-action, action, reaction. Like a coiled snake or an alert cat, we are transfixed by such acting.

The Elephant in the Room

By Paul

There are very few actors who are ready or willing to commit themselves to working with one theatre company for most of their career. Peter Brook managed two: Yoshi Oida and Bruce Meyers. Grotowski had several but that arose from the peculiar circumstances of Communist Eastern Europe. Stanislavski could not hold onto Meyerhold, and there is the danger that a weaker performer looks for the security of a stable company.

Overall if we want to create new theatre or even good theatre we need an ensemble. The world we live in (capitalism again) militates against this. TNT has been blessed with many actors who have stayed the course for years: Christian Flint joined us to perform in 'Brave New World' in 1998 and as I write this is playing Scrooge in our unusual 'A Christmas Carol'. Richard Ede and Natalia Campbell went one stage further and for seven years only toured with us, living together in hotel rooms. They created some extraordinary work, and it was no accident that one British national newspaper called Richard "the funniest man alive"; constant performance is the best training of all. Their swansong was a revival of 'Taming of the Shrew'. Natalia played Kate and Richard played Petruchio. At the curtain call at Shanghai's Lyceum Theatre, Richard went down on his knees and proposed. Natalia accepted and hundreds of Chinese burst into tears. (Me too). But they needed to move on, or actually move in, since they had bought an apartment in London partly on the proceeds of seven years' frugal touring, and now pursue successful careers in Britain.

Some actors such as Dan Wilder stay with us, surely his skill and looks (tall blonde Viking) could have established him in conventional theatre, but Dan is a rebel, a post-punk hippy hybrid. With us he can kick back against it all. At times this has been a brutal choice. A long tour is mentally and physically demanding (and lonely) and a short tour makes no financial sense. And then we can cast the wrong person.

It's New Year's Day and I receive a phone call. An actor has not arrived at Heathrow airport. His mobile phone is switched off. He has gone to ground. In 36 hours time he should perform as Lord Henry in Wilde's

'Picture of Dorian Gray' in Strasbourg. 36 hours later I am performing the role of Lord Henry in Strasbourg. The lines are being fed to me in an earpiece by a German stage manager who reads English rather poorly. The missing actor is surely an alcoholic. I once caught him pouring half pints of cheap whisky into his beer. The rest of the cast are shocked but delighted to lose such a disruptive and selfish performer.

In the final scene the broken Lord Henry bursts into a chapel and confronts the ever youthful Dorian, hypocritically praying. I lean over Dorian and fix his eyes with mine. The actor almost jumps out of his skin. Why? Because for the previous ten weeks of touring Lord Henry has spent his acting time showing off to the audience and ignoring his fellow actors on the stage. How could I know when he was cast? This selfish drunk gave one of the best Shakespeare auditions I can recall. His CV did not include "heavy drinking" in his list of interests.

Many actors go to any and every audition offered. Either to gain practice or to please their agent. After a rigorous audition process some actors turn down the job. Others accept the job without truly wanting it. Some actors are so beaten down by the insecurity and randomness of trying to earn a living as a performer that when they are employed they find the reality does not live up either to their fantasy or their aspirations. So, despite sending out detailed information about the tours, we find that actors complain about long drives and morning audiences. While some actors simply don't look at the map, others more seriously fail to think what it means to be on tour with the same people in strange countries for months on end. Touring is tough. Then sometimes it gets tougher.

Theatre is a social art. We need each other and we must enjoy the company and work of people who are different from ourselves. Those that can do that prosper, but it is surprising how many cannot tolerate the 'other'. The present cast of 'Pygmalion', despite spanning ages from early twenties to mid-fifties, are bosom buddies and as a result not only enjoy their eight-month and twenty-nation tour, but this is manifest on stage. Their evident give and take brings this complex comedy to vibrant life. But, it is not always like that...

The East German city of Neustrelitz. I have come to watch our 'Streetcar Named Desire' at its fine old theatre. It is the last performance before the Christmas break. I know there are problems with our Stanley. The American actor playing the role simply *is* Stanley in real life. Sadly, Stanley in Tennessee Williams's masterpiece is impossible to live with; all vanity and masculinity. No wonder I cast this actor, he looks great, pecs and all. He is from the South, he moves in a way no British actor could. He is 'easy' as well as being difficult. He has a bad case of self-love. He likes pranks such as handing props to the Blanche actress on stage whilst stark naked. He finds it very amusing to open the sliding side door of the van while speeding along an autobahn at 90 miles an hour. For much of the tour and rehearsals I have got on well with him. He is not a bad person (see 'Lord Henry'). He is a child locked in a rather handsome adult body. Phil Corbett, the marvellous actor and number one human who plays Mitch, has been his mentor. Stanley looks up to Phil, but becomes insanely jealous when Phil's girlfriend comes to visit. The tour manager is tired of Stanley's antics and suspects there is heroin abuse in the mix.

When the tour manager takes Stanley to task shortly after I arrive, Stanley feels humiliated and punches the tour manager. He leaves swiftly to sulk in his dressing room. He has to go, but how to do it? Replacing a leading actor is expensive. I need to contact the producer. We patch things up as best we can and drive through the night to Berlin. We are booked into a hotel near Tegel airport and then each is to fly to our different homes for the break. Stanley has a return ticket: Berlin - Miami - Berlin. Luckily we are able to check into this anonymous hotel in such a way that Stanley has no idea who is in which room. The rest of the cast and me gather in Phil's room, which unbeknownst to Stanley abuts his own.

I ask the cast what they want to happen. They all say that Stanley must go. I phone the producer in the middle of the night. Not a popular move. After some pressure he agrees to replace the actor. Then in a democratic discussion it is decided that I have to pass the news on to Stanley and somehow get him to the airport. The tour manager will not drive his attacker anywhere. So it's me in a taxi.

I am certainly no match for Stanley in a fist fight, but I still have some aura of paternal authority that this man-child respects. I leave the room. As a gesture towards my safety Phil places a cup against the thin hotel room wall and prepares to leap to my defence. Phil is a big man. I make Stanley a cup of instant coffee, knock on the door and wake him from his untroubled sleep. I tell him I will take him to the airport. Then I drop the bombshell: "The rest of the cast no longer wish to work with you".

He tosses the coffee on the floor, starts to rage like a second rate De Niro, banging the walls and table top. I keep calm and sip my own cooling coffee. He rants against the cast, he rages against life. Very gently, I get him to pack his bag and I call a taxi. Now he is weeping, but he is still hitting the table as he does so. Will he attack me? Will Phil get here in time if he does?

At last I manoeuvre him through the door into the corridor. He is suddenly sweet: "Paul, which rooms are they in?" I cannot tell him, so he flings down his bag and races up and down the long concrete corridor screaming with fury: "You can run but you can't hide. I am gonna come back and kill you all. Kill you all!" It is six in the morning, a Turkish room cleaner cowers in a doorway. I pretend not to know this wild man. Then grab his bag and dash down the stairs to the taxi that will take us both to Tegel airport. Stanley needs his bag so he joins me at the taxi. Later, I sit down in a departure lounge café and buy him more coffee. He moans out his victimhood to me. I nod and try to offer words of comfort. I worry he will return to the hotel and do some dreadful deed. Time crawls by. At last I can escort him to security and thank him for his work. He grips my hand. I suppose I am the better actor at this moment. He trudges off. Miami awaits. I know it is easy to buy a gun in Miami. He has a return ticket. I wave and walk sadly towards the taxi that will take me to the station and my train home. We replaced Stanley, the tour continued until May when we laid the production to rest in Tokyo. But we never truly replaced our Stanley. He was the best because he was utterly truthful in his role. He failed in life and so ruined his art. Our art. One does not work without the other; break one and eventually you break both.

A director needs to understand and factor into their work the almost unbearable pressures that the professional actor faces. If it is tough for men it is far harder for women. It is a sad fact that there are more women chasing fewer roles. Of course the new theatre can and must do what it can to change that. TNT has continually cast women in strong and unusual roles – the Countess of Derby, Winnie Mandela, Angie the paramedic in 'Crooked Letter, Crooked Letter' – not merely casting blind but casting for dramatic effect (which is our overall policy on race and gender).

So Prince Malcolm in Macbeth is played by a woman. This makes sense because if Malcolm is a young man in medieval Scotland he must be a young warrior. If so why does he not fight the murderer of his father? A woman playing Malcolm emphasises his vulnerability and allows us to guess that he must be a clever youth of sixteen or so years. Little wonder he suspects Macduff when that warrior comes to woo him in exile in England. "There's daggers in men's smiles" – Malcolm is not yet a man and a woman can portray that.

The entire cast of our 'Lord of the Flies' (recently, 2019, remounted in Spanish in Costa Rica) are women. Without women playing boys the whole tale collapses; for this is a story about innocence corrupted. This is not a tale of testosterone fuelled youth, but of pre-pubescent naivety corrupted by the brutality of the English Public School system. Well, that is our take; others might blame the inherent barbarity of humanity for the savagery of this modern myth. It is up to the audience to decide. But that audience will see children, not adults pretending to be children. So much so, in fact, that audiences were sometimes unable to accept that the women clearing the stage after the show were the same persons who had been the boys a few minutes before. So the stylisation of women playing boys brings us closer to truth or even to reality (which may not be the same thing).

Malcolm crowned by the weird sisters in TNT's long running 'Macbeth'

I think it was the collaborator of Grotowski, Eugenio Barba, who said that an actress can achieve a profundity of feeling on the stage that few male actors can match. An angry woman is so much more terrifying than an angry man because she breaks out of type. Men have squandered the currency of anger. Hence the everlasting popularity of 'Macbeth'. The scenes where Lady Macbeth screws her husband's courage to the "sticking point" are perhaps the finest every written. "If we should fail?" pleads the warrior husband. "We fail?" replies his wife in a devastating riposte. Our own Lady Macbeth from the play's premiere to a tour some ten years later was Gail Sixsmith. This performer only knows how to give one hundred per cent in either rehearsal or performance; she dares any cast not to match her fierce commitment. She came into TNT to play the murderous Jack in 'Lord of the Flies'. A slight bundle of energy, she dominates the stage with her extreme physicality and glinting eyes. If she can frighten me, actors and audience, she also terrified the Royal Shakespeare Company who cast her in several good roles before each fled from the other. Her special creativity had no space in that institution. So Gail and TNT were and are a natural fit. She now spends most of her time teaching physical theatre in London. Many of her ex-students come to work for us. Any director, but especially a male director, needs to be aware of the special pressures and needs of female performers. If male actors tend to turn to the bottle, many of our best female artists have turned to anti-depressants. We try to play some small part in helping them keep work and life from breaking. But no one should come into this profession without realising that it is a 'matter of life and art' affair. The stakes are sometimes very high.

Some six hundred professional actresses applied for our recent production of 'Romeo and Juliet'. It is almost impossible to wade through the applications. Actors whose surnames begin with a Z may be at a disadvantage. But the very deluge of applicants tells us about the need for expression that these young artists possess. Yet how deeply frustrating it is to confront the lack of opportunities there are to express that need. Then there is maternity. So many of TNT's finest female artists have chosen not to have children. There is nothing a modern international touring theatre company can do to accommodate children on tour. There are no rock star tour buses, and the old family-based touring company, moving a few miles between gigs in a procession of mobile homes, does not compute with tour schedules that bound between continents.

When I directed 'Julius Caesar' in German in a fixed venue I had the chance to briefly rectify this: I cast the striking Lara Körner as Portia and Octavius (another wise youth best played by a woman). Lara is a single mother with three small children and could only rehearse during school hours. The producer was set against this compromise, but I persisted and was rewarded with a strong performance. One maxim of TNT is that it is better to be under-rehearsed doing the right thing than to slickly present the wrong thing.

So why hasn't TNT cast a woman as Hamlet? Here we have a conundrum: many of our audience are not regular theatre goers. For them the narrative is essential. We are story tellers. If we go too far in undermining the story – whether for reasons of formal or political innovation – we can end up placing the needs of the artist above that of the audience. And that we cannot do. If it is our job to make sense of 'Hamlet', to elucidate the text for a worldwide audience, then Hamlet's sex and sexuality are crucial. Hamlet's first soliloquy is his most troubled. The Prince's jealous disgust at his mother's passion for his uncle is transferred onto the helpless Ophelia. Hamlet actually becomes more rational and measured after the Ghost reveals that his father was murdered. Everything springs from that first great tortured speech and it is the speech of a male who cannot accept an older woman's passionate sexuality.

This theme is carried through to Ophelia's own madness, one that stems from a trauma inflicted by a male Prince. I may be wrong, and there are surely other ways of looking at this greatest of roles (and some may argue that a good female actor can portray all of the above gendered qualities in Hamlet), but that is my understanding and I need to pass that on to an audience who may have no knowledge of the play. This is not a fixed principle, but it is where we are in seeking to go beyond realism without falling into abstraction.

Where we are in control we can do better. And in plays such as 'My Sister Syria' and 'Dracula and the Eco-Warrior' we place women in the foreground. In our 'Free Mandela', Winnie rather than Nelson is the focus and dilemma carrier. But in some modern dramas this is not so easy; how does one present a play about Martin Luther King without a mainly male cast? I wish it were otherwise, especially as female performers are often more creative than men, less blocked. *Mea culpa.*

So here is a sequence from the finale of our 'Oliver Twist', where three of the five cast are women, and which remains TNT's most performed production.

Nancy is murdered. The mob is pursuing Bill Sikes, her killer, through the streets of East London. He leaps across the rooftops to arrive at Fagin's den. The game is up. Fagin and two boys wait for Bill and their own doom. Oliver and the Artful Dodger are played by women.

BILL: Let me in, damn you! Let me in, damn your eyes. (FAGIN lets in BILL. BILL searches the den.) Have you nothing to say to me? They're after my blood! (Pause) Do you mean to sell me, or let me lie here till the hunt is over?

FAGIN: You may stop here, if you think it's safe, my dear.

BILL: Is Nancy buried? *(All shake heads).* No? Why isn't she? Why do you keep such ugly things above the ground? *(All silent)* Say something can't you? Dodger, Dodger, don't you know me?

ARTFUL DODGER: Don't come near me, monster!

FAGIN: We have all been made into monsters.

ARTFUL DODGER: All I ever done was steal handkerchiefs! *(Police whistles, howls of the mob).* Listen to them: Blood! They'll have our blood, damn you *(To Bill:)* Get back, Bill! I ain't afraid of you. Witness me Oliver, I ain't frightened of him. *(Breaks out of the Den.)* Murder! Murder! Help! Sikes is here. Bill Sikes is here! Help! Murder!

FAGIN: *(Sadly)* Now, Oliver Twist, it is time for us to die so you can live happily ever after.

ARTFUL DODGER: *(From rooftop)* Here, in here, Police! Murder!

Only a woman can play the man-child Dodger with the right mix of energy and pathos. Savage punishment awaits him but all he ever did was steal handkerchiefs…

The director must have the support and cooperation of the cast. This will only arrive if the director treats the actors as artists not as puppets. And the director needs to understand that every actor will bring the problems of being an actor to their work. Theatrical institutions and subsidised companies must by their very nature be part of a system that ensures actors are mostly poor and undervalued. Their usual solution is hierarchy and discipline which draws on the power of the employer in a saturated labour market.

The new theatre must draw the actor into the valued place where they too are a creator; one who asks for advice from an outside eye without bowing down to that eye. I give one example: in every rehearsal room we establish a 'bad idea corner'. Anyone in the room can come up with an idea or interpretation or movement. If that idea is poor they can either walk into or be placed in our 'bad idea corner' and emerge unscathed. The joke encourages creativity which has to be based on success arising from the lessons of failure.

And finally, every TNT production includes company veterans. Some productions, such as the current 'Macbeth', are fully cast from previous TNT companies. These are actors with whom we have an affinity, part of an extended family that will give them work for the foreseeable future. In this way we can release the actors from the servility and resentment that too often accompanies the job insecurity of their calling. So we go full circle. The best director enables other artists, offers them an outside eye and is first among equals. And the next step for the new theatre? The ideal director probably abolishes themself.

Chapter Eleven: 'A Streetcar Named Desire', 'The Crucible', 'Death of a Salesman' and 'Pygmalion'

By Phil

In 1997 TNT did something that might be considered contrary to the very spirit of the company. We staged an existing play! The adaptation of classic novels, begun in 1994 with 'Oliver Twist', took a risk with the identity of the company's aesthetics. Performing from a text not only in existence, but regularly performed and considered authoritative, looked more like wilfully self-inflected damage. The company had been founded as a devising and writing company, producing new work; TNT stands for The New Theatre!

As with our move into adaptation, this new development began with an offer from producer Grantly Marshall. To make a performance of Tennessee Williams' 'A Streetcar Named Desire'. An invitation that we accepted, but in our own way.

In making a performance of 'Streetcar', we approached the published script as if it was a first draft that either Paul or I had produced. Though dead, or distant, the writers of this and subsequent plays were to be our collaborators; at least in *our* minds. Although very little of their scripts would be changed, we would always add plenty in terms of unusual staging; in ways that some of our playwright-collaborators might not have anticipated.

So, at the beginning of 'Streetcar' we showed an incident which in Tennessee Williams' script is only described in retrospective dialogue late in the play. This is when Blanche Dubois discovers her young husband in a sexual encounter with another man, triggering a disgusted response from Blanche that leads to her husband's suicide. In its time – the original play was first staged in 1947 – this revelation was shocking. Such things were not shown or discussed on the Broadway stage in those days. In 1997, however, while the story remains powerful in its impact on the character of Blanche, the script's hinting at a dreadful secret seems now more tabloid salacious than seriously themed. Few taboos are broken by such a revelation now.

Rather than encourage the audience to seek for such a single revelation of Blanche's tragic psychology, we uncovered this at the very start of the show, so that the audience could watch the extraordinary character of Blanche (played, for us, by a very talented performer) unfold in all her many aspects, rather than be hanging on for a doubtful 'final explanation'.

Similarly, in 2005, in Arthur Miller's 'The Crucible' we staged the innocent dancing of young women, in silhouette behind a white screen, which triggers the accusations of 'witchcraft'. As with Blanche's back story, at the play's very beginning we sought to 'give away' the solution to its mystery. This dispensed with the canny skill of the commercial realist playwright, who builds narrative 'hooks' into his play by which to hold an audience in suspense. By passing this hidden information across to the audience early on, any temptation on the part of the audience to imagine a supernatural or non-material basis for the panic of the 'witch hunt' was diminished. The audience are then invited to observe calmly, albeit engrossed, the unfolding of the subsequent horror of the Salem persecutions, rather than worry about the historical veracity of its narrative. The play is not a history class; it is an emotional and ethical parable. This same white screen of gauze, which enabled us to defuse any issue around 'what really happened', was redeployed at the very end of the play. It allowed us to stage in silhouette a tableau of modern characters from fundamentalist religious and extremist movements in the USA, repeating actions and attitudes from the seventeenth-century 'witch trials'.

Arthur Miller had used the events of the Salem 'witch trials' to discuss the McCarthyite witch hunts of the 1950s, when large numbers of radicals and innovators in politics, government service, science, arts and entertainment were accused of treasonable communist sympathies and aggressively investigated and publicly interrogated. In our final tableau, we indicated that the same authoritarian attitudes still survived in the USA; remember this was just a decade prior to the election of a US President with overt support from his country's Far Right. The gauze enabled us to substitute the spontaneous dance of innocent victims at the beginning of the play with the conspiratorial choreography of those in the present day who would like to see the return of a similarly draconian America.

The formal experiment we began in 1980 we were testing once again, almost two decades later, in a way we could never have predicted. Tentatively at first, we deployed to pre-existing texts an approach and stylistic tactics from our practices of devising and adaptation. The precedent for the gauze tableau at the start of 'The Crucible', and for the revelation at the beginning of our 'Streetcar', was right there in the opening of our second ever production ('1945!', still being performed as late as 2010), when, in an almost agit-prop documentary style, the traumatic event behind the hallucination that constitutes the play was explicitly revealed: the accidental killing of a German civilian by a gunner in a British tank.

By deploying and refining the formal experimentation begun in 1980, we could undo and reassemble the dynamics of realist texts. By exposing concealed hooks within the narrative structure, we could redirect the texts to explore wider and more complex webs of desire, behaviour, causation and consequence. By acknowledging and eliminating the 'cause' of the play at its beginning, the audience could see it not as an explanation, but simply as the condition necessary for the action and its dilemmas unfolding before them. In many cases, this was the intention of their writers; an intention sometimes obscured by slavishly naturalistic productions or their use as star-vehicles.

Our staging of Arthur Miller's 'Death of a Salesman' in 2002 was a radical reworking, embracing Miller's dislike of 'method' acting and his interest in the fantasy-life of his characters. Something that is not only evident in his prose, such as his novel *Focus* (1954) – the symbolist style of which influenced our approach to 'Salesman' – but in his initial sketching out of 'Salesman'. He had begun with an image of the unpeeling of the face of the salesman, revealing his inner workings. We staged Miller's text in order to bring out both his own preferred non-naturalistic performance of character and the physical animation of significant symbols.

Willi Loman's memories come to life in TNT's production of 'Death of a Saleman', with John Moraitis as Willi

Without resorting to a postmodern mash-up, we became increasingly aggressive in our approach. So that in the 2018 production of George Bernard Shaw's 'Pygmalion' we transferred events to new locations, re-locating a crucial scene at the conclusion of the play from a drawing room to Covent Garden market. We returned the psychodrama of upper-class tutor and working-class pupil to its earthy social context, while highlighting the extent of the subtle violence inflicted on the pupil, Eliza. By looping back to Eliza's former place of trade, it was evident to the audience that her training (perhaps even brainwashing) to imitate the manners of upper-class women makes it impossible for her now to 'go home'. Stripped of her working-class identity, but without the means to sustain a middle-class, let alone an upper-class, one, she is left without the possibility of an economic role. Previously she could sell flowers, but now the only thing Eliza has left to sell is herself.

In itself, this is a horrific narrative, within the body of a 'much loved comedy'. But it got worse. We identified in the text evidence of the playwright's anti-materialist 'Gnosticism'. Shaw had once even attempted, very unsuccessfully, to found his own 'Gnostic' religion. Now we found evidence of his surreptitiously inserting his ideas in 'Pygmalion'. So, while he might have exposed the social violence inflicted on Eliza, he was undermining his critique by championing a belief in the lesser reality of the material world through his main character, the monstrous Professor Higgins. The giveaway is Higgins' use of the phrase "spark of divine fire"; the 'divine spark' being the Gnostic idea that all material being whether just or unjust is wholly depraved, the only thing of worth in a human being their tiny spark of godly fire.

Given Shaw's interest in esoteric belief, the use of this term was clearly not accidental. His character Higgins's indifference to good manners and the feelings of others is founded on a Gnostic-influenced hatred of the ordinary and the fleshly and an indifference to everything human. Higgins is interested only in the abstract and the ideal. No wonder Eliza calls him a "devil"!

Many who have approached Shaw's text have sought to find and express some sublimated romance between Higgins and the flower girl, Eliza – thus reducing the play to a sentimental banality. Just as the mistaken game or the revelation of homosexuality belittle both 'Crucible' and 'Streetcar'. By our identifying of George Bernard Shaw's hidden Gnostic agenda, we were inspired to remove any hint of the pleasing prospect of an 'oddball' romance. This shifted all the focus of the play to the machinations of Higgins and his collaborator Pickering and their consequences for Eliza.

In pursuing these clues within the text, it had not been our intention to do anything more than address the meaning of the words and actions in the text written by George Bernard Shaw in 1912. Yet, in the context of the #MeToo movement of 2018, and particularly for young audiences, our extraction of all 'romance' from the narrative laid bare the malevolence of a kind of manipulation that was high on the news agenda of the time.

We began the performance of 'Pygmalion' – equivalent to our openings of 'Streetcar' and 'Crucible' – with a prologue in which all of the cast together show and tell the audience the classical myth of Pygmalion, a sculptor who, in disgust at the desirous behaviour of real women in his sophisticated city, creates his own ideal woman in stone. Then falls in love with his image. From classical Greece in our prologue, by the end of the play, we moved Shaw's Edwardian comedy onto uncompromisingly contemporary territory, laying bare the misogynistic and anti-sexual narrative it manifests. By responding to an existing and authoritative text as if it were raw material, we were able to transform a crafted and 'crafty' piece of idealism, which both celebrates and critiques bigotry, into its own undoing. In its own words. And meanwhile entertain its audiences.

Much to our amazement, where we feared a talkative Shavian script might be met with (at best polite) disinterest, our 'Pygmalion' generated a welcome outrage, fury and resolve from its audiences. The production demonstrated – in realisation of a proposition that Meyerhold had sustained in his 1926 production of 'The Government Inspector', but that we had never experienced with such intensity – that a text is only ever a pre-text; that in the workshops, production preparations and in the rehearsal room, a text, any text, becomes something that is never itself again, and sometimes becomes almost its opposite.

Chapter Twelve: China

By Paul

This is Chairman Mao's theatre. At the height of the Cultural Revolution, Madame Mao would invite her husband to view Socialist ballets on the very stage where TNT is about to start our own Theatrical Revolution. In less than a decade our company will establish itself as not just the most popular foreign theatre company to visit China but the only true nationally touring theatre in China performing in any foreign language. More than that, we will collaborate with Chinese artists to create a performance and touring base for TNT productions in Mandarin. There will be single performances such as those of 'Othello' on an open-air stage near Canton or in the Great Hall of Peking University that will hold more audience members than saw entire tours in Britain in the 1980s. The Great Hall holds 2,400 people. We often perform for two nights and fill the space. Our outdoor audience for 'Othello' numbered over 3,000 people on one sweaty night. It is easy to be seduced by numbers when talking about China; there are, for example, 22 exits to the People's Square Underground station next door to our usual theatre in Shanghai! There are twice as many people in Shanghai as in all of Scandinavia…

TNT has toured to China at least thirty times since 2005. I was reliably told that audiences in Shanghai believe TNT to mean "The National Theatre". We were in China at the right time; just as the country was examining its relationship with theatre. Our breakthrough production was 'Oliver Twist'. It is the very essence of TNT theatre: it is set on a gallows, its furniture is a coffin, its holding form is a speech before an execution. Yes, Dickens hangs Fagin but nobody else in film, musical or theatre wants to address that uncomfortable fact. We do. We place what is ignored in the very forefront of our production and ask "why?". The theatrical style of the production swerves from comic grotesque in the workhouse to heightened realism for the tragic fates of Nancy, Bill and Fagin. Sung music will underscore each death, Fagin's hanging accompanied by a Yiddish lament as he cries out: "If I am so evil why am I so poor?"

It is this relation between poverty and crime that fascinated the young Dickens and which now strikes a chord with our Chinese audience. Tom Johnson's haunting score is sung *a cappella* by the cast. This is not a musical, it is too dark for that, it is music theatre sustained by the human voice, which moves as Brecht suggests from speech via heightened speech to song. The ghost of Brecht's composer, Kurt Weill, lingers in Tom's savage harmonies.

The Chinese know 'Oliver Twist'. Dickens was always held in great esteem, both before and after the Communists took power in 1949. I find it touching that the same reverence is given to Charlie Chaplin; two boys from that part of London that I know best (south of the river). They both knew the prison, the workhouse and poverty and used grotesque humour to change the world through art.

In China, our own 'Oliver Twist' has had a double effect: its economy and athleticism astonished an audience accustomed to ponderous theatre with vast casts and huge sets, and it showed that music and theatre could combine without being superficial and shallow. It spoke to an audience which has itself experienced a rapid transition from poverty to wealth that has left many behind. Touring our 'Oliver Twist' in China, we joked that we felt like the Beatles in Hamburg. We were surfing a wave that we had not known existed. Some of the performances our canny Beijing producer, Cui Yang, has managed to pull out of the hat have been extraordinary. Initially booked to perform only in Beijing and Shanghai, we were suddenly offered the grand theatre in Hangzhou and when we responded expeditiously found 800 audience members waiting for us in a building the size of a cathedral.

Our 'Oliver Twist' has become a staple on the Chinese theatrical scene. In 2012 I was invited to restage the production in Mandarin at the Shanghai Dramatic Arts Centre. Once again it swept the board and now regularly tours China. I have no idea when it is performed as I am seldom told. Sadly, the royalty agreement is another joke in this grotesque comedy. But then that is China too: hard-nosed and uncompromising. I let it ride.

> TNT is China's Shakespeare champion; as the most established and compact group, it has the broadest touring circuit, which includes second-tier cities and countless universities.
>
> (Nancy Pellegrini, *The People's Bard: How China Made Shakespeare Its Own*, Penguin, 2016: p.110.)

If the Chinese value Charles Dickens, they adore William Shakespeare. I cannot prove it, but I believe there are more statues of Shakespeare than of Mao Tse Tung in China today. I think it is crucial to understand that there is no clear distinction between religion and literature in China. This ought not to be such a shock to us if we reflect that in ancient Greece it was much the same.

Shakespeare has his own history in China. His works influence modern Chinese literature. There is even a classic debate as to which of the three best known translators of his work are superior: Bian Zhilin and Lian Shiqiu who claim accuracy or Zhu Shenghao who aims for the poetic. I think we need to go further than say that this love of Shakespeare is all a part of China's fascination with the West. Rather China is confused by the West. As the Middle Kingdom, the centre of the earth, China felt able to reject the West as late as 1800. When the British sent an embassy to the emperor with the finest and most modern products of the Industrial Revolution, the Chinese replied that they simply did not need the artefacts. The Middle Kingdom had nothing more to learn. Indeed, China had a greater GDP than Britain at that time, so advanced was its own science. But the next century went horribly wrong for China. The country became the victim of the West in a way that even India never did. It was rape, followed by mayhem. There simply were no benefits to Western and Japanese interference for the Chinese.

It has taken 150 years for China to emerge from the horrors of a period when more of its people died violently than those of any other population in history. It did this by adopting Western technology and philosophy; for what could be more Western than Marxism? When Marxism stuttered, the Chinese turned to capitalism. Their extraordinary success, however, masks an insecurity: for the Western values they have embraced are not the same as the old Chinese values. The deeply cultured Chinese turn to literature for some understanding of this conundrum, and so it is natural that the Chinese reach for the West's greatest poet in order to understand not only the West but themselves.

A curious proof of this is a production of 'Much Ado About Nothing'. TNT has enjoyed considerable success with our own version, partly because 'Much Ado' is the single clearest marker for the start and end of Mao's Cultural Revolution. In 1961 director Hu Dao produced 'Much Ado', complete with elongated 'Western' noses for his actors. In 1979 he restaged the production in Shanghai, which was then broadcast on state television. What was remarkable was that every single actor from the 1961 production reappeared on stage, even those who had been punished or exiled during the Cultural Revolution. The noses also made a reappearance. It was as if the Chinese public knew the nightmare of the Cultural Revolution was over because they saw Shakespeare on the TV again. The other proof of the pudding was Dickens's 'David Copperfield', which was serialised on the same national TV channel, and which TNT toured in China in our own version in 2011.

Dickens's novel and Shakespeare's play both deal with forgiveness and reconciliation, using humour to express sympathy for the underdogs such as Hero or Mr Micawber. Just as the Cultural Revolution used culture to humiliate and crush the more sensitive members of society: teachers, artists, intellectuals and even lofty party members such as the much-loved Deng Xiao Ping (the true creator of modern China), so culture came to the rescue. It helped reconnect China with the West. Deng himself used poetic metaphors to express his key policies, such as his memorable, "It does not matter whether the cat is black or white as long as it catches mice", which signalled the end of ideology and the start of the pragmatism that has taken China to its present stage.

It is important to remember that TNT is not bringing Shakespeare to China. We are finding him there. Not long ago, I travelled with our company of 'Midsummer Night's Dream' actors, driving into a sprawling boom city larger than either Rome or Berlin. Our first performance was miles from the centre, in an industrial zone obscured by smog. At the city limits we were greeted by a new construction: a semi-circle of vast Doric columns linked by classical arches (reminding me of a recent visit to the Temple of Zeus in Athens) set against a backdrop of tower blocks, pylons and smoke stacks. Later that day, well over one thousand students packed into a lecture theatre to see our performance; many stood for almost three hours, even the stairs were used as seats. It would be impossible to ask for a better audience. They laughed and shouted their approval, interrupting the Mechanicals scenes with constant applause and cheering when the lovers were finally reunited to their true loves. There was no irony in their response which was entirely fresh; I felt as if I had been transported to the Globe on the play's premiere.

So the question is: how do the complete misunderstanding and misuse of Western classical culture represented by that columned monument and the astonishing passion for genuine classical art – Shakespeare's 'A Midsummer Night's Dream' – co-exist in such proximity? I asked a Chinese friend why he thought a set of classical columns and not a Chinese monument was built. He replied that "the Chinese lack self-confidence". This at first seems strange, given the extraordinary developments of modern China in fields from economics to sports. Yet modern China seems more at home in its present than with its past. Dislocation is a key word. Here is another example: in Shanghai there is a fascinating private museum of

Maoist posters and propaganda paintings. There is nothing critical of the Communist Party and although the museum is in the basement of an apartment building it is clearly not clandestine. You can find directions to it in the Lonely Planet guide. Much of the art work is exceptional, and its historical value is immense. Yet, when I told a different Chinese friend about this museum, a young bilingual and well-travelled artist, he said: "What do you want to go there for? No one is interested in that old stuff any more."

So, if the "world is out of joint", does Shakespeare offer China a way of dealing with cultural dislocation? How else can we explain the status of Shakespeare in China, when four thousand people come to see TNT's 'Othello' in a medium size city near Guangzhou, crowding into an outdoor arena as if at a rock concert. And this is not a general desire to see Western performance. We have on occasion struggled to raise an audience. Having filled the National Centre for Performing Arts in Beijing for 'Romeo and Juliet' we were disappointed to see half empty houses at the same theatre one week later for our highly accessible 'Gulliver's Travels'.

The position of Shakespeare in China is exceptional. The first translation of a Shakespeare play into Mandarin was made less than a hundred years ago. Yet here is the astonishing rise of Shakespeare to the status of a core writer in a culture that is so ancient and successful, but so ambivalent about its rapid rise and shifting identity.

"And nothing is but what is not…"

Perhaps what is most crucial for understanding Shakespeare in China, is that the country underwent a ten-year-long Cultural Revolution, beginning in 1966. The phrase 'cultural revolution' is now so well worn that it is in danger of losing its meaning; but in 1966 this ancient civilisation experienced a total break with its past, a cutting off of its cultural lifeblood, and all this is within the memory of many people alive today. Today, the connection is re-growing, but the trauma remains. How similar this is to the savage break with the past that Shakespeare himself experienced within his lifetime! The Reformation destroyed not only the continuity of religion but also of popular theatre and other arts. The repertoire of Catholic mystery plays was destroyed forever. They were consigned to the archive, with an occasional revival today. The same with many folk customs which were suppressed or went 'underground'. Shakespeare's fear of civil war and chaos, an ever-present theme in his plays, from 'Henry VI' to 'The Tempest', is also a preoccupation of the Chinese as they look back on the period from the Opium Wars to the fall of Madam Mao.

The cultural dislocation of Elizabethan England was the background and starting point for Shakespeare's revolutionary idea: that the individual could explore the answers to the conundrums of the age without recourse to fixed beliefs. As Hamlet points out: "There is nothing good nor bad but thinking makes it so". Shakespeare's genius was to span the cultural divide; retaining the 'balance' of an old hierarchy, while sampling the fecundity of its folk poetry and pastimes, at the same time as defining the emerging modern individual consciousness. Shakespeare expresses this emerging 'mind' with greater clarity than most philosophers or religious thinkers, and he does so in a form that is accessible to almost anyone.

There were many Chinese children in our subtitled performances of 'Dream' in Beijing. They were always held to the very end, howling with delight when Titania fell in love with the ass or Pyramus over-acted his suicide. However, beyond the entertainment offered by Shakespeare's stories and characters (and it was Charles Lamb's *Tales From Shakespeare* that first made an impact in China, according to Alexa Huang, Professor of Comparative Literature at Stanford), Shakespeare is gloriously incomplete and wonderfully unspecific. Michelangelo's Sistine ceiling may be a work on a par with 'King Lear', and equally well known around the world, but it is, first of all, finished, and, secondly, it requires an understanding of Catholic mythology to make any sense. Both of which are stumbling blocks to entangling with the Chinese consciousness. 'King Lear', on the other hand, is set in an invented Albion that has more in common with China in 1900 than with any modern Britain. A dying and betrayed Sun Yat Sen (founder of modern China) is much closer to King Lear than any modern British politician. How often in the first half of the twentieth century did ordinary Chinese people feel that they were "as flies to wanton boys", that gods killed them for their sport? And what gods? Fill in as you wish.

Somehow, by spanning cultural divisions and meshing samples of traditional forms, then mashing them up with the emerging 'bourgeois' individualist consciousness, while still holding on to such old coherences as 'a world in balance', these plays are able to contain modern and even hypermodern anxieties. Providing for us the perfect material for a theatre aesthetics that is serious, literate and grotesque.

Thoughtful writing has not been so divided between art and philosophy in China as it has in Europe. From Confucius and Mencius to Mao's own poetry, there is a long tradition of the artist as a guide to living. "To be or not to be" is quoted to me with such regularity as I travel China that it clearly means something special to modern, educated Chinese. 'Hamlet' grips their Chinese imagination; this most dislocated of Shakespeare's creations holds up a special mirror to their minds. Ones in which the world is shifting and uncertain; a world where love, power and life itself is only ever provisional and uncertain. This world is built on sand, and humanity is Hamlet's "quintessence of dust". Dust settling on unsettled sand. Only an extreme life-affirming action can stand against these shiftings of the tide; hence, perhaps, the massive popularity of 'Romeo and Juliet', our most visited play nationwide.

At the same time, let us not forget the comedies, whose profundity operates in an equal but different plane. They seem to promise that, finally, extreme commitment to love and all the apparent foolishness that goes with it can result in lasting happiness. In a China of fractured families split apart by the move away from agriculture to the big cities, and single children, true love is a relationship that can hold real promise. Or, on the other hand, may turn out to be much ado about nothing.

TNT does not claim to be expert on China. But we have witnessed the extraordinary impact of Shakespeare on this modern country. The upheavals of the twentieth century may be past, but Shakespeare and the productions we are lucky enough to make of his work offer an antidote to the tawdry globalisation and fake classicism that sweep across East Asia. They also, perhaps, offer a moral compass for a turbulent future; for everything we have learned from producing his plays suggests to us that once Shakespeare had plotted out his opening situation, he let the writing form the characters, let the words and actions unfold their choices and uncage their desires. He was not writing actions to fit any fixed moral code – check out the pansexuality of the opening of his 'Twelfth Night – instead, everything had to be renegotiated and re-navigated by his characters as they passed through the turning points and crises of the play. Morality is a thriller, a cliffhanger in Shakespeare's hands. In an overly digital world he always promises a good night out. Live theatre – with plenty at stake – shared with other people. It's a potent mix.

TNT touched the hand of history when we received an urgent phone call from the British Embassy in Beijing during our first Chinese tour of 'Hamlet'. It was curious enough to be performing on Hainan, China's largest island and southernmost point. The view from the hotel window reminded me of Thailand, although the view changed radically when one afternoon the city council blew up the tower block opposite. I suppose it was not high enough. Unlike most of China, Hainan has a warm winter climate. Many senior cadres retire to the island. There was no more senior cadre living than Ji Chaozhu. Ji was Mao Tse Tung's translator and stood beside him on the balcony of the Forbidden City when the People's Republic was triumphantly proclaimed in 1949. He went on to become ambassador to Britain and the UN. In 1972 he translated and mediated between President Nixon and Premier Chou En Lai at the crucial meetings that changed the dynamics of the twentieth century. While abroad he cultivated a love of Shakespeare and attended many productions in London and New York.

TNT's visit to Hainan was an unusual event even for us. Giant banners welcomed us to the hotel and the local press hovered around us as if we were minor rock stars. One thousand people were booked to see the single performance at a cavernous auditorium. But it was that one guest who caused the panic-stricken call from Beijing: Ji Chaozhu was coming. He had not phoned the venue box office for a ticket, but the British Ambassador! We had a few hours' notice. I hastily found a tie and went to meet the great man. Hands were shaken. I expected a few halting words from the frail but elegant old man who greeted me; his unaccented English put me to shame. He was courteous and urbane. After the performance he congratulated us all and was led away by his entourage. I had shaken the hand of a man who had often shaken the hand of Chairman Mao and who had probably heard the words "To be or not to be" for the last time in a long life spent at the cutting edge of the twentieth century.

The key to our tours of China is flexibility. The cast and I travel by high speed train from, say, Shanghai to Guangzhou (Canton). We are accompanied by a bilingual Chinese tour leader and a technician. Each actor carries hand luggage of personal effects (just 10 kilos for seven weeks in Asia) and a suitcase of props and costumes. The sets are built in Beijing to our design and travel by van, covering vast distances on deserted Chinese motorways with a team of two drivers. The motorways are deserted because few Chinese drive their cars anywhere except around the mega city in which they live. Sometimes we have to fly, for example from Beijing to the world's largest city, Chunking. TNT is popular in Chunking which is famous for its highly spiced cuisine. It really is the largest metropolitan area on earth, home to around 30 million people. Chunking has built two theatres to prove it is at the cultural forefront of China: a concert hall at the confluence of the Yangtse and a new theatre in the centre of the town constructed, it seems, from giant chopsticks. We perform in the latter.

One product of the rise of China is the competition between major cities to build the swankiest theatre. This has helped us enormously since the municipalities are then often unsure how to fill their prestigious new buildings. We are able to offer 'Hamlet' or 'Oliver Twist' at an affordable price and with a reputation for being accessible. Unlike the infrequently visiting Globe or Royal Shakespeare Company, we can build a loyal local audience as we return twice a year to most venues. TNT also responds to sudden interest. 'Hamlet' went well in Beijing in May; by November we were back, responding to an urgent phone call to Grantly at his Munich office asking if we could take a newly available slot at the same Beijing venue.

There is also a question of style. TNT does not make theatre for foreigners. We make theatre for everyone, including young people. Families pack into a theatre in distant Chengdu (population a mere 8 million) for a Sunday afternoon performance of 'Hamlet'. Kids run up and down the aisles. Adults munch sunflower seeds. Loud laughter accompanies Rosencrantz and Guildenstern's sycophantic antics. At the finale, shock waves pass around the audience as Hamlet dies; surely, he was about to kill King Claudius and avenge his Dad? But no, our hero dies! Consternation sweeps through the audience. They had no idea, nothing prepared them for this. Some are sobbing as Hamlet expires in the arms of Horatio and the "the rest is silence". Black out. A moment's hush, even the kids are quiet and the sunflower husks no longer hit the floor. Then, as the cast bow, the audience rise in a standing ovation. Where did they learn to do that? I have never seen one before or since in China. As for old, so for new; as for Ji Chaozhu, so for the children of Chengdu: Shakespeare and TNT Theatre.

Our key intention is always to elucidate Shakespeare rather than interpret Shakespeare. I have written elsewhere in this book about the need to ask "what does it mean?" rather than "where is it set?" Our 'Hamlet' is not turgidly traditional; it includes a live score by Thomas Johnson that sings to the text. Hamlet may be on drum, Ophelia plays the violin. The costumes are stylised, yet historical. The King wears a crown. There are sword fights. The set is an abstract crescent of wood, Rosencrantz and Guildenstern are clowns and the dumb show is realised with giant puppets. But, above all, the storyline is clear. We are not performing for audiences who have seen so many 'Hamlets' they want it set in a giant dolls' house, or with the bizarre doubling that I saw recently in Berlin. Shakespeare wrote "the play's the thing to catch the conscience of the King" and not the director's ego. We are not performing for our peers nor for the critics. I am not trying to make my name to move on to greater things. I am too old to be an *enfant terrible*.

And what of the other China, the country that is not embracing the values we in the West hold dear? Well since this is not a nostalgic memoir but the account of an ongoing and intimate relationship with the world's most populous nation, I am not prepared to bite the hand that feeds us, (especially given my love of its cuisine). Sometimes we have brushed up against a harsher world, such as when we were ushered offstage before a performance to some 3,000 students because of nearby unrest. But, all in all, our experience of China has brought us into contact with the positive: we have felt the effects of 300 million people being raised out of poverty while our own country, the UK, sees nothing but increased inequality. At midnight in Shanghai I walk alone along deserted streets and fear nothing.

It has always been the aim of TNT to move beyond touring theatre and create theatre with artists from the countries in which we tour. Our first co-production was with TamS Theatre in Munich in 1987, and since then – despite a misfire with a small Polish company (a little too nationalist-mystical for our tastes) – we have created work in languages other than English with Greek, Russian, Italian, Spanish, French, Costa Rican and above all Chinese artists. I have immersed myself in China in a very special way, spending many months in an exclusively Chinese environment. I joke that no other non-Mandarin speaker may know China as well as I…

The bizarreness of the situation is such that I fling my arms round my old friend and collaborator, the musical director of the Shanghai Dramatic Arts Centre, without ever having exchanged a word of language with him; we have worked together on three productions. The actor Shen Lee is another example, having performed both Petruchio and Sherlock Holmes for me with precision and passion. He is a man of great integrity and almost ruthless skill. He threatened to walk out of 'Taming of the Shrew' because another actor was habitually late to rehearsal. He is so well known in Shanghai from his film and TV work that the audience applaud him on his entrance, but he is always humble and seeks to expand his range and learn from me as I learn from him. We recently worked together on 'The Murder of Sherlock Holmes', an old TNT hit that I created anew in Shanghai some twelve years after its last European tour. Shen Lee watches a DVD of my performance of the great detective and copies my mannerisms and timing with such precision that I feel I am watching my younger self in some strange dream world where I speak Mandarin.

Although a few artists do speak English or a halting version, most do not. I hold rehearsals with the aid of skilful translators. The best is Lin Qian. She is herself a playwright but earns her living as a specialist arts translator across many mediums including the minefield of orchestral conducting. We have become good friends.

The Shanghai Dramatic Arts Centre is the hub of theatre in that great city and I have been fortunate to have been invited to direct there after the success of our touring productions. The theatre stands on Anfu Lu at the heart of the French Concession, the leafy former-colonial hub of sophisticated Shanghai. Theatre is so cool and hip in the city that Anfu Lu has benefited by the presence of the theatre. Wine bars and French bakeries rub shoulders with craft beer bars and fancy boutiques. Is this a good thing? When I first worked at the SDAC there was a cheap and cheerful Szechuan restaurant in an old building by the theatre. The building now houses a sterile boutique. A glass of wine and a sourdough pizza on Anfu Lu costs more than its equivalent in Milan. But we should not mock this 'progress' too much. That theatre is hip activity in modern Shanghai points to a bright future for our art. A place for wired and serious live performance to speak directly to the conscience of huge numbers of people at the heart of the world's fastest growing economy.

The SDAC has a wide repertoire. Recent examples I have seen include a fine production of Tennessee Williams' 'Glass Menagerie' and a homegrown musical about Karl Marx. The SDAC is housed on the first six floors of a tower block, with rehearsal rooms added on the 22nd floor and three different performance spaces. There are 150 actors under some sort of contract. The theatre is the only recognised production house in Shanghai. The complex is run by a troop of young administrators overseen by Nick Rongjin, one of Asia's leading playwrights. The theatre regularly hosts foreign companies and enjoys a healthy competition with Beijing's Capitol Theatre for the mantle of China's leading theatre. Nick is trusted by both the artistic community and the authorities, no mean feat. It was Nick who invited me to direct at the SDAC and together we decided upon 'The Taming of the Shrew'.

TNT's version of the play had been a success in China. I was quietly confident we could repeat that in Mandarin, but I wanted to do something more than imitate a TNT show. So, I transposed the setting to 1930s' Shanghai, the golden age of the pre-Revolutionary city. In 1930 Shanghai was the biggest industrial city in Asia, a strange boom town run by a consortium of colonial powers and finance houses. As there were five jurisdictions, a gangster could commit a crime in the French Concession and nip over the border to the British Concession for afternoon tea. Appalling poverty rubbed cheeks with staggering wealth. There are still more Art Deco buildings in Shanghai than anywhere outside of New York or Chicago.

As Shanghai was not a state, no one required a visa to enter or live in its modern limbo. White Russians fleeing from Stalin rubbed shoulders with Jews fleeing the Nazis. Most bizarrely, Chinese Revolutionaries fleeing the Chinese Republican government felt safe in Shanghai. Indeed, the Chinese

Communist party was founded here. The building where the first meeting was held is now a museum. Above it towers a huge billboard advertising Calvin Klein underwear. Of more practical interest to me was the invention of a uniquely Chinese form of Jazz, helped along by the unsegregated clubs and cabarets where many Black American Jazz musicians played.

In my 'Taming of the Shrew', Kate is from a conservative Chinese family who dress as traditionally as their father wishes them to act. Kate's suitor and extrovert manipulator, Petruchio, comes from another world. He leaps from his motorbike in a double-breasted suit. The score, all of which is live, uses traditional Shanghai songs and some of the extraordinary Jazz written in the Art Deco high rises of what was then surely the wildest city in the East. The transposition involves some fairly major changes, for example with the wedding scene; I find myself taking lessons on traditional Chinese marriage ceremonies and then comically subverting them with the aid of my cast. At other times the culture clash is an almost insurmountable one. The most famous line in the play is clearly "kiss me, Kate". Her reply is "what here in the street?" And indeed, they do kiss. But not in China! No one kisses in the street in China (except prostitutes). The cast are firm. A public kiss is unthinkable nowadays and ten times more so in 1930. I can only persuade them to agree once we see that Petruchio is prepared to break every rule in order to tame his Kate and that Kate is a rebel so wild that she is prepared to break the same taboos. And the audience are included, asked by Petruchio to give their assent. The Chinese adore audience participation. They also know how to laugh. A total contrast to the behaviour of a Japanese audience. In China comedy is king. Almost every Beijing taxi driver will be listening to stand-up comedy on his radio, rather than music.

'The Taming of the Shrew' speaks directly to the current confusion in gender relations in China. Strong women are traditionally seen as threats. The Cultural Revolution is usually blamed on Madam Mao. The collapse of Chinese power in the nineteenth century is placed at the feet of the Empress Dowager, one of the few women to have ruled China. The Communist Constitution gives equal rights to men and women but the reality is that few women rise to powerful positions, especially those that involve commanding men. But there is another force at play here; one that springs from the 'one child' policy.

Young Chinese women tend to be better educated than their male counterparts. They are often the family breadwinners. Many refuse to marry in order to preserve their independence. The pressure from their families is also to remain single, lest they lose their income to a son-in-law.

From my perspective, young women make up a high proportion of our audience. Shakespeare's battle of the sexes resonates. And before the reader accuses us of reinforcing sexism, I should add that in both our European and Chinese versions of the play, a little research – as so often has been the case with our Shakespeare productions and classics adaptations – turns the play on its head without traducing it. In the Folio version of Shakespeare's works 'The Taming of the Shrew' has a prologue: aristocratic huntsmen come upon a drunken man, Sly, in a country pub in Warwickshire. They play various tricks on the drunk, persuading him that he is a Lord who fell into a long sleep and now must be returned to his noble life (and wife). They even engage a group of travelling players to perform a play, which is the 'Taming of the Shrew', set in Italy.

This Folio version ends with the (rather sexist) conclusion of the Italian play-within-a-play. But there is another, older, text called 'The Taming of the Shrew'. In this version, at the conclusion of the travelling players' story, we return to the Warwickshire pub where the drunken Sly wakes up and tells the landlady that he has had a marvellous dream in which he taught a woman how to behave and respect him. The Hostess taunts the drunken tinker: "Your wife will thrash you when you get home!" In both of our versions this "Lady Wife" appears, throws Sly over her shoulder, just as Petruchio mistreated Kate, and carries him off for his thrashing. Blackout. The play is not simply rescued, but it is restored to balance; a score draw in this cruel but hilarious battle of the sexes.

This Mandarin 'Taming of the Shrew' has become an audience favourite and remains in regular repertoire some nine years after its first run. It has toured across China including to the National Theatre in Beijing and is probably the most performed Shakespeare production in Mandarin in the last ten years or more.

During rehearsals for my next Mandarin production, 'Oliver Twist', I am invited to give a talk to designers and senior engineers at the largest car plant in Shanghai. I am told that they are well prepared, speak good English and my talk is part of a package that includes a forthcoming backstage tour and a reception after seeing the play. A car is sent to pick me up on Anfu Lu. I grab a coffee, which is a good idea as the journey lasts almost two hours. We snake through the suburbs of the megacity, fly over flyovers and once out of the centre drive along almost deserted six-lane highways. The Chinese are building for the future. We eventually pull into a huge factory complex and I am led by a pair of uniformed security guards to a hall, passing draughtsmen at work on large computer screens. I am utterly alone. I feel like an albino ant in a giant nest of frantic activity. At length I am led into a carpeted hall. Applause breaks out from some two hundred be-suited engineers and designers. An English speaker welcomes me and leads me to a lectern on which stands a plastic bottle of water.

I am introduced and assured that the audience speak a high level of English. Declining the microphone, I begin. I may not know the life and works of Charles Dickens as well as I know those of Shakespeare, but I have dramatised (with Phil Smith) three of his novels, read the biographies and drunk a pint or two in his hometown of Rochester. So, I start. After about twenty minutes exploring the similarities of the world's first megacity, London, with Shanghai and placing 'Oliver Twist' within that context I begin to realise that the eyes of my audience are glazing over. It dawns on me that this is a captive audience in the worst sense; their grasp of spoken, let alone literary, English does not match that of the technical language in which they are no doubt fluent. So, what is to be done? Is it ruder to continue or to stop?

I test the water with a rather random insertion of a verbal joke that usually goes down well in Asia. Nothing, not a titter. And this is China where comedy is king. (It's a joke about a rabbit on a motorbike, it even has some relevance to engine design). This all has to stop in mid flow. I pretend that my talk is complete and that it had always been my intention to get the audience on their feet and play theatre games.

None of the games I know has the slightest relevance to 'Oliver Twist', but what am I supposed to do? Run a pick pocket workshop? We clear aside two hundred chairs and form a wide circle. My repertoire of theatre games has never been tested on such a scale. Nor with Chinese engineers in suits. My favourite game is Dwarves, Wizards and Giants, which is loosely based on scissor, paper, stone. I have adapted this to feature three types of physical theatre role, structured around a simple movement sequence ending in an explosion of competitive tag. No one gets knocked out. A losing Dwarf simply joins the Giants.

You may have noticed that every one of these designers and engineers is male, so no one is going to fall over their high heels; except perhaps the woman whose job it was to replace my plastic water bottle and present me with a bouquet of flowers. The massed engineers and designers seize enthusiastically upon the game, there are squeals of delight as at last they are allowed to become mythical creatures and play tag. I say "at last" because I had the impression that the game had liberated a long-suppressed love of play. Which returns me to the idea I discuss in the theoretical sections of this book: that play and plays, playing and players are all linked. Good theatre releases the playfulness in both artist and audience, after the most enjoyable activity of childhood has been banished from our adult lives or channelled into competitive sport.

In the West I believe that such a group would have held onto their inhibitions or relinquished them more slowly. Here the Chinese technocrats fling themselves into the games. Time is forgotten and we run hopelessly over my allotted slot. My reward is to hit the Shanghai rush hour, but as I sit in the back of my limousine nursing a huge bouquet of flowers and sipping at my water bottle I feel it was a day's work where once again I had learnt as much as I had taught.

'Oliver Twist' repeats the success of 'Taming of the Shrew'. It tours widely in and around Shanghai and enters the theatre's long-term repertoire. We are becoming something of a force in the cultural world of this megacity. At which point we attract the attention of the Chinese Army. A year later, I am leaving my comfortable apartment above the theatre on Anfu Lu by taxi and arriving at a tower block in a rather rougher area of town. No cappuccinos here. I take a lift to the sixth floor and am ushered into the presence of Colonel Lin. She is both charming and forceful. Hers is the hand of command. Beside her stand two leading members of the local Communist party. This is the committee of the People's Liberation Army Shanghai Farce Troupe.

They 'invite' me to direct 'A Midsummer Night's Dream'. Refusal is not part of the equation. The only problem is that I am already contracted to direct 'The Murder of Sherlock Holmes' at the SDAC at the same time. We arrive at a compromise, I will cast the play, adapt it and direct the first three weeks of rehearsals. My long-term TNT colleague Eric Tessier-Lavigne will complete the work while I shift over to rehearse 'Sherlock Holmes'. Directing the production will prove a new type of challenge; the Army Farce Troupe have never worked with a foreign director and they expect much of the dialogue to be in the local dialect, which is almost a separate language to Mandarin.

The process will be helped by the presence of two rather extraordinary actors who will play Oberon and Puck; one a master of traditional opera and "First Class Artist" and the other a graduate of Gaulier's clown school in Paris. One resembles a fading matinee idol, the other a mischievous Hobbit. Both are Party members and hold military rank. Many a lunch break is extended while the Committee meet. Ironically, directing at the SDAC can be quite a lonely experience; Chinese actors certainly do not have a drinking culture and the city is so large that most vanish after rehearsals. Besides which there are other foreigners buzzing around the SDAC and indeed in the coffee shops of Anfu Lu. The Farce Troupe are very warm people; on the first day of rehearsal the Colonel arrives with a giant cake to celebrate my birthday, which is only four weeks away... I get to grips with some startling names in the army: Echo, Melon and Maud are the three women who translate or help deal with the bureaucracy. Chinese people are very content to choose their own Western names. Where 'Melon' and 'Echo' came from, I have no idea. Maud is one of the best translators I have worked with, an arts student of great sensitivity whom Eric and I enjoy introducing to craft beer.

The Amazons attack at the start of the Army Farce Troupe's 'A Midsummer Night's Dream', directed by Paul Stebbings in Shanghainese and Mandarin

The production itself allows us to have as many Fairies and Amazons as we could ever wish for! The Fairies play traditional Chinese instruments such as the two-string violin. Bottom and the Mechanicals use heavy Shanghai dialect. The Farce Troupe has a noble purpose, preserving the traditional culture of Shanghai, a city that invented its own dialect and hybrid culture as it sprang from fishing village to a hub of the modern world in less than two hundred years. Short farces in heavy dialect became the calling card of Shanghai culture in the 1920s and were seen by the Party and the People's Liberation Army as part of the Folk Culture of the People (quite correctly) and something to be encouraged, even on a military level.

Asia abounds with giant cities whose similarities can grind the visitor down. Shanghai is different, not least because about half its centre is made up of elegant rows of houses and villas from its golden epoch. But Shanghai is also different because it has an energy that comes from being China's greatest city, while not its capital. Globalisation dilutes its individuality, but Shanghai fights back better than Seoul or Jakarta. So I salute Colonel Yin and the People's Liberation Farce Troupe for defending the soul of this grand city in an increasingly soulless world.

Meanwhile TNT shifts its own touring performances to the much larger Shanghai Grand Theatre on People's Square. From the square it is a short walk to the Bund and the astonishing view over the Huangpo river as it heads towards the mouth of the Yangtse. On one side of the Bund stand the grand Edwardian buildings of Shanghai's British heyday, a sort of Liverpool of the East. On the other bank rises the largest collection of skyscrapers on earth. This view, which reaches its apogee at night when the lights of the skyscrapers match the floodlit domes and columns on the opposite shore, can be seen as a metaphor for our own work in Shanghai: British and Chinese, rooted culture and futuristic forest, West and East. And the twain do meet.

Paul Stebbings in front of the new theatre in Chongqing China, about to host TNT's 'Hamlet'

Failure

By Paul

Any book by any artist about their own art is likely to focus on their successes. Theatre is a very cruel way to make a living. For decades, newspapers have featured theatre reviews far more than the criticism of other art forms because a review that tears a performance to pieces makes for entertaining reading. There are so many things that can go wrong in theatre. I recall a great review of our 'Romeo & Juliet' from Buxton Opera House that decided to praise everything to the heights, yet savaged the set. TNT has even used bad reviews in our publicity, such as the *Colchester Evening Standard's* rather thrilling assessment of an early show as: "a tedious evening of sadism and transvestism". Clearly, a critic with a boisterous social life.

Failure in theatre is not only a matter of poor reviews. It is also the consequential matter of poor audience figures and the judgement of funding bodies and promoters. And when a tour is booked, the failure must still take the road. The depressed artists must drag their wounded production around the circuit like a dying bird on a string.

TNT has had its fair share of failures, mostly and crucially in our early days when we needed to learn from experiments but also had less of a reputation to fall back upon. An artist can only develop if they do not repeat and the new is always risky. However, a company that calls itself The New Theatre must take risks. There is no gamble without the potential to fail. No rock face that the climber assaults without the fear of falling. We are not alone in this. Shakespeare himself wrote 'Timon Of Athens' between penning 'Hamlet' and 'Macbeth'. How could he do that? Beethoven's Fourth Symphony anyone? They were human, they were experimental, they were artists.

One very useful failure was our early production called 'Don't Look Back', loosely based on Russell Hoban's far better novel *Kleinzeit*, which is itself flexibly modelled on the Orpheus myth. This show had followed hot on the heels of two of our early hits: 'Harlequin' and 'English Tea Party'. We also had the addition of the performer we most wanted to join the company:

the French Circus-trained Mark Heron. How could we go wrong? We even had a grant. Kleinzeit, played by me, was a lisping failure who encounters love and death on the London underground. Death was played by Simon Clews as an ape that only spoke medieval English, gleaned from Mystery Plays. Wisdom or Orpheus was a juggling tramp played by Mark. It sounds wonderful but it wasn't. It did not gel.

I recall a particularly disastrous night in Croydon where the set fell down mid show and the hugely influential 1980s' London magazine *Time Out* gave us a big thumbs down. We lost some of our grant money and had to mount our next production on even less money. But what we did learn from this failure was just how effective the integration of old English poetry within a modern play could be. So when we created 'Cabaret Faust', our biggest British hit, we integrated text from Marlowe's 'Doctor Faustus' within our story of temptation and betrayal in the 1930s.

After 'Cabaret Faust' the company suffered another shock. This time the problem was our own success. Sudden darlings of the Arts Council and feted by Britain's main music festival we set out on a new play 'Tempest Now'. This could have been a fine production but it was undermined by a coup, orchestrated by a good actor who shall remain nameless. In a series of bureaucratic manoeuvres, he persuaded us to turn TNT into a cooperative and then proceeded to collect the votes of newcomers to the company to exclude the veterans who had built it up. The victims of his purges included our composer John Kenny and our faithful administrator. Then the play itself became subject to writing by committee and was pushed towards realism. (I took my stand by portraying the Latin American dictator Supresor with non-realist relish). 'Tempest Now' was not a disaster; the *Financial Times* liked it, but many people were disappointed after the vibrancy and down-to-earth tragic-comedy of 'Cabaret Faust'.

In the closing phases of the 'Tempest Now' tour the company split. The manoeuvrer took over the rump and Mark Heron and I fled to Germany to take up an invitation from TamS theatre in Munich. When the rump applied to the Arts Council they were put on hold. Without the certainty of pay, the actors refused to commit to the project. A few weeks later the Welsh Arts Council came riding to our rescue and commissioned a new piece of music theatre that became 'The Wizard of Jazz'; our (let's be immodest) global success.

There were structural lessons to be learnt. We veterans had allowed our general beliefs about democratic social organisation to damage the production of art. Eight writers are not eight times better than one. Yes, share, yes, be open, yes, give weight to the opinions and ideas of fellow artists, but art is for the audience and an audience is made up of individuals. In order to reach that audience at the end of the process, there had to be some individualism and individual responsibility at the front end too. I can understand if some people disagree with the conclusions that this failure suggested to us. But when the company was formally restructured we always included on the contract: "While every effort will be made to reach decisions by consensus the director shall have authority over the production".

Does this go against what I have written about wanting to abolish the director? I don't think so, because that is an ambition. I would honestly like to be able to work in that way, but in the meantime we have an audience and we need to allow the impulse towards co-operation into our art without paralysing our art.

Perhaps the crucial point here is that in 'Tempest Now' we had, understandably, some actors who just wanted a job and others who were committed to our long-term ensemble with all the sacrifices that that would involve. There was a need for a structure that could accommodate both levels of commitment, not just one. How can we expect it to be otherwise? Few will commit to something so transient as a theatre company. They are probably sensible. There is a kind of absurdity in our commitment to the future; somehow we have got away with it so far! We even dramatised this dilemma in 'Cabaret Faust'. The play follows the fortunes of two socialist actors in 1930s' England, one who sells out to the theatres of smart West End London before joining fascist-backed tours of Germany, the other who stays true to his principles and Northern working class community, and then attempts and fails to assassinate the British fascist leader, Oswald Mosely. The real-life socialist actor who played the would-be assassin was himself offered a West End role during our long tour of our 'Cabaret Faust'. He took the job. He was poor; he used to slip his dad a ten-pound note when they met. I understand why he left our company.

No one should get too high and mighty when commenting on the choices of actors. The level of attrition is extraordinary – only coal miners and steel workers have had it as bad. Who has survived from the subsidised British touring theatre circuit of the 1980s? Théâtre de Complicité, Forced Entertainment, Kneehigh and TNT. Are there many others? We all adapted and changed and only did so because we learnt from failure.

Nor did we stop failing when we expanded and joined hands with Grantly Marshall's ADG Europe. But by then we had learnt how to make more of our productions consistent. Our failures since have come more from putting the plays in front of the wrong audiences, or casting the wrong actors, than from the production process.

Dhera Dun, India. We have been invited to perform 'A Midsummer Night's Dream' in two Himalayan hill stations. We cross the Punjab by train, dangling our legs out of the carriage door and watching the eternal India of bullock carts and peasant farmers working the land with little more than their own strength. Dhera Dun had moved with the times; most of the hill stations near Delhi have lost their charm and sunk beneath a sea of cheap bars pumping out Bollywood pop. A forlorn Victorian church, its fabric rotting under the lash of a hundred monsoons, looks on like an old aunt at a teenage party. We check into a hotel on the quieter edge of town. I feel at home, reminded of my backpacking days many years ago. There is a scream. Natalia has found a giant reptile in her bathroom. The Queen of the Fairies is reassured and a houseboy evicts the monitor lizard.

The next day, after breakfasting on fresh mango, we head for the venue, a modest sports stadium. We are told to expect an audience of between two and three hundred. We are asked if we want microphones. We decline, confident our voices can carry. It is only about an hour before the performance that we find that we are not the main attraction. Two events are to precede our play. The first a blessing by Hindu priests in the presence of a senior politician, once the Chief Minister of Uttar Pradesh (India's largest state). The second event is a traditional dance by a child prodigy. She and her mother share a dressing room with the Queen of Fairies. The girl dancer is loud and precocious, indulged in everything by her doting mother and her minder. We should have guessed by now that we were in trouble.

The sports hall is set on a hill. We can see the road leading up to the hall. Although it is dusk it is clear that there are a great many people on the road and all heading towards us. A kind Sikh gentleman, who will do his best for us all night, warns us that five hundred chairs have been put out and that many more will stand. Then the Chief Minister arrives at the centre of a motorcade. The Sikh man informs us that this Minister single-handedly revitalised India's car industry and as a young man was a *confidante* of Nehru and Ghandi. On his entrance the crowd, now literally hanging from the rafters, go wild. After the blessing and a rather long speech in Hindi, we are pushed onstage to meet the great man. He is utterly charming and invites us for morning tea at the State Bungalow. We are already almost an hour past our supposed starting time. Then they bring on the dancing girl.

"Never act with animals and children" is an old theatrical adage. The girl is dynamite and I fear we will be a damp squib. The crowd yell, cheer and clap in time to her extravagant dance that soon switches from the traditional to pure Bollywood. At last it is our turn.

The Chief Minister sits politely in the front row surrounded by acolytes and officers. The crowd continues to increase as passers-by drop in; there seem to be no tickets nor any other form of control. We try our best, but hardly anyone can hear us. After about twenty minutes the kind Sikh rushes in and takes the small microphone that the Chief Minister used and sticks it centre stage, running naked wires across our props table to do so. Sparks literally fly, but not on stage. The performance *is* a damp squib. At the interval the dancer's mother asks if we really need to perform the second half as assorted grandees want to go home but cannot until the Chief Minister rises. We hurriedly edit the second half, axing most of the lovers' scenes and pushing on to Bottom's comic tour de force. We manage to raise a few laughs and then stop as soon as we can. When we bow only the front row applaud, no doubt relieved that now they can leave. The rest of the audience seem not to notice us at all. When we get back to the hotel, drenched in sweat and so humiliated we can hardly speak, we find the bar has closed early for religious reasons.

The tour could only get worse and it did. The next performance seems promising. The theatre belongs to the Indian Civil Service staff college in the Himalayan foothills at Mussoorie. We will perform to an educated, Anglophone audience. The High Himalayas even play their part in raising our spirits by emerging from the post-monsoon clouds. Unfortunately, those same clouds are far from harmless. The first half goes well, with laughter and applause after each scene. The second half begins with Oberon telling Puck to find the lovers so they may observe "what fools these mortals be". Then we hear a tinkling on the metal roof as if someone is throwing small stones... The sound intensifies, it is a hail storm. But not a normal hail storm; this is a Himalayan hail storm. Soon no one in the audience can hear a word we say. We virtually mime the rest of the play, cut to the end as at Dehradun, and slink back to our hotel.

The next morning I complete the contractual formalities. We are supposed to be paid in Euros but I am handed our rather modest fee, in non-exchangeable rupees. I spend a hurried hour finding a man in a backstreet to give us hard cash at a terrible exchange rate. Wondering which is most likely: mugging or arrest.

On the train back to Delhi, Natalia starts to feel sick. I am next. One by one all seven of us succumb. We are due to fly to China the next day. I confess that I projectile vomit across Delhi Airport departure lounge. In Beijing we are forced to cancel the school preview and the next day we play to over 2,000 people, with the precaution of buckets stationed in each offstage wing. This time we have microphones and no hail. It all works.

India is a wonderful country, one where I spent many memorable months of my youth. But frankly, I think it was a tour too far for TNT; we failed.

Are the above examples a true confession? Is there some element of justifiable failure? Simple bad luck? If I am going to be truly honest I am going to have to mention TNT's own 'Timon Of Athens'. Why did we do it? Why when we had a production about Russia, Communism, art and dictatorship that had been lauded from Moscow to Edinburgh did we make a truly second-rate production about...Russia, Communism and dictatorship? Why did Phil Smith not tell me it was a terrible idea? Can I blame him for my dreadful idea? Or can I blame the Arts Council for forcing us to do new work rather than allowing us to develop a repertoire? Or was the Leningrad State Comedy Theatre to blame?

'The Dragon' by Yvgeny Schwarz was one of the most significant Soviet plays premiered at that theatre. A theatre where I and TNT were very much in vogue. It was probably my vanity that steered me in the direction of 'The Dragon' – after all, it was tempting to revivify a play in the theatre from which it had been banned by Stalin's censors; taking elements of the play and reworking them to look at contemporary Russia. The problem was that the play was not contemporary. The USSR was falling to pieces. Although we called our new production 'Gorbi and The Dragon' it was neither about Gorbachev nor (Stalinist) Dragons. It was just a mess. Our bad fortune was to present it at a London press night after some small success in Germany persuaded us that it was worth a shot. If only we had performed 'Harlequin' to the same critics; but we didn't and we were savaged.

I think at that point in our development we should probably not have used an existing play as a basis for our work. Later, as Phil Smith describes, we were ready for the transition. But 'Gorbi and The Dragon' was the worst of both worlds, neither an original play nor a sensitive interpretation of an existing one. However, we were chained to an Arts Council tour and some foreign dates. The show, no matter how unfit for purpose, had to go on. And, as we had fine performers in the production, the performance began to rise above the limits of the material. That summer we were invited to return to the Ukraine for the third time and offered a three-play repertoire of 'Harlequin', 'English Tea Party' and 'Gorbi and The Dragon'.

It was 1991 and Gorbachev is still in power. We were back in the USSR. After a fascinating week performing in Kiev at the venerable Podol theatre we are taken for a picnic on the wide Dnieper river by the energetic director of the theatre. He disdains vodka and swigs neat spirit from a bottle while his charming daughter splashes in the warm and muddy river. Chernobyl is not so far away; they still won't eat fish from the river. The director says he knew something was wrong when his daughter came home from school and told him that her school had given them red wine to drink. Red wine contains iodine; it was given to combat radiation sickness. Little wonder he pulls on the spirit bottle.

The director asks if we would like to perform in a small town a hundred kilometres from Kiev, called Bogoslav. We always say 'yes' to "would you". I assume we should take one of our two classic TNT shows to Bogoslav but the director suggests 'Gorbi and The Dragon'. He starts to praise our ugly duckling for its clear story and Russian themes. We are not going to argue with our host. A week later we climb aboard a bus built before any Cosmonaut circled the earth and rattle our way to Bogoslav.

We first drive to the house of the only person in Bogoslav who speaks English, a teacher in her sixties. She lives in an idyllic clapboard house, painted cloud white and sky blue, with a garden full of flowers. She pours us tea from a samovar and chats away in archaic English. This might be a scene from 'The Cherry Orchard'. After tea and pleasantries we drive into the centre of town, arriving at a 1970s' concrete complex of public buildings on a broad square. There is a band. The mayor is here to greet us. Our photographs, blown up in black and white, adorn a large billboard next to be-medalled heroes of the Soviet Union. I start to wonder if our play is suitable. Do they know? Should they be told? I think we might be risking something worse than a poor review. Yet everyone seems perfectly happy in the summer sunshine. I shake hands and smile. There is a press photographer. We wave good bye to the Mayor and his committee, assured by the teacher that we will meet again after the performance for a civic reception and buffet. "Vodka!" Our host grins, as if this were a metaphor for lasting happiness.

We unload the bus, set up and prepare for the performance. It is a Saturday matinee. Two to three hundred people file into the theatre and fill about half the large auditorium. Off we go. It is a performance I will never forget and from which we were lucky to escape unharmed. I am performing. We have no crew or back up. We are all onstage. About thirty minutes into the performance I notice some disturbance at the back of the auditorium. Because it is not a purpose-built theatre but a Hall Of The People, there is no proper blackout. I can see much of the audience. And they start to move. One or two men in black leather jackets are slowly walking along the rows of seated public. I wait until there is a long scene in which I do not appear and leave the stage through a side door. I want to find an usher. What is happening? But there are no ushers, nor any box office staff. It is a ghost building. They have all run away. What can I do? I have to be back onstage.

When I return to the stage I can just make out that a large group of leather clad heavies have now taken over the back of the auditorium. Many of the audience have fled but a core of over one hundred people are gathered around the teacher who is giving a running translation of the play. What a hero! We cannot abandon her even if we want to; there is a play on, we cannot communicate with each other. Have the other actors even noticed? Perhaps they think that some of the audience are as bored as the London critics and have gone home. We carry on. OK. We all know now. We exchange worried glances, stumble over text. It is up to me. But I am paralysed; worried that if we suddenly stop it will provoke a reaction that we cannot control.

The audience begin to form a tight knot of rebellion, while the leather jacketed heavies spread out and start to softly hiss. The play ends, we quickly bow, I shake the teacher's hand and we rush backstage. Our driver is sitting in the reception room drinking the mayor's vodka. The buffet is abandoned, the mayor has vanished. The driver shouts at us in Russian, we know what he means. "Go, just go!" So we grab a loaf of bread and, yes, a couple of bottles and run for the bus, dragging our suitcases behind us. We speed out of town looking nervously behind us for pursuing cars.

One month later the same dark forces will attempt the coup against Gorbachev and bring down the Soviet Union; a failed state whose brave citizens witnessed our failed play.

Directing Theatre

By Paul

Do we really need directors to make good theatre? This is the Dodo questioning his right to be. But am I sure I really am a director? Maybe we need to stand back and question assumptions of how we make art if we are going to make new art and if TNT is going to earn the right to its name: The New Theatre.

There is and always was a great deal of excellent performance made without the help of directors or designers. Shakespeare never met either. The ancient Greeks had chorus masters but no drama director. Japanese Kabuki and Javanese Ramayana dramas are story-driven and highly accessible theatres, but there is no director. I would rather spend the day with a bento box and a beer watching Kabuki than an evening in most European theatres. And if that sounds highbrow, my favourite recent Kabuki was called "Samurais raiding the bath house"! TNT's early work, from 'Harlequin' through to 'The Murder of Sherlock Holmes' had no director. Phil Smith would sit in on later rehearsals and focus on meaning but there were no note sessions or even plans for the rehearsal day. This included complex productions such as 'Cabaret Faust' with a mix of actors, musicians, masks, puppets and complex text ranging from political thriller to chunks of Marlowe's poetry. No one ever wrote that these productions were 'imaginative but chaotic'. I created the concepts, wrote the dialogue with Phil and did most of the administration. But I was only first among equals in rehearsal. We recruited excellent performers and paid them little enough. They needed to feel that they were participants not puppets.

I needed to act, not just because it was in my blood but because it was the only way to make a (bare) living. We could not have afforded a director, but even if we had suddenly come into possession of the required funds, we would not have spent them on one. At best, for example on 'The Murder of Sherlock Holmes', we had two actors in the company who had considerable directing experience. We would give each other notes straight after each performance; Greg Banks (who co-founded his own highly successful company Dr Fosters) would say "take the note". And we did. We trusted each other so we could criticise each other and we always changed and improved the production.

The creative process continues right to the end of the last day of the tour. I recall the final performance of 'Cabaret Faust' in Cheltenham. After eight months of touring we changed a scene, rehearsing until the moment the audience came into the theatre. In many professional theatres, things are rather different: the director vanishes after the first few performances. The production is fixed in aspic. I have given up going to transfers of National Theatre or RSC shows in London's West End to watch stale productions limping towards their final curtain call.

I cannot blame directors; the only branch of the theatrical profession with a worse unemployment rate than actors. Freelance directors keep moving to stay in work; 'in house' directors stay put until a board or a funding organisation prises them out. These realities affect how and why directors direct. Success with an audience is secondary if critics and professional peers have the greater say about a director's employment. It was like that for TNT in our early days; if the *Guardian* critic and the Arts Council assessor praised the current production we were safe for a year.

If my comments seem cynical, I am simply repeating lessons learned from my friend Andy Hay who ran the Bristol Old Vic for ten years. What should have been one of Britain's top creative jobs was often a nightmare of political and financial pressures with little time or space for actual direction. In such institutions directing becomes a symptom of hierarchical creation and controlled, risk-free environment-making, where mere actors have little or no input. The director becomes a guardian of public funding, the sensible one in the room.

And *this – these last few paragraphs!* – is what happens when you try to write about the art of direction! Instead, you end up writing about hierarchies! Or capitalism! Like professional football managers when the off-pitch part of the job distracts them from the game itself. There is too much money in football and not enough in theatre, but the effect is identical. Yet, despite their oppressive structures, the magic of both the stage and the pitch remains. Because the fans and audiences still gather together and feel alive in the presence of the live.

I think it is very difficult to change what happens on a stage without changing how the event is brought to the stage. TNT began as a company without subsidy. We gained minor subsidy very early on (thanks to Helen Flach of East Midlands Arts). We existed on the lowest rung of UK Arts Council support for thirteen years, touring to every nook and cranny of the British Isles. But from our first year we tentatively dipped our toe into commercial touring; no subsidy, just live or die by the box office takings. First in Europe; by our third year we were in New York. By the time we were collaborating with TamS Theater in Munich and had been recruited by a tours agent in Hamburg, in 1987, we were at last swimming in the waters into which we had dipped that nervous toe a few years earlier.

This change enabled us to keep successful productions in repertoire, something the UK subsidy system discouraged and at times actively prevented. Our long-term repertoire developed through performance; shows changed titles; 'The Mystery' became 'Funny Money' and switched its theatrical vocabulary from English pantomime to German fairy story; and '1945!' became 'An English Tea Party' and then 'Hitler Killed My Canary'. The last title was clearly an improvement, and so was much of the dialogue in this final version.

For a while, this approach worked well enough. It enabled us to present a three-play repertoire across Europe: 'Harlequin', 'An English Tea Party', and 'The Wizard of Jazz'. We even put on all three in repertoire in Leningrad in 1990. But the fatal flaw in all this was that I was an actor in all of the productions. I also ran our administration and the burden was too great. It was also inefficient: we might have been able to perform the three productions in three different places on the same day if I had not appeared in all three.

Then the Russians asked me to direct. Actually it was the Soviets but that changed half way through the job, which caused a few headaches! I will pass on too explicit a description of that extraordinary time (it includes the KGB and MI6). At about the same time, Grantly Marshall of the American Drama Group Europe began collaborating with TNT. I offered him a new play based on the world's most famous detective, an old-style TNT production in which I acted and co-wrote the script: 'The Murder of Sherlock Holmes'. After a successful tour of that production, Grantly Marshall asked for another. His proposal was an adaptation of Charles Dickens's novel 'Oliver Twist'. The tour that followed was to last for many, many months with performances from Singapore to Paris. The problem was, I already had acting commitments with 'Wizard of Jazz'. There was no choice in the matter, I had to direct. So it was that I suddenly found that I was a theatre director, having to work out what that meant and trying to keep artistic continuity with our early work, the heart and soul of TNT.

I went back to basics. Which start with Stanislavski.

Quite how Russia, on the edge of Europe, managed to define modern theatre is a conundrum I have no answer for. Whatever the reasons, it was Konstantin Stanislavski, an actor, right there in Moscow, who was asking the big questions; like, 'what *is* acting?' and 'how *should* we act?' He decided he could only answer these questions by getting off the stage and becoming a director. Now, in my own humble way, I was following him, only able to give my own answers to these questions by giving up what I loved: acting.

Thus I was promoted to the sidelines. The football manager is jealous of his players but knows in his heart that he can no longer play. The theatre director has no such brake on his vanity. I could still act, but I must not, because I required a wider vision.

I suspect that Stanislavski's acting was far better than his directing. When he produced Shakespeare's 'Julius Caesar' he went to Rome to study the ruins. That says it all. He should have stayed home in Moscow and read the play. His production of 'Uncle Vanya' included a complex soundtrack of frogs and crickets that drove Chekhov wild with fury. Yet, despite his fetish for the trappings of authenticity and realism, Stanislavski was onto something about character: he talks of the big arrow and the small arrows. The big arrow is the overall aim of a character in a play; the small arrows (the subordinate aims of the character) which must all build towards the trajectory of the big arrow. The different arrows can syncopate rather than just support, but they must all shoot towards the one target. This is good. This is practically useful; a model that can sustain paradox and unevenness without everything falling apart.

Stanislavski rehearsed plays for ten months and more. That was also good, because it demonstrated the need for rigour and seriousness.

Stanislavski was the first great interpreter of Ibsen and Chekhov. Put up a 'fourth wall' theatre space with a proscenium arch and no one could fill it as well as Ibsen and Chekhov. But today that is the problem; their theatre is completed, finished, all been done. Where do you go after 'The Cherry Orchard'? How do you write a symphony after Mahler's Ninth? When forms have been exhausted, everything after their apotheoses is going to be a poor copy. So everyone needs to change the form. Thank you, Stanislavski, you may have nailed the poetry of realism, but you also ended it. After you, no one could honestly pretend that 'fourth wall' realism was not the most extreme stylisation of them all!

Actors can pretend they are being real, but a director must not – cannot – entertain the same fantasy. She knows that the actors must not speak upstage and that she must create space where the furniture is carefully arranged to enable the actors to gather downstage centre and speak to the "wonderful people out there in the dark" (as Gloria Swanson famously called the audience). So while the actor pursues one goal the director enables it by doing the diametrical opposite.

Rather like his contemporary Sigmund Freud, Stanislavski asks all the right questions but comes up with some very peculiar and unhelpful answers! When he talks about the "Magic IF", I rebel. To worry about 'what would my character do IF s/he were real' is absurd. Similarly with his idea of offstage continuity (keeping character and intention while not onstage). It is simply mistaken to take the focus off what is happening onstage to imagine what a missing character is up to offstage. The actor who plays Macduff, for example, about to enter in 'Macbeth', must not ignore the drunken comic performance of the Porter onstage in order to fantasise about his offstage attitude to Macbeth. The Porter's bawdy comedy has interrupted the dramatic flow of the thriller-tragedy and Macduff's role is to play straight man to his funny man, setting up some of the best gags in Shakespeare. While all the time the public knows that the King lies offstage in a bloody heap. Stanislavski's method loses sight of this audience, fixated as the method is on invisible psychology. He misses the grotesque combination in the interests of a numinous innerness. In later life, Stanislavski's passion became the training of young professionals in rehearsal periods that were so long they struggled to reach performance. This is where Realism, when disconnected from the compromises of mainstream production, leads: the abolition of the audience and liveness.

The character of Meyerhold speaks a line in TNT's 'Harlequin': "when we go to the theatre we want to see the actor show off his brilliant skills to the public!" Vsevolod Meyerhold was Stanislavski's star actor; he created the character Konstantin in the premier of Chekhov's first masterpiece, 'The Seagull'. Konstantin, the troubled artist, the raker of his own soul. Just as Stanislavski was the cool Trigorin in real life, so Meyerhold was the incandescent Konstantin. Meyerhold was everything Stanislavski was not, but they were drawn together as magnetic opposites.

Meyerhold would spend much of his life running from Stanislavski in both art and politics, but he often looked over his shoulder. Since fiction is not real we exaggerated their conflict in our 'Harlequin'. My Stanislavski was vain, pompous, fixated on realism and always trying to creep beneath the political radar. Stanislavski was Pierrot, the sad faced elegant clown. Meyerhold was the masked and cheeky Harlequin and this interpretation reached its apotheosis in the USSR in 1990 when the quicksilver *commedia* clown from Naples, Enzo Scala, played our Meyerhold.

Our production's aim was to perform the life and death of Meyerhold, the great director, in the style of his own theatre. The story of a great director killed by a great dictator. Stalin murdered Meyerhold in 1940 despite, or maybe because of, the fact that Meyerhold was one of only three people to have responded to Lenin's 1917 appeal for artists to join the Revolution. Did Meyerhold really split from Stanislavski over an argument about the opening of a wine bottle? He certainly grabbed the moment when the "world turned upside down" in 1917. He reached for the stars and found that they were Red. He drew together great talents that were fired with the same enthusiasm as himself for the new society and the new art it might make possible. Shostakovich was his music director, Eisenstein his assistant director, Prokofiev his collaborator and the greatest of Soviet poets, Mayakovski, was his ally and inspiration.

So, what went wrong? Mayakovski sensed it first, like a dog who sniffs the oncoming storm. Mayakovski the poet of the Revolution blew his brains out in a fit of political and personal despair.

> Horse don't cry,
> Dying in this life is not so hard
> Building a life is harder.
>
> (Mayakovski, quoted at the finale of our 'Harlequin')

Meyerhold was a hyper-technician of theatre, he wanted to understand all of its mechanics. When he invented a physical training programme for actors he called it Biomechanics. This was very different from Stanislavski's psychological delving. Meyerhold reached back over his shoulder in order to spring forward into action, into the future. His biomechanical exercises teach a triple pattern:

- Pre-action
- Action
- Reaction

His pre-action – the energised readiness of an actor to move in any direction, respond in any way, both relaxed and tensed at the same time – took liberally from *commedia dell'arte* and laced it with a little Kabuki.

As soon as Meyerhold put a mask on an actor the whole system of Stanislavski collapsed. All *commedia* characters are masked. Heavy and colourful make-up can be a mask. The mask forces the whole body, not just the face, to express complexity. We are so used to the face giving us all the information, we forget that the limbs and hands can also tell us what we need to know; indeed the limbs and hands find it hard to lie. How many actors express themselves only from the neck up? Yet Meyerhold starts with the feet. *Commedia* can be close to ballet, but is rougher, harsher. When Meyerhold was to be tortured to death, they started on his feet, beating the soles black and blue and returning the next day to beat the bruises. We know this from his last letter, recently unearthed in the KGB vaults. Would Meyerhold have found that curiously funny? That would be grotesque. And 'grotesque' was Meyerhold's favourite word; one we borrowed from him with humble thanks to one who gave his body for our privilege.

The grotesque is at the dark heart of all essential theatre.

Try:

Alexander Blok's Harlequin squirting stage blood from a bottle all over his white costume and through his clown tears crying: "Don't worry, dear audience, I'm bleeding cranberry juice!"

Or:

HAMLET: Whose grave is this?

GRAVEDIGGER: Mine, Sir.

Or:

Frankenstein's Monster claiming his stitched together bride.

Macbeth's Porter whose drink stirs his desire but undermines his performance.

Petruchio's taming Kate with a raw potato.

Quasimodo's laughter as he pours molten lead on his attackers.

Willy Loman's boasting about his sons to the waiter at the final catastrophic dinner party.

Don Quijote convincing Sancho that a pig farmer is his princess Dulcinea.

The alarm clock ticking crocodile as it eats Captain Hook.

The 'blacked up' Lithuanian Jew Al Jolson performing Gospel music with an African American choir.

And:

Stalin shooting Meyerhold with a football rattle.

All the above, except the first, are examples from our repertoire. All impossible without the springboard of Meyerhold and the dizzy somersaults of his imagination, which we still try to find new ways to follow, not in theory but as practice, not following rules but taking as inspiration. And, of course, perspiration. For Meyerhold always moves first. Words follow. "All text is pre-text" is one of his most valuable axioms. Talk, talk,

talk; how often theatre drowns in words. Following Meyerhold, the text is always a means to the theatrical, never the outcome of it.

In Meyerhold's theatre, a play like Gogol's 'The Government Inspector' was transformed into something akin to a political ballet inside a satirical cartoon. Gogol's words are all there, but their role is to follow the action and support the image. That is why it is in the work of Eisenstein (who called Meyerhold a god) that we can best understand the master's work today. Films such as 'Battleship Potemkin' or 'Ivan the Terrible' are cinematic tributes to Meyerhold's art. Eisenstein invents 'montage' (modern film editing), and he knows how to do it because Meyerhold invented modern theatrical editing. Meyerhold's actors people Eisenstein's films; his spirit can be heard in Shostakovich's tortured harmonies. And what a showman Meyerhold was in life as in art! While Stanislavski looked like a bank manager, Meyerhold, in long leather coat and a jaunty cap above his jagged profile, looks a little like Leonard Cohen, but he probably packs a pistol.

So was Meyerhold always playing Konstantin? A bullet ended both their lives, but Konstantin's was fired from his own revolver.

> KONSTANTIN: I've talked so much about new forms of art, but I know my work is slipping into the same old clichés. I'm starting to understand that good art is not about new or old forms, but of ideas that rush freely from an artist's heart, without tormenting his brain about form at all. [A knock at the window.] What was that? [He looks out.] I can't see anything. [He opens the door and looks into the garden.] Who is there? [Nina enters.] Oh, Nina, Nina!
>
> (She lays her head on Konstantin and weeps).
>
> KONSTANTIN: Nina, Nina! It is you--you! I knew you would come; my heart has been aching for you. My darling, my one love, you've come back to me! We mustn't cry, we must not cry.
>
> NINA: There's someone else here.
>
> KONSTANTIN: No, we're alone
>
> NINA: Lock the door, please.
>
> KONSTANTIN: No one will come in.
>
> NINA: Your mother's here. Bolt the door.
>
> KONSTANTIN: There's no lock. I'll put a chair against it. [He does so.] Don't be afraid, no one can come in.

NINA: Look at you! Have I changed too?

KONSTANTIN: Yes, you're thinner, your eyes are larger too. Oh Nina, it's so incredible to see you! Why didn't you let me go to you? Why didn't you come to me? I know you've been here nearly a week. I have been to your house every day. I've stood beneath your window like a beggar.

NINA: I was afraid you hated me.

KONSTANTIN: Nina! You're crying again. Oh Nina!

NINA: Don't worry. It will all pass.

KONSTANTIN: You're going away. Aren't you? Why? Why!

NINA: I have taken an engagement in the provinces for winter. The theatre is…well. Konstantin, it's time I left here.

KONSTANTIN: Nina, I've cursed you, hated you, torn apart your photograph, but I've known my heart and soul belong to you forever. I can't stop loving you. Without you my life, my work, has become unbearable. My youth has suddenly been snatched away, I feel so old. I have cried out to you, kissed the ground you walk on, everywhere I look, I see your eyes, your face, the smile that lit up the best years of my life. I beg you to stay! Nina!

(Nina shakes her head and goes…Konstantin tears up his manuscript, opens his desk and takes out a gun).

I performed these words, while trussed up and spun around on the end of a rope by the triumphant Bolshevik Harlequin, forced to perform his new art of theatre, but struggling to keep within me the heart of the old. Meyerhold directing Stanislavski. Nina was not only Nina, she was also Columbine, she was also Russia, she was the Revolution that simply went away. At the end of 'The Seagull' a shot is heard and Konstantin's mother rushes towards his study. At the real end, in the cellars of the Lubyanka prison a shot was heard. No one rushed towards the door. It was just another execution.

And the blood was not cranberry juice.

Curtain.

I am making a pilgrimage. Wrapped in a Chinese Air Force greatcoat against the bitter February cold, I came here by clanking tram. Just one more metal track on a journey that started east of Siberia. This is a Berlin graveyard, East Berlin, well behind the watchtowers of the Wall. There are two rough hewn slabs of stone, one to the superb actress Helena Weigel and the other to her less than faithful husband, the greatest theatrical force since Shakespeare: Berthold Brecht. Brecht is as annoying as he is brilliant; where all the other directors I praise in these notes are wrestlers and warriors, he is a chameleon. He writes one thing and does another, in art and politics, in love and life. He stood up to Hitler but stood down to Stalin. He published reams on how to act, direct and write for the theatre and then produced work that contradicted much of what he claimed to be true.

After the War this devout Communist moved from Hollywood to conservative Munich and took over the city theatre. "Act with passion," he yelled at the actors, "Move the audience!"

"But Berthold," replied the actors, "you wrote we should never do that?"

I am told, by those who should know, that his reply was: "Oh forget all that stuff, it was just words". So why is what Brecht wrote so important?

Well, first of all he wrote some of the finest plays ever written, though I do wish they were shorter. His heroines and heroes are refreshingly practical, cynical and world weary. If sentimentality is the curse of theatre then Brecht is the antidote. He learns from Meyerhold and the expressionist German film directors and adores the grotesque. 'The Threepenny Opera' features a callous Highwayman who woos the daughter of his jailer while on Death Row. Brecht nails the connection between capitalist exploitation and crime in the same way that Dickens had done a hundred years before. "What is the difference between robbing a bank and owning a bank!" cry his characters. After the fall of Lehman Brothers how do we disagree? But Brecht is not a simple Leftist preacher; he creates landscapes where character, narrative, politics, poetry and song are arranged in jagged contours. Where most fiction forces us to feel, Brecht forces us to think through our feelings. His plays are anything but dull, his rogues delight, his heroes are flawed and his soured love affairs remind us of our own.

As directors, we can learn much from this curious theatrical poet. He asks actors to observe themselves while acting, to know why they are acting, to work from the outside in, rather than the inside out: a total reversal of Stanislavski or Lee Strasberg. I find this very useful. I ask an actor not to pretend to be someone else but to know why at that moment in the performance they are imitating someone else. The answer is in the impact on the audience. And if that impact is merely emotional then it is self-indulgent and tending to sentiment (or soap opera). But great art forces us to think, to be aware, to use our brain. Hamlet is not known as the philosopher prince for nothing. And when we think about life we must think about politics.

Is there any play with more contemporary resonance than Brecht's parody of Hitler's rise to power set among Chicago Gangsters: 'The Resistible Rise of Arturo Ui'? But Brecht, like Shakespeare, is a poet not a news reporter. Beauty moves him, especially the beauty of the ugly. It is no coincidence that Charles Laughton defined Quasimodo before performing Galileo for Brecht. Brecht frees us from the frivolous but allows us to laugh at the same time. Brecht the stern Stalinist is also Brecht the sensualist poet with his boots on the grubby earth. He notes that "when I go to the theatre I want to put my feet up, light a cigar and reach for a beer!" Cheers, me also!

I turn away from the slab stone graves humming 'Mack the Knife'. East Berlin is a forbidding grey. For such a colourful character as Brecht to come home to this must have been shocking. Even when the Soviet tanks rolled in to crush the East German uprising in 1953, he kept his trap shut and carried on extolling the virtues of the state that fed him. After so many years of struggle and exile perhaps he simply lost faith in his ability to change things, to change himself?

To the cities I came in a time of chaos
Cities ruled by hunger.
I sheltered with the people as battles raged above
Then I joined in their rebellion.
That's how I passed the time that was given to me on this Earth.
I grabbed meals between fire fights,
I slept rough among murderers,
I didn't care too much for love
And for nature's beauty I had no time....

Our forces are slight and small,
Our goal lies in the distance
Clearly there in sight,
But for me, far beyond my reach.

A guard hands me back my passport, the exit stamp is a hammer. I walk through the Wall and on towards Checkpoint Charlie. West Berlin breathes colour. Good bye, Comrade Berthold, this is not your world, it was beyond your reach.

So, how do I talk about Jerzy Grotowski? He changed my life.

And here my own story intersects with that of a great director; a tiny wheel within great wheels. Because in 1979 I had stood in line in the Polish snow to buy black market carrots and cabbage to feed Grotowski's iconic actor, the mighty Ryszard Cieslak. The actors of Grotowski's Teatr

Laboratorium had to rehearse and train; the least I could do was make sure they lived on more than vodka and salami. Grotowski gave me a lot. I gave him a carrot.

Without Grotowski this book would not exist. Nor the company it documents. But my relationship with this iconic figure was not one of pupil and master and I resisted the temptation, to which many succumbed, to treat him as a guru. Indeed, perhaps the greatest victim of that tendency was Grotowski himself. TNT later defined itself not by imitating the great man and his company but by testing ourselves against his ideas, a Luther to this most Catholic of modern artists. So although now I will try to explain some of his ideas and practices I cannot separate them from my own personal experience. My encounter with his ideas was woven in with tender and difficult feelings. In the interests of candour, I should now confess that whereas many Westerners were besotted by Grotowski and his Laboratorium, I was rather haplessly in love with an actress in his company. And for a few precious months it seemed she shared my feelings.

It is quite extraordinary that a rather shy artist working in a provincial Polish city behind a very iron curtain should manage to become the most famous theatre director of the late twentieth century. Grotowski ended up in Wrocław and started in Opole; not even fashionable provincial towns within Poland. But Grotowski was in the right place at the right time, because there he found the space to create a disciplined mystical theatre of enormous physical, even visceral, power just as the West was rejecting theatre (or any art) as lazy spectacle for the comfortable. His book of almost scriptural power is called *Towards a Poor Theatre*. The word 'Towards' is important. It is a journey and Grotowski invites you to be his follower and follow him down that road, that Way. The road itself is the actor's body.

All of us who work in theatre envy dancers and musicians. They train and that training produces tangible results. An unemployed violinist may practice their art in private and perform spontaneously to family or friends. The dancer hones their body and attends 'class' as often as they can. The unemployed musician can prove they are a musician. The unemployed actor is just a woman on the dole who might be able to crack a joke slightly louder than the next out of work woman in the queue. So Grotowski addresses this, influenced of course by Meyerhold's bio-mechanical training. But where Meyerhold talks of the influence of Henry Ford and the industrial production line on his work, Grotowski invokes the spirit, the 'organic' actor who will, through the absence of materialism-fixated inhibitions in mind and body, achieve a transcendent performance. And he did it. Unlike Artaud's wild theories of a Theatre of Cruelty, Grotowski's

Laboratorium created astonishing pieces of performance which took theatre to a new level of experience, or perhaps to an old one that had existed in Asia for centuries but was thought impossible in the rational, commercial modern Western world.

For better or for worse, Brecht, Meyerhold and even Stanislavski believed their art served a Soviet future. Grotowski was very much a product of the deeply Catholic and spiritual Poland that would bring down the Soviet Empire. One of his actors once said to me: "You know, Paul, I spent three years in the Polish army. When World War Three breaks out and the forces of the Warsaw Pact head west, the Polish army will cheer and head east for Moscow. The Russians know this and have kept all the heavy weapons under their own control." Culture was Poland's heavy weapon and it expressed itself through resistance to the idea that humanity is what we see. Grotowski created terrifying performances: there they are, his actors, in their Auschwitz uniforms, singing the poetry of Romantic Poland. In physical ecstasy they climb into a giant metal oven and slam the crematorium door behind them. Bang. The end. How can any other performance stand up against this howling wind, this storm of art?

Ryszard Cieślak was the Spanish 'Constant Prince', tortured yet impassive, resisting, always resisting the Satanic forces of brutal power. That production swept New York off its feet. And just to make sure that his theatre was poor, Grotowski refused to play large theatres or audiences. Grotowski built audiences of less than one hundred into his stage sets. So that in his extraordinary production of Marlowe's 'Doctor Faustus' the actors and audience are all seated at three long tables. Faustus invites actors dressed as monks onto the tabletops to perform his fall from grace before the eyes of the audience, who are diners at a Last Supper that Marlowe creates before Mephistopheles drags the host to flaming Hell. In another production, set in a psychiatric hospital, the audience sit on lower cots as the actors/patients lie howling in the bunk beds above them.

Grotowski's final production dramatises the end of the world. In 'Apocalypsis Cum Figuris' there are no seats. Actors and audience share a room lit by candles. After the bread of life is broken and eaten the candles are snuffed out one by one and the World Ends. It is not something you can applaud and then go for a glass of Chablis. And it is not a form of theatre where you can rub your hands over the box office receipts. Poor theatre. Grotowski inspires but he also makes sense. He asks: "What do you really need for theatre?", noting that you can take away set, lights, costume, music, words and that what is left is the actor and the audience. So that must be the essence. There is something attractive and Quakerish about this. Finally,

Grotowski will abolish even the actor himself. The audience will get up and come to the stage and join together with the actors in a theatrical experience. This is the 'Tree of People' project in which I was involved. By then the guru had started to swallow the director. The poster for the project was a beautiful watercolour of Grotowski with a long staff striding through the Himalaya. Cieślak tried to go along with it all but after a while he ran away to (re) join the Circus – or, in his case, Peter Brook in Paris. I too left Wrocław alone. But for now we are discussing the art of directing, not the art of falling apart.

Directing is about controlling structure. About taking care that the detail contributes to the overall purpose or 'gestus' of a work. Whether I like a piece of theatre or not is a personal decision. To be able to decide how to direct one must ask the question: does the piece achieve what it sets out to achieve? And is that achievement a worthy one? I might believe that the musical of 'Les Misérables' is a miserable travesty of a great radical novel, but I can appreciate that the production is skilfully achieved. Yet, 'Les Mis' remains tainted by its dumbing down of greatness. We have to discuss purpose as well as practice. Or else we bump into Leni Riefenstahl whose marvellously directed films celebrate the Nazis and their monstrous gods. It would be foolish to fix the moral compass in one direction. Grotowski and Brecht were on different sides in the Cold War, but each of the above and many more fine directors keep a moral purpose as part of the 'gestus' of their work. The finest directing I have seen: Richard Eyre's 'Comedians', Lev Dodin's 'Stars In The Morning Sky' or Pina Bausch's '1980' were all morally driven. Politics might or might not be part of that morality. An actor can feed off passion and commitment but a director has to think as well as feel. As Hamlet notes: "There's nothing either good nor bad but thinking makes it so".

Which returns me to my opening thoughts on directing. Is the director at some point a modern imposition, even a capitalist manager of exploited actors? The list of artists under discussion tempts me to suggest that there is another role: which for want of a better word I call the 'auteur'. Not in the sense of 'autocrat', not in the sense used in cinema to denote the bending of all to a single vision, but in the sense of one whose work is to bring together, with neither division nor singularity, all the different elements of the performance. Most of the directing in the modern world tends to be a craft rather than an inspired calling; because this work is in realisation rather than creation. In contrast, the 'auteur' in my sense, is not fenced off from the text or any other area of creativity. "All text is pre-text!" thundered Meyerhold. And I think Shakespeare would agree. Hence the constant revisions of 'Hamlet' in the various folios and quartos that have come down to us. Shakespeare is after something, it is hidden within the stone of the idea of the perfect Hamlet. It is fascinating that in the shortest version of 'Hamlet' that we have, in the first Quarto, there is an extra scene that never makes it to the full version. In it Horatio tells Gertrude of Hamlet's escape in a clearer and more dramatic manner than the clunky letter and pirate ship sequence in the final Folio. TNT always performs this scene in our long running production of 'Hamlet'. So, Shakespeare was clearly 'hands on', but was he a director? Brecht and Grotowski control their texts. Brecht is clearly a playwright but is Meyerhold? And what about TNT? Dare I discuss our practice in the presence of such Titans?

Phil Smith is a founder member of the company and writes his own version of our journey. We call him our Dramaturg, a German title that is very useful. A Dramaturg is different from a literary manager; Phil is not looking for texts that TNT might perform. The TNT Dramaturg is responsible for the textual 'gestus'. Phil keeps us on the rails. Sometimes he drafts a first version but usually I will draft and he will shape, comment and even demolish. We hardly ever sit in the same room to do this. We play digital ping pong with versions of scripts and edits of classics. Any text can be changed or added to in rehearsal. When I give notes to actors after a run they may well include new lines of dialogue.

Even on tour we change and develop dialogue. Often we cut. Because dialogue can be like the pencil drawing that enables a painting. Words often need to be rubbed out to allow the performance to breathe, to enable the action which is the essence of theatre. Hence the word 'actor'. Classic plays are not sacred texts. Grotowski wrote that in order to justify performing the classics we must confront them.

A case in point is the fifth act of 'The Tempest', one that needs careful attention. What happens to Prospero's murderous brother? If this, Shakespeare's last play, is about forgiveness, where and when exactly does it happen? If the text is played straight, this question cannot be answered. But if the text is cut up and reassembled, every word being that of the Bard's, then it is possible to construct a satisfying answer and, aided by clear visual imagery, deliver a 'Tempest' that does not fudge and flap as it moves towards the resolution of the lesser plots of Caliban and Ariel. So *as a director* I am stuck with the unsatisfying Fifth Act, but as an *'auteur'* I can slice into the text and make it serve the overall big theme: how do you forgive a brother who would kill your daughter?

So that is what we did. No one I heard ever complained that this was not 'The Tempest' and we have toured it from Britain to Japan. I suggest that this 'auteur' approach mirrored Shakespeare's and freed the play to be itself.

Just as Ariel liberates himself by destroying himself; for, in our production, Ariel dies when Prospero burns his books and breaks his staff, because the spirit dies when the magic ends.

Then our grieving Prospero bends over the mortal corpse of our lost and loved Ariel and delivers a blend, an edit of some of the most beautiful speeches ever penned:

> PROSPERO: My Ariel, chick, Please you, draw near *(They embrace).*
> To the elements
> Be free, and fare thou well!
> *Prospero breaks his staff. Ariel collapses.*
> Our revels now are ended. These our actors,
> As I foretold you, were all spirits and
> Are melted into air, into thin air:
> And, like the baseless fabric of this vision,
> The cloud-capp'd towers, the gorgeous palaces,
> The solemn temples, the great globe itself,
> Ye all which it inherit, shall dissolve
> And, like this insubstantial pageant faded,
> Leave not a rack behind. We are such stuff
> As dreams are made on, and our little life
> Is rounded with a sleep.
> Now my charms are all o'erthrown,
> And what strength I have's mine own,
> Which is most faint: Now I want
> Spirits to enforce, art to enchant,
> And my ending is despair.
> Unless I be relieved by prayer,
> As you from crimes would pardon'd be,
> Let your indulgence set me free.

Well, I too would like to be "pardon'd" for this editing, and I hope that if Prospero speaks for Shakespeare we speak for him, who grappled with the world as something between a director and a writer and ended with a plea for forgiveness on the lips of his last creation.

Chapter Thirteen: Latin America

By Paul

The town of San Isidro El General sits in a valley on the border between Costa Rica and Panama, accessible on a highway that snakes across the highest peaks in Central America before plunging into the rainforest that stretches from here to the Panama Canal some 200 miles away. San Isidro is the last town before the forest takes over. Indigenous tribes live both sides of the unmarked border. For many years they resisted taking citizenship of either country, insisting they were their own nation and had no need of any other.

It is six in the evening. The sun is setting across the nearby Pacific. I take a stroll from the hangar-like evangelical hall towards the forest. It has rained as is usual in the afternoon. I dodge puddles in the red mud. When I reach the trees I stand still and listen to the most extraordinary natural sound I know: the waking of the rainforest to welcome the night. Birds, insects, bats and howler monkeys hoot, chirp, squawk and, of course, howl. A humming bird flits by. I look back towards the building and notice a Roman senator in full toga smoking a cigarette. It is Cassius.

Brutus addresses the crowd in TNT's 'Julius Caesar' on tour in Latin America with surtitles. Note the Roman grave portraits.

That night we perform 'Julius Caesar' to about three hundred people of all ages and backgrounds in the hall. We aid understanding by projecting subtitles in Spanish onto a wall. But it is the theatre that carries the evening, the sheer rush and release of this extraordinary play, first a thriller then an epic. Firstly, a triumph for Brutus and then a tragedy as his world, built on an impossible morality, collapses. And in the middle a manipulation, a horribly contemporary swaying of the gullible by the powerful and 'elite' figure of Mark Anthony, who pretends to be a simple man unversed in the powers of persuasion. TNT's style is on display: the togas are not white but coloured according to the nature of the character; the soldiers have stylised Roman armour. We suggest but reject realism. The crowds are created with placards of Roman faces taken from tomb and wall paintings. Caesar dies in an explosion of red ribbon, the battle scenes are dynamic but only one army is present. Metal shields become complex percussion instruments as they are hit and scraped with swords. The whole is held together by Helen Beauchamp's powerful score, using cello, human voice, drums and French horn (all performed live). The Roman Republic falls, dictatorship triumphs. The audience are swept along on a wave of energy and emotion.

Afterwards we sit on the edge of the (sort of) stage and talk to the audience, who have no intention of leaving. One says: "I never in my life thought I would see something like this in my town". We promise to return. A few days later I follow a local guide through the forest not so far away. We come across a bright yellow snake, frozen in defence mode: a Z shape of coiled danger. It is an eyelash viper whose neuro-venom is especially deadly. I ask the guide: "How can this snake be on the defensive, what could frighten or eat this creature?". His reply: "Other snakes." It seems a metaphor for 'Julius Caesar'. The killers are killed, the assassin's dagger is the one Brutus takes to end his own life. Democracy dies when it uses violence to defend itself. Once released from the moral code, that same moral code can no longer defend Brutus. You cannot express your humanity with the tip of a dagger. In Shakespeare's plays murderers become beasts, but there is always a bigger snake than them.

Latin America has become TNT's frontier. A continent and a half where we have steadily developed our work for over ten years and where, as in China, we have gone from visiting artists to becoming a part of the local theatre scene. Costa Rica has been the key to unlock this vast area. Curiously this all began in Berlin.

In 2005 we were touring 'King Lear' in Germany. The production used live music, creating, for example, the storm with cello and violin while dancer-actors cracked and flapped long strips of cloth. In the audience was one Steve Aronson, who had seen a poster and was intrigued that a British company could perform Shakespeare in the original in Germany. After the performance Steve walked onstage and asked the cast if they would like to tour to Central America. I received a hurried phone call and very soon Grantly Marshall and I met Steve in Neustrelitz, where we were performing 'Lord of the Flies'. There is no question that TNT attracts eccentrics and Steve is a unique individual. In brief: Steve was in Germany to follow the footsteps of his parents, Lithuanian Jews whose family were murdered in the Holocaust and who met in Dachau concentration camp, which they survived together. They emigrated to New York and their son grew up with a keen interest in coffee. In the 1970s Steve broke the Costa Rican government coffee monopoly by buying most of their best export beans and reimporting them to Costa Rica. Suddenly it was possible to get a decent cup of coffee in the country where it was grown. Business boomed and Steve set up the Café Britt company which soon expanded throughout Latin America and then diversified into everything from handicrafts to airport malls.

On the Café Britt home plantation Steve built a theatre to enable their famous coffee tour, a tourist magnet that took the visitor from bean to cup via every process along the way. What was unusual about the tour was that it was run by actors who then performed a history of coffee in the onsite theatre. Those same actors then performed a repertoire of plays in the evening for a general public. Steve invited 'King Lear' to Costa Rica and his energetic sidekick, Eduardo, organised further tours to El Salvador and Guatemala. For many years we have presented TNT's Shakespeare productions at Steve's theatre and at the beautiful National Theatre of Costa Rica, modelled it is said on the Opera de Paris. (Echoes of Herzog's brilliant movie 'Fitzcaraldo'.) In 2008 I was invited to direct a Spanish language version of our 'Christmas Carol'. Very soon this became a staple of the Costa Rican theatre season and is performing for ten days at that same National Theatre, as I write these words at the end of 2019.

A notable co-production was 'Don Quijote', for which we found Spanish actors in Madrid. We created the piece with the TNT team in Munich. I also had the assistance of my good friend Pablo Morales, director and actor from Steve's Café Britt theatre. He then returned to Costa Rica and mounted the same production with local professional actors. While we toured Europe with one version, he toured Central America with another. 'Don Quijote' is ideal material for a TNT show: as wise as it is absurd, as grotesque as it sad.

A few years later Steve opened another theatre in downtown San José, the capital, setting up his own ensemble called Teatro Espressivo and adding an extraordinary café in the foyer – organic volcano roast anyone? There we brought our touring shows and I directed 'Romeo y Julieta', wrestling with

Pablo Neruda's far too beautiful translation which prudishly removes both the sexual and the comic from Shakespeare's original! Other plays followed including 'Lord of the Flies', which transferred to Peru, and a memorable 'Brave New World' (appropriate, as Aldous Huxley was fascinated by Central America and spent a long time in Guatemala).

El Salvador: I enter the cathedral through a gap in the razor wire fence. We have come to see the chapel where the Archbishop was gunned down by right wing paramilitaries. Part of a cycle of violence that swept Central America from the Sandinista Revolution in Nicaragua until the peace accords of 1987, when Óscar Arias (President of Costa Rica) negotiated a regional peace settlement despite the best efforts of the US government. Óscar Arias won the Nobel Peace prize, and one evening in Nicaragua he would sit down to watch TNT perform 'The Taming of the Shrew'.

Back in El Salvador the tension is rising; we return to our van. We are driving to a market. Our driver turns and yells at one of the actors to wind up the window. We pass the boarded up presidential palace. This is the only city in the world where there is no curfew but everything shuts at dusk. The darkened streets of the city centre will be left to the police, the gangs they fight and the death squads that wear no uniform and switch allegiance with the wind. A Coca Cola truck overtakes us, to the right of the driver a man cradles the barrel of a weapon, riding shotgun. The next day we arrive at the theatre, which is inside an international school. The school is arranged so that the students are dropped off and picked up in a high walled car park topped with the usual razor wire. We perform once in the day for the students and once in the evening for the general public. Between shows a teacher drives me to a shopping mall to buy bottled water for the actors. The mall has shot gun guards at the car park gate. But what is truly alarming is the metal tower in the centre of the parking lot, where a bored man in uniform leans over a heavy machine gun.

It is a pleasant sunny afternoon. Salvador City is, like many Central American capitals, set high on the central plateau. The place is teeming with families enjoying the weekend in a safe mall, lit by neon light and bright shop window displays. They feast on Taco Bell, Kentucky Fried Chicken and Burger King. Gallons of coke are consumed. Kids run riot. There are a lot of smiles and quite a lot of wobbling flesh. And the music is fabulous; Reggaton and Cumba, Salsa and a Mexican ballad. I like to play the game of seeing how long you can listen to a song in Latin America without hearing the word 'corazón', which means heart. There is so much open emotion in Latin America, a total contrast to East Asia. How strange that these bizarrely reversed cultures, where one has great food and terrible music and the other terrible food and great music, both love Shakespeare. Rehearsals start in Costa Rica with everyone kissing; the actors like to hit the town hard at weekends. Rum fuels the long nights and even sponsors the company. It was at the hotel complex of the king of Nicaraguan rum (Flor de Caña) that we performed for Óscar Arias and assorted grandees. But we also perform to school kids, not just the privileged. They flock to our 'Lord of the Flies', chattering and laughing as they enter the theatre but silent as the actors take the stage.

These young people were hooked in by a theatre concerned with young characters; of young boys marooned on Golding's tropical island, revealing both the best and worst of humanity. Then the best is slaughtered in an orgy of violence. In post-show discussions the pupils talked of their own experiences of violence and bullying. One child had been kidnapped and spent weeks hidden in a barrel. Given up for dead, an informer tipped off the police who raided the hideout. Gangsters were shot. Miraculously the boy was unharmed. He chose to return to school just a few days after his ordeal.

It would be unfair to characterise Latin America chiefly by violence. It is also a land where many marvels can occur. None more extraordinary, perhaps, than a visit of the cast of 'Much Ado About Nothing' to a Mayan ruin in El Salvador. There are no tourists in El Salvador, so they were greeted with surprise by the local shaman. He performed for them and explained his role in a modern world still linked to its ancient foundations long before the gringos came. One TNT veteran present that day was Gareth Fordred, a fluent Spanish speaker, who not only acts but helps develop our circuit to include Chile, Peru and Colombia. It looks to Mexico next...

Still in El Salvador; I am alone in a village square. I choose to ignore a few glue-sniffing youths at the end of the plaza, and some Marxist graffiti. I have come to see the church, built less than a hundred years after Cortés murdered Montezuma and collapsed the Aztec empire. It captures the spirit of that Age. Indeed, statues of conquistadores in their distinctive conical helmets adorn the west front. I push open the heavy side door and am greeted with a scene from a long-gone world. There is no artificial light; shafts of sunlight pick out the dust in the warm air. Giant strips of cloth hang from the ceiling, I presume to be flapped from side to side when the congregation fills the aisles for mass. At the transept sit a band of musicians, playing instruments the Conquistadores brought with them: guitars of varying shapes and sizes including a giant one that a man can hardly lift. They play the softest, saddest music I can imagine, pulling at the heartstrings in this hallowed place where time has stood still. Artists performing for themselves and me. Why do we do it? Maybe because we have to. Because it makes sense of everything and without it, outside this special place, life is still nasty, brutish and short.

A few of the nuts and bolts of directing

From Stanislavski to Grotowski, the pressure from theatre's progressive theorists has been to replace inspiration with technique, to bring the actor and director in line with the dancer and musician. None of which is to deny the importance of passion and raw ability, but these elements are nebulous and can be shaped but not taught. Discussions about directing can easily be hijacked by extreme examples of the art, such as lovers lying on a piano flying into a winter sky! But theatre direction is also about the arrangement of actors on a stage, the enabling of text and image by careful yet fluid positioning of people in a space.

John O'Mahony, our Captain Ahab in 'Moby Dick', appealed to me and his fellow actors with these words: "Only you can make me the captain of this ship, all of you must give me the absolute authority of the man who stands between you and God." The actor must feel that the director will arrange the stage so that the audience sees this. Personally, I start from visualising a scene. Everything else follows. Too often directors start with text and psychology. But the audience will react and understand through their eyes before any other sense, let alone intellectual interpretation, intervenes.

A designer and lighting designer can provide frameworks but this frame can easily result in a blank canvas. The director has to grapple with the play as if neither design nor lighting exists. This is why Peter Brook wants an empty space.

There are certain mechanics available to directors. I will suggest a few, (and apologise that many are related to front-on proscenium arch stages, for most travelling theatres have to accept this as the most common and most practical set-up).

Three tips on stage movement

1) The triangle is your friend. As in geometry, the triangle is the strongest arrangement of one to four lines. The horizontal line is the weakest. Squares are weak because they are symmetrical. Where there are less than three actors on a stage then the third element is the audience. Where there is one actor on the stage, direct address is also a triangle as the actor gives their performance from a single point that expands into the auditorium in a triangle. One of the most effective triangles on a stage is to position an actor in the downstage corner. From there they can speak to both stage and audience, the triangle being formed by the two other points: one in the top corner of the stage opposite the actor and the other in the top corner of the auditorium. Because movement and image upon a stage should be fluid and

active, which actor forms the fulcrum of a triangle should change. Triangles can also be formed on sets that answer to Meyerhold's call for "machines for acting". Raising an actor on a podium will create a more dynamic triangle, an actor standing on a chair will always be more interesting than one sitting on a chair. Triangles do not have to have equal sides. Symmetry should be used sparingly, as in architecture it can be oppressive. If the director wishes to draw attention to hierarchy then symmetry has its place, but most plays are about the disintegration of hierarchy and hence of symmetry. This means that the best theatrical triangles are created without a corner stood at upstage centre.

2) Exits and entrances. One of the great drawbacks of front-on proscenium arch theatre is the tedium and predictability of the entrance from the wings (sides) of the stage. The Royal Shakespeare Company felt much the same and I admire the layout of their new Stratford stages with a thrust stage and entrances through the audience. My favourite Asian form of theatre, Japanese Kabuki, has a raised walkway spanning the auditorium for actors to storm onto the stage. Where this is not possible, Italian *commedia dell'arte* offers a solution: a screen at the rear of the stage behind which the actor changes or waits to enter. We often use this device: in productions such as 'Harlequin' or 'Gulliver's Travels' we actually build a *commedia* screen and keep as many entrances and exits behind a simple square some two metres high and three metres wide. Entrances and exits become circular. The actor commands the stage from the moment of their entrance. Exits are faster from centre stage. An added bonus is that bits of an actor can appear before the whole person; for example, a horse's head in 'Gulliver's Travels' is followed by a human body. A Shakespearian 'arras' or curtained space upstage can have exactly the same effect. An actor can enter through the curtains, or around the sides of the curtains. Circles of movement on the stage replace horizontal lines.

Where it is not possible or desirable to use a *commedia* screen, then it is worth questioning the age-old tradition of actors leaving the space upstage right and left. This has the effect of pulling those actors who remain on the stage in the wrong direction, since exits are powerful. Parting shots of dialogue may well be delivered upstage but the result is that the poor actor who remains on the stage has to reply or even simply react with their face away from the audience. I encourage actors to leave downstage, that is exit into the "wings" as close as possible to the audience. Once again a triangle is created: the actor who remains on stage being one point, the actor leaving downstage another and the audience the third.

3) Actors like to stand up or sit on chairs. Question this. Getting rid of chairs helps. Actors sitting on steps, on podiums, on each other – anywhere that is not at a comfortable or usual height – is strong. If an actor takes a chair, turns it around and sits with their hands over the chair back this is clearly a powerful image. (See Liza Minelli in 'Cabaret'.) A table set for afternoon tea invites dull theatre; standing on the same table is exciting theatre. Even in a realistic scene a break away from the usual position can be powerful. For example, in our production of 'Death of a Salesman', the emotionally tortured Biff sat on the floor at his father's failed dinner party. An actor lying on their back on the lip of the stage will always command attention. An actor turning their back to the audience and fellow actors will command the stage.

The most astonishing and satisfying movement of performers in space that I have seen was not the result of direction but choreography: Pina Bausch's '1980'. Anyone wishing to understand how to move people around a performance space should watch Wim Wenders' 3D film documentary of her work 'Pina'. She demolished the fixed roles of choreographer and director, dancer and actor. Her dancers speak. Their movement arises out of nothing at all, just life. She writes "there is no book. There is no set. There is no music. There is only life and us. It's absolutely frightening to do a work when you have nothing to hold on to". Which bring us back to Peter Brook's 'empty space' and Jerzy Grotowski's 'poor theatre'.

As a result of these and other influences, TNT has usually worked with a choreographer and that choreographer has had a more important role than any set designer. For many years this has been the Canadian Eric Tessier Lavigne, who has often performed leading roles for the company. A multilinguist who grew up in Belgium, his most realised role has been Don Quijote in our production of that name. This iconic character was created as much through dance as text (which was in Spanish). Eric shapes scenes after I have created a structure. For example, in 'Macbeth' I decided that the Witches (or rather Weird Sisters) must dominate the production and every scene in which they appear was rehearsed before the rest of the play with Eric creating extreme movement patterns within the dialogue. Is this choreography? Is this direction? Does it matter?

Recently we have been working with another Canadian, Jasmine Ellis, who turned scene changes in 'Pygmalion' into dances with furniture and even ran action through scene changes (such as Higgins pursuing Eliza to Covent Garden). The choreographer teaches us that the performer can be skilled and stylised, that movement on stage is at best a fluid pattern. The choreographer is the essential visual collaborator in the new theatre.

Actors and Spies

By Paul

In 1991 TNT received a grant to bring the director of the Leningrad State Comedy theatre to Britain to promote cultural exchange with the USSR. It was a small grant. I had to mobilise friends and family to host Yuri Gubanov and his young translator. I drove the two Russians from London to the Bristol Old Vic, to Stratford Upon Avon and the RSC and then to Nottingham, to the Playhouse where I had cut my acting teeth. On arrival back in London I knew I could not put Yuri up in my down at heel apartment. So we delivered him to the house of a university friend, Colin, who was now a British diplomat. Little did we know that this arrangement would cause some excitement in the higher echelons of British Intelligence. For Yuri Gubanov was given control of the Leningrad theatre after loyal service as a colonel in the KGB. He had been head of station in Istanbul at the height of the Cold War. What I also did not know at the time was that my old friend Colin was a high ranking officer in MI6, a spy prominent enough to later be outed in the famous 'Spycatcher' revelations. So, in the interests of cultural exchange, TNT had, rather dramatically, brought the KGB and MI6 together!

All of which reminds me of Julian Beck's brilliant book 'The Life of the Theatre', a history of Beck and Judith Malina's company, the Living Theatre (founded in the 1950s), a company with which TNT shares some traits and much sympathy. In his book, in short thoughtful paragraphs, Beck analyses society as theatre, naming spies as the best actors of all.

Chapter Fourteen: TNT and Islam

By Paul

One of the most fascinating and rewarding elements of TNT's work has been touring to Moslem countries or countries with large Moslem populations. Given the level of misinformation and prejudice that surrounds Islam as a culture (not just a religion) in the West, it is sometimes difficult not to allow our own experience to be overturned by the negative myths and half-truths peddled by politicians and media.

Islam is founded upon a book of poetry; in its pursuit of abstract beauty it stimulates the imagination and arrives at a sublime beauty that few cultures can match. Of course, there are exceptions, and no theatre company wants to tour to an Isis-controlled area of Iraq. But TNT has tried to connect with the Islamic mainstream and has been rewarded with extraordinary experiences from Tehran to Istanbul and Kuwait to Jakarta.

Rather than link observations and anecdotes from these theatrical travels, what is written here is a series of impressions and memories with some conclusions which may or may not be correct; the personal opinions of someone who was there. We try to travel with humility, we offer questions not answers and we expect of ourselves a respect to be shown to all, but especially to those who are deeply different from ourselves. The art is the bridge, our physical presence is the pledge.

We land with 'Hamlet' in Tehran in the middle of a freezing January night. We are met by a smiling Iranian who is our guide. He should feel at home because he is an air traffic controller. Each year he takes his holiday in January so he can care for foreign theatre companies who visit the 'Dawn Festival'. He has never left Iran, but as an air traffic controller he speaks fluent English. Here at the heart of the "Axis of Evil" is a man of such courtesy and kindness I can write nothing that does him justice. He will be our guide not just to Tehran and its Festival, but to Iran itself, of which more later.

We drive through the strangely dark streets of the megapolis. Our hotel is a grey concrete block. The exhausted actors retreat to their rooms; they performed last night in London and rose at dawn to fly to Central Asia via

Amsterdam. Our guide, Ali, informs me that we need to set the theatre lights in four hours as we have a busy day ahead of us before the evening performance of 'Hamlet'. I sigh and realise that the actors must be left in peace while I tackle this task alone. (Actually I am an actor too, I play Second Grave Digger and will have to rush from the lighting box to make my brief entrance). More alarming is the gently worded threat that follows: "You will need to show the entire play to the Morality Police before you are allowed to perform tonight."

"All?" I reply with alarm.

That is three hours of performance. Ali can only pass on the news. I snatch some sleep in my bedroom of chipped and peeling grandeur and rise three hours later to take an ancient taxi to the theatre. In the grey dawn, huddled figures brave the ice-cold wind; most but not all are women shrouded in black. The taxi's radio is locked on a Mullah's prayer. Ali translates, adding, without sarcasm, that there is no music on Iranian radio. So, no DJs in the audience tonight…

For two hours I manipulate heavy East German lights that would better belong on a perimeter fence than in a theatre. At noon the actors arrive. They are chipper. Breakfast at the hotel was a feast of exotic flavours from goat's cheese and honey to flatbreads and fresh herbs.

Then I tell them about the Morality Police.

The two actresses, suitably headscarfed, are particularly alarmed. We did know that we had to adapt the performance. We have half-heartedly rehearsed scenes so men and women do not touch. This is not easy in so passionate a play as 'Hamlet'. Gertrude and Ophelia are amongst Shakespeare's most tactile females (although Ophelia has to go mad to release her more sensual self). We set up props and costumes, busy ourselves in the dressing rooms and sip sweet tea from bulbous glasses. Then the Morality Police arrive. There are three of them. They wear drab ill-fitting suits and smile disarmingly as they shake our (male) hands. One of them speaks English. The other two are presumably experts in visual morality.

Time is short – we have to perform at seven. I appeal to the Chief Officer: must we perform the whole play? Our actors are tired and should save their best for tonight when they perform to the people of Iran. There is a muttered and lengthy discussion as I stand and smile inanely. The actors sit grumpily on the stage. It is, of course, all my fault, as I persuaded them to come to this festival, and only later broke the news to them that there would be no pay. Not a penny or a dirham. But breakfast, lunch and dinner are free. Claudius is already missing his beer. Ophelia is a staunch feminist and is in no mood to mollify these policemen who avoid all eye contact with the women and address only myself, the silver back male.

We reach a compromise. We shall perform only those scenes where there are men and women together on stage. Ophelia bristles and bites her lip. After about an hour of improvised distance between male and female we conclude this bizarre drama. The Visual Morality police nod to the Chief Moralist and we are given the green light. Then a panic seizes me: "What about the men?" Horatio and Hamlet have one of the warmest bromances in dramatic literature. I gently pop the question to the Police Chief. He laughs, slaps me on the back with alarming force and exclaims: "Men hugging, men kissing on stage? No problem!" Yes, he said that. I shake hands and pretend to enjoy sharing a cigarette with one of the Visual Policemen. The show will go on. The first professional performance of 'Hamlet' in English in Iran since its Revolution. Ali tells me the performance is sold out tonight. But then there is probably not a lot of competition. Even backgammon is banned in public.

Seven o'clock and the stage is set, the actors in costume. I am at the lighting board also in costume, which rather alarms the technician who must think we English are very poor (the Second Grave Digger is not a well-dressed man). I have a shovel which I prop up next to the redundant sound desk: all our music is sung and played live.

The audience are packing in. Many of the young women sport headscarves rather than the usual head to toe black cloth. They wear strident make-up and their scarves are carefully positioned to reveal as much hair as possible. The Morality Police are nowhere to be seen. When I see the seats are full, I ask Ali if I can alert the cast to start. "No, not yet," cries Ali, with some concern. I suddenly see why. Once the thousand seats are full, the ushers let in those who have queued for standing tickets. Soon every aisle in the stalls and balcony is packed tight with fans of William Shakespeare who rush for the privilege of standing still for three hours. I assume there are no fire regulations. This is Iran, this is Islam and this is 'Hamlet': the man who questions everything and everyone and turns in on himself to find a conscience far removed from any scripture.

TNT's 'Hamlet' has a simple but striking set: a large semi-circle of wood about one metre off the floor, tilting towards one end and rising to the other. Actors can stand on the curved wood and suggest the battlements of Elsinore. They can sit on the edge of the curve and create an interior. Ophelia can be buried behind the set, Polonius can hide under the set (and be strangled when his head protrudes). Hamlet can race to the higher end and arrive at a "sterile promontory", balanced on a cliff edge above a raging sea.

The semi-circle set for 'Hamlet', the ghost on the battlements

The action of the play is never slowed down by tedious scene changes (which we know never took place at The Globe). The play that catches the conscience of the King is a puppet show, at first lyrical then melodramatic. As in Shakespeare's day, the one embellishment is music. Tom Johnson's epic score is chiefly sung in complex five-part harmony by the cast but augmented by drum and violin. Much of the music underscores the text. The costumes are stylised Elizabethan. The colours drained of life: all reds, black, grey, purples and gold with no hint of natural green, yellow or blue. There are fast and furious sword fights. The drowning of Ophelia is presaged in her madness when she offers stones not flowers to the King and Queen, stones taken from a deep wooden bowl of water into which the actress plunges her head. In contrast, Rosencrantz and Guildenstern are clowns, grovelling grotesques and the audience in Iran howls with laughter just as they have laughed from Berlin to Tokyo. We humans are far more similar than we like to think. As the dying Hamlet collapses in Horatio's arms, the stage littered with the dead, he inhales and speaks the best words to ever end a play: "the rest is silence". The lights slowly fade. A single sustained violin note diminishes and dies. Total darkness in Tehran, no safety lights in this theatre. A few seconds silence. The audience erupts. No one knows how many people are in this auditorium, but those that are not already standing rise to applaud, then stop suddenly and leave. No second curtain calls in this culture. But then perhaps we should have applauded the audience who, without subtitles, have hung on every word for three long hours.

After the performance, sipping alcohol-free beer, a massive moustached figure places his hand on my shoulder. I turn. Ignoring introductions, he makes a bold invitation: "I want this play in Iraq". This would be tricky at the best of times but a war is raging across that country that very night. He sees my look of alarm and attempts to reassure me: "Do not worry, I talk of Kurdish Iraq. We will make sure you are safe. We Kurds love Shakespeare". We arrange to meet the next day, but this giant warrior does not appear. I will never know why.

The following day I meet an even more impressive figure: the chief of the Iranian International Theatre Institute. Very few of you reading the last sentence will have imagined that this is a woman, and a very special one. About seventy years of age she is fêted as one of the country's great theatrical minds. A collaborator with Peter Brook and a guest director at the National Theatre of France, she is back in Tehran to review the Festival. We speak for a long time and I immodestly have to write that she called this 'Hamlet' her favourite of the very many she has seen in half a century of theatre-going. I have seldom felt more humbled. She goes on to write about the production for the I.T.I., but sadly my Farsi is non-existent. How far away from the contemptible clichés of an Iranian woman is this sophisticated individual, her mind as sharp as her wisdom is broad.

Later that day it was announced we had won a prize at the Iranian 'Oscars'. Under a large portrait of Ayatollah Khomeini, I went on stage and collected a heavy metal statue that was clearly modelled on the 'real' Oscar. I never got to thank my mother, but I did wave the Oscar to the crowds (and passed it on to Martin Christopher who played Hamlet). As the Dane says to Horatio: "There are more things in heaven and earth than are dreamt of in your philosophy."

Salaam alaikum.

Days later, after crossing the desert, with snow-capped peaks either side of the highway, we arrive in Isfahan. We are sitting on the steps of the Imam Mosque. Behind us rises a dome that puts the Taj Mahal to shame: a dazzling sky blue and gold cupola encircled by calligraphic quotations from the Koran. The mosque sits on a square built four centuries ago by the greatest of the Iranian shahs. The winter sun warms us, but in the shadows the fountain ponds are solid ice. A group of women approach us. Students? They have the 'headscarf look', a hair covering so flimsy it seems to mock rather than obey the law.

We have one actress with us: Suzie Marston who plays Ophelia. The women gravitate towards her. "May we ask you a question?" says one, in flawless English. "Of course", we reply. I will never forget her question: "We are great fans of literature in English, our favourite author is Raymond Carver. What is yours?" So here in deepest Iran, a random group of young women sit reading the finest short stories written in the USA. As we are touched by the complex and subtle Iranian art around us, so they are touched by the complex and subtle literature of our culture. Ali guided us through the glories of Isfahan for several days. The only payment he asked was that we might return to Tehran via the Holy city of Qom so he might pray.

We flew out of Tehran at midnight on KLM. The minute the seat belt signs were off almost every Iranian on the flight ordered an alcoholic drink. We too raised a wine glass to Iran.

Comedy

By Paul

Why do we accept the idea that tragedy is somehow grander than comedy? Looking back over this book, are we trying to prove how serious and deep we are and forgetting our roots in the theatre of laughter? I remember Phil asking us to run 'Harlequin' for a few kids before the premiere. It's a clown show. It works like a 'Punch and Judy' puppet show at the seaside, as well as examining Stalinism and betrayal in art and revolution. World War I is an ice hockey match (no ice). Rasputin on beer crate stilts tries to seduce the audience with sweeties. TNT productions like 'The Canterville Ghost' have scarcely appeared in this book, perhaps because they are rather low brow. Yet the sheer release of performing this hyper-comedy to a packed audience can be as satisfying as the catharsis of the most profound tragedy.

Indeed, I recall having to step in for a whole week of 'Canterville Ghost' playing Ma Otis. The actress had had a tiff with another cast member and had simply run away. The show had to go on. We had a week of sold-out shows before we could get another actress into the role. So, I put on a wig, learnt the words over the weekend and was Ma Otis on Monday morning in front of 500 teenagers. By Thursday evening we were playing the main stage of the Leipzig Schauspielhaus to an adult audience... we had a standing ovation. There is a kind of exhilaration unlike any other when an audience reacts together to comedy.

Animals cry, animals protect their young and gather in protective groups. But only humans laugh. Laughter is what sets us apart and to laugh together, to be 'played' by an actor or comedian, is one of the most life-affirming and communal experiences that a human can have. Is it any wonder that comedians have recently replaced singers as the prophets of our time? If I could go back in time, I would choose to watch Max Miller rather than Laurence Olivier. Shakespeare felt much the same way: after writing the finest tragedies the world has seen... he stopped. Shakespeare returned to comedy. He understood that human life is often 'much ado about nothing'. He knew that comedy heals, that laughter and forgiveness are allies. This is why he put the Gravedigger in 'Hamlet' and the Porter in

'Macbeth'. This is the great achievement of his final work and one of my favourite TNT productions: 'The Tempest'.

We are quite rough with 'The Tempest'. We make sure the comedy is truly funny. We engage a clown to play Trinculo and we add a long umbrella sketch to the play. We also cut Gonzalo (blasphemy) to try and rescue the last act of the play which is frankly a mess (more blasphemy). We want to explore why and how Prospero forgives the brother that tried to murder him and his child. As this complex drama unfolds, the clowns and Caliban stage their attempted coup. Prospero's spirit, Ariel, sees it coming and distracts the plotters with fine robes. But in our production, there are no robes, just the idea of robes on an empty line: Emperor's new clothes. Despite the best efforts of Caliban, the would-be murderers strip naked and put on these invisible garments. They attempt their coup in the nude. It is funny, honestly....and so is Shakespeare, a man who chose to end his life's work with a play where two clowns escape to paradise on a barrel of wine.

From 'Wizard of Jazz', a TNT joke:

BARMAN: "I say I say I say, my joke's got no punchline."

DRINKER: "Your joke's got no punchline! How does it end?"

BARMAN: (Silence).

(You will have noticed that a TNT joke ends, like 'Hamlet', with silence; high or low the same, from comedy to tragedy at the wink of an eye.)

Sir Toby Belch and Sir Andrew Aguecheek (Glyn Connop and Alistair Hoyle) reveal their disguise in TNT's production of 'Twelfth Night'

The Gulf

By Paul

"No one brings theatre to Kuwait." This is the British Council Officer for the Gulf advising our producer, Myriam Woker, to abandon her wild idea of taking TNT to a country for which no tourist visas are issued. The country is still traumatised after Saddam Hussein's recent invasion and expulsion. Well, three months later TNT is in Kuwait, myself playing Sherlock Homes, and the audience packs into the Shamiya Theatre. At least, I think it is called the Shamiya Theatre because there is no sign or indication that this is a place of performance. Islam is uncertain about theatre. Does it imitate life? Is it a painting of the real world? Is our performance a blasphemy? Most of the local organisers are Lebanese, as if this somehow makes it all alright.

Myriam has single-headedly enabled this tour and will bring more of our productions to the Gulf over the next decade. This achievement would have been impossible, but that she is the wife of the Swiss ambassador to the Gulf. TNT attracts just the right sort of 'oddball', not just as actors but also as promoters. Myriam is a French Swiss whirlwind and has bullied and cajoled for us from Geneva to Dubai, from Brisbane to Singapore.

Our greatest triumph in Kuwait is 'Macbeth'. Even in this cultural desert over two thousand tickets were sold in advance. One Arab in full traditional dress told me: "I do not like theatre. I believe it is forbidden by the Koran, but Shakespeare is the greatest of poets and we Arabs have a deep love for poetry." But even Shakespeare is not allowed a poster outside the Shamiya.

This is not a ban that affects fast food advertising. There are twenty-one McDonald's in Kuwait. Of course there are no bars. The bored and rich young Kuwaitis race motor bikes up and down the sea front before screeching to a halt at the next burger bar. The city is not so much artificial as non-existent. The shopping malls hum with air conditioners but little life. French lingerie shops stand next to burka outfitters. The desert itself is off limits as no one has been able to dig up the many thousands of mines that Saddam's troops laid. The horizon is flat in every direction. In our spare time we build sandcastles and sip soft drinks. The bored wives of bored expat engineers read airport novels by the side of tepid swimming pools. Each morning, as we emerge from our hotel rooms, we notice the room service trays all along the corridor, each overflowing with empty bottles of illicit Russian vodka and smuggled Scotch whisky. Since no one drinks in public, everyone smokes. The men, that is. The women pass by as black as shadows. Alarmingly, they often catch your eye. We all experience this and guess that this is an act of rebellion rather than an invitation.

Myriam explains to us how Saddam took Kuwait. He invaded in August when every sane Kuwaiti was in London or Geneva. Even now in autumn the heat hits you like a hammer. I imagine this fake city in high summer and wince. Mostly it was the slaves who were there in August; once the Iraqi army had brushed aside the border guards, the Palestinians and Pakistanis who watered the lawns, swept the floors and grovelled to the great, all ran onto the streets and cheered the liberating army of the tyrant. There were almost no Kuwaitis in Kuwait to resist the Iraqis. There were only the slaves and the oil. Saddam knew that. When the Kuwaitis returned on the shirt tails of the US army they turned on their slaves. Now there are only Indian workers here, their passports confiscated and their pay a pittance. The Palestinians and fellow Moslems are all gone. The rulers are just as hated by their new slaves, but the Kuwaitis no longer care as the Indians are infidels, and besides they have had their revenge.

Do I sound cynical or ungrateful? Our audiences were warm and appreciative and I met many cultured and intelligent locals, but nothing could alter my discomfort. Looking back, the time I spent touring from one end of the Gulf to the other is fascinating, a learning curve: not about Islam, since usually I saw only a parody of that great Faith, but about the corrosive effect of unearned wealth. The oil wells had only just stopped burning when TNT first arrived in the Gulf. But the pollution of oil is nowhere darker and deeper than in these lifeless city states built on its sticky wealth.

A few years later we are circling above Abu Dhabi airport, unable to land as US fighters are blocking the runway. This is day one of the Second Gulf War. For some reason no one has bothered to cancel TNT's Gulf tour of 'A Midsummer Night's Dream'. This is ironic since our overall setting is inspired by Operation Desert Storm; Theseus's army, who overcome the Amazons, are dressed in desert fatigues. The lovers Demetrius and Lysander swagger around the forest of Athens in 'butch' uniforms. It is our answer to the often feeble portrayal of the lovers and Amazons that grace this wildest of Shakespearian comedies. Ours is a battle of the sexes in a war zone.

We land at last and transfer to the hotel. That night we decamp to the hotel bar in this mostly dry state and witness one of the more extraordinary scenes of the wide travels of TNT. The bar is a microcosm of all that is wrong with both the Gulf and the war that is consuming it. The layout of the bar is crucial: the serving counter is at one end of the large room away from the door. The bar is reached by a special ramp up the side of the hotel so hookers do not have to pass reception en route to the rooms. Those prostitutes who are not already upstairs gather by the door. They are mostly from Moldova or Ukraine. None is Arab. On a podium in the centre of the room a Russian cover band churns out popular hits. The singer is not too bad; in a cigarette and vodka drenched voice he intones: "Down a durk desert highvay, cool vind in my haar". In front of the band are two girlie dancers in high boots and bikinis. They barely dance, just flapping their arms and nodding their heads off beat. No one cares, least of all them. Their performance is rather wonderful, expressing their total contempt for their gawking audience.

The clientele is split between Indian managers, Arabs in full robes and European businessmen. There are so few bars in Abu Dhabi that many of the clients are not hunting girls so much as chasing a cold lager. We are the only theatre company there for sure. Our actresses are the only unavailable women in the bar and are not amused. But it is hot and we all need a beer. What turns this sordid scene into an extraordinary landscape of grotesquerie are the televisions. There are three large screens on the wall opposite the dancers' podium. They are tuned to Al Jazeera. Almost no one is looking at them as they find the dancers and hookers more interesting. But this is midnight on day one of the Second Gulf War. The bombardment of Bagdad has begun. Shock and Awe. The screens are right in the eyeline of the two bored dancers. This is Al Jazeera not CNN. The violence of the attack is shown in graphic detail and shocking colour. With every explosion the bored dancers react with random jerks and looks of panic. Their bored flapping is suddenly enlivened. But no one turns to see the screens, save us, the thirsty artists. The hookers hook, the ex-pats sip, the Indians sidle up to the Moldovan girls and negotiate. It is 'Babylon'. Utterly corrupt. Despite the heat we never return to the bar, even our Theseus, who loves his beer, quenches his thirst with pomegranate juice for the rest of the week.

The shows go rather well, comic distraction in the desert. Before our open-air performances I check for escape routes. Each night the bombers and cruise missiles roar off. For Iraq there is neither laughter nor escape.

Then the final Kuwait performances are cancelled. What do we expect? And then a reprieve. We are invited to perform in the security of the American base. So off we go. We do not just perform to those who agree with us. Taking 'Hamlet' in past wire, guards and tank traps. GIs gather in an improvised theatre. The performance takes on a significance of the like

Horatio could never dream. "To be or not to be" is no longer theoretical. At the play's conclusion a soldier comes up to Martin who plays Hamlet and says how much the performance means to him, tomorrow this GI deploys into Iraq. He will carry Hamlet's tortured wisdom with him.

Istanbul more than a decade later. Our host theatre, the Kenter, is struggling as its subsidy has been cut for supporting the anti-Erdoğan demonstrations in Tahrir Square. It carries on, holding the light of culture. We are performing 'Frankenstein, the Monster and the Myth'. Our version includes scenes from Mary Shelley's flawed masterpiece, a lot of Boris Karloff, a dash of 'Young Frankenstein'-style japes, and much original material. I wonder how any version can ignore the line: "Throw the switch, Igor!" since it seems to me that this might be the second finest line in English dramatic literature, (after "To be or not to be"). When Igor does throw the switch, the Monster wakes and the modern world is born, the internet is upon us, A.I. is already here. And it is very funny. The audience seem to think so. So it is.

10 am. The theatre is packed with Turkish teenagers. Many of the girls wear headscarves and hijabs. Then disaster strikes. A power cut. The Kenter is underground. There are no safety lights. It is pitch black. Then a miracle. First one girl raises her mobile phone and flicks on its light, then another follows. Soon three hundred mobile phones are held aloft. The performance continues to its grizzly end lit by the phones: the Monster gets his bride, Victor fries. In any Western theatre the teachers would have led the students out to safety. Here the young Muslim audience cares so deeply for theatre that they rescue us with their own ingenuity. How we are humbled. Bless them all.

We are rehearsing 'Don Quijote' in Spanish in a university hall in Munich. Every night the students leave the corridor and toilets awash with broken glasses and empty bottles. We pity the cleaners, nearly all are Turkish women in headscarves who speak little German and no English. The production picks up on Cervantes' conceit that his great novel is written by a Moor named Cide Hamete Benengeli, a Muslim. This extraordinary device is usually, perhaps always, overlooked in stage and film versions of the epic. So TNT makes this the frame of the show, the focus, the lens through which the narrative is fixed.

Cervantes understands that Islam is a European religion, part of our civilisation, far older and more firmly rooted than any Protestant sect. That morning in the University we rehearse with the first music cue: a powerful and melodic call to prayer, which will be interrupted by agents of the Inquisition. But instead of actors breaking into the Moor's chamber as his quill sketches the opening lines of 'Don Quijote', the Turkish cleaner, mop in hand, rushes through the door. Her eyes lit up with joy. We share no language, nothing but this recorded track. We make her tea, invite her to sit down and play the track one, two, three times. Marginalised, excluded, exploited as she is, us with the shabby but real privileges of Western artists – theatre brings us together. Like Cervantes' imaginary Moor she is a part of our lives on this our shared continent. Next day she brings us all Turkish sweets. We learn her word for thank you: Teşekkür!

The final development that TNT seeks in its work with other cultures is to cease to 'perform to' but to 'perform with' that culture. In 2017 we premier 'My Sister Syria', a thriller that responds to the terrible and ongoing war in Syria, aiming to break down some of the myths surrounding the refugee crisis it has provoked. To do this we recruit some extraordinary Arab artists and create a play in English and Arabic, which tours Europe for seven months. Our key audience is older teenagers, although most performances are open to the general public too. Many of these performances take place in the 'dragon's den' of Eastern Europe, where hostility to all things Arabic is rife.

Our key collaborators were Lama Amine and Nafee Mohammed. Lama grew up in a Beirut orphanage after both her parents were killed in the Lebanese civil war. She began to dance and thanks to her great tenacity arrived in London to take a course in 'Movement for the Theatre', teaching herself English at night. We found her at an open audition. Getting her a visa to tour with us was a nightmare, but one from which we woke with the necessary documents, though only by the skin of our teeth. Nafee Mohammed's story is even more extraordinary: a senior officer in Saddam Hussein's army he fled to the West during the Gulf War. A master Oud player and man of great learning, he is now Professor of Middle Eastern Music in Edinburgh. He told us that it is only his music that saves his sanity and blocks out the horror, which, like Colonel Kurtz, he faced with open eyes. Ali Nakeeb and Lana Miller completed our Arabic cast.

'My Sister Syria' is very loosely based on Conrad's *Heart of Darkness* and is influenced by Coppola's reworking of the novel in his film 'Apocalypse Now'. Rachel, a British aid worker, slips into Syria to bring out a wounded female rebel general at the prompting of MI5 and the CIA. Rachel's journey into this particular heart of darkness is a lesson in kindness and fear, brutality and joy, rebellion and cowardice, *jihadi* and Sufi Islam. The soundtrack (scored by John Kenny) is gunfire, calls to prayer, Syrian rap and classical Oud music. There is betrayal and a key deception: MI5 have misinformed Rachel, the rebel general does not wish to escape, she only wants to get her traumatised son out of Syria, and then die in battle. When the aid worker agrees to take the son, she infuriates her Western minders who abandon her. Rachel keeps her promise to the Kurtz-like general. Alone now, she takes the boy along the refugee route back to Germany via leaking life rafts and sealed trucks. Back in Syria the wounded general finds calm and walks out into the desert to her certain death at the hands of Isis. Oud blends with trombone as the sun rises. The aid worker and the general's son arrive at last in Germany but there he rejects her further help and retreats into a closed world. Rachel is left only with the gift of the dying general, a poem of the Sufi master Rumi:

> Inside this new love, die. Your way begins on the other side.
>
> Become the sky. Take a hammer to the prison wall.
>
> Escape. Walk out like someone suddenly born into colour.
>
> Do it now. You're covered with a thick cloud.
>
> Slide out the side.
>
> Die, and be quiet.
>
> Quietness is the surest sign that you've died.
>
> Your old life was a frantic running from silence. The speechless full moon breaks from a cloud – now.

TNT's original script, 'My Sister Syria': an Isis Jihadist approaches the Sufi General's hideout

Chapter Fifteen: 'Brave New World' and 'A Christmas Carol'

By Phil

In 'Brave New World' (1998) we looked to the future and attacked the present day 'Spectacle'; that tendency in our hypermodern lives to privilege the image of a thing over the material thing itself. When it was suggested that we consider an adaptation of Aldous Huxley's dystopian 1932 novel, we were fearful that it might be seen as 'old hat', out of date. But once we got to work on the detail we discovered a vision that remained remarkably prescient, and was becoming more so every day. In 1998 the Iron Curtain police states were in disintegration (though some would partially reassemble themselves in new guises) and 'Brave New World' was far more relevant than its perennial companion piece: Orwell's 'Nineteen Eighty-Four'.

In his attention to body modification, virtual reality and the technological invasion of private and subjective spaces, Aldous Huxley was clearly ahead of the game. The threat to freedom at the end of the twentieth century lay as much in the exploitation of pleasure, obsession with twisted ideas of 'health', and recreation, as it was in imprisonment, propaganda and slavish obedience to the state. As public services and institutions fragmented in the so-called 'developed world', social solidarity and community seemed to stumble before an explosion of manipulated individualism and consuming-subjectivities, while giant corporate entities swelled to fill the void.

Drawing on our physical theatre origins, inspired by Meyerhold's biomechanics, we were not only able to portray the complex and alien psychologies of Huxley's future selves, but also the physical synchronicities into which they had fallen or been programmed. The media portrayed in our adaptation were recognisable. Indeed they became ever more so as access through the internet to US-influenced media became global. But what seemed to grasp our audiences was the play's assemblage of hedonistic shape-shifting and subjectivity wed to mind-numbing conformism. In a consumerist world where everyone could buy rebellion and weirdness from big corporations delivered via Amazon direct to their door or screen, there was nowhere to go to be a rebel. No space left to be unconventional. Rather, to be nonconformist was to fit in. Identities slithered and slid. On the one hand there was the great social liberation, first flowering in the counter-cultures of the US and Western Europe in the 1960s; but, on the other hand, those hippies were now running or funding the social media corporations and what had begun as handmade was mass-produced; what had been mind-changing was now mind-shaping.

'Brave New World' secured our work with younger audiences. It played to large numbers of teenagers. We were still performing our vital physical and visual theatre. Our set was another acting machine: a climbing frame able to whirl bottled homunculi around the heads of the characters. But this time the content hit home directly at the personal and social concerns of young audiences. There was nothing literary about this learning. This was scholarly watching and learning through the body and emotions. Our subsequent prioritisation of that audience – and our reliance upon it – has continued. The privilege of having time with young people at a formative moment in their lives, and learning to win their attention and directing it to vitally and physically entertaining matters is a serious business.

In 'A Christmas Carol', in 1996, we created a Christmas phenomenon which continues to play every 'festive season', often in multiple productions and languages. It is a shining example of learning from mistakes and not repeating them. What we originally got right was the sense (returning with 'Brave New World') that a familiar literary classic might hold contemporary relevance that was hidden by most adaptations. Not a modern 'interpretation' placed over the original, but a contemporariness that lay within the material and simply needed sympathetic staging to coax it out.

Dickens and his work have suffered from the popular assumption that he has mostly sentimentality to offer as the contrast to the excesses of his exaggerated characterisations. Given our indifference to realism, we saw this as a useful quality rather than as a problem. Our grotesque aesthetics put us in tune with Dickens. We were just as happy with the extremes of heartstring-tugging and eye-watering sentiment as with the twisted satire of Victorian death-dealing and poverty-cultivation. Indeed, we were willing to push both aspects of Dickens's art to extremes.

In 'Oliver Twist' we emphasised the greed of the workhouse Beadle, siphoning off funds meant for his starving inmates, by having Mrs Corney, the matron, make a pot of tea *in his mouth*. With 'A Christmas Carol', it was almost as if we were staging a myth or folk tale, not a Victorian melodrama. The prevalence of ghosts and dreams let us depict metamorphoses that were corporeal but impossible, moral, social and absurd but also recognisable.

'A Christmas Carol' is about extreme change. It concerns a miser, Scrooge, who becomes a benefactor; a small redistribution of wealth transforms the lives of the Cratchits, a sickly family facing imminent death, into happy ones with a bright future. All pretty much within the Aristotelian unities. As with many original texts of the classics, we found that 'A Christmas Carol' held radical, unconforming, gritty contents that were usually watered down in modern adaptations, apparently incompatible with the 'Christmas season'.

Ross Mullan as the ghost of Jacob Marley appears in Scrooge's safe in TNT's 'A Christmas Carol', with Anthony Pedley as Scrooge

So it was that we could restore the green (pre-Coca Cola red) of the suit of Father Christmas – the Ghost of Christmas Present – to make him more the folkloric 'green man' of the natural world. From his sack of presents, despite his warnings, Scrooge would pull a ventriloquist's dummy of a child who claims to be the future and that Scrooge is his father. The monstrous infant spouts Malthusian indifference and quotes Scrooge's own words about the poor back at him: "Let them die!" The Ghost of Christmas Present names this child "Ignorance". This was our grotesque version of Dickens's two emaciated children, 'Want' and 'Ignorance'; but they were not passive objects of pity. We had returned them to the active malevolence of 'Ignorance' in the Dickens.

Unfortunately, our enthusiasm for the grotesque and the past success of framing devices, emphasising the folkloric nature of storylines and pointing to themes rather than representations, led us astray. In our original production (see the chapter, Writing for TNT) the ghosts of 'A Christmas Carol' performed Scrooge's story to the miser. While this created an immediate frisson, there could be no real redemption into life at the end. All the invention and sharp satire with the chilling dummy-child or the mumming with an over-sized stuffed turkey or the mimed rides through the London night sky were undermined, when there were only ghosts in the mix. If the Cratchits were ghosts how could their prospects change? They couldn't.

Here was a revelation for us: in the strange world of theatre, the ghosts were not a formal device. They were the reality. In the eyes and hearts of our audience, our frame was not just a dramatic structure, but the real presence of spectral, tragic characters for whom life was over. By addressing and removing that frame in future productions, and replacing it with a simple opening in which Bob Cratchit opens a Christmas-wrapped copy of the novel and begins to read, the production came alive and now runs year after year.

The production was also exemplary for the way we solved a problem at its climax. Dickens's story introduces many new characters to bring about Scrooge's transformation from miser to benefactor. This is a problem in the theatre, particularly with our tiny casts. But, rather than seek a solution by changing and trimming the story, we found one in the very act of theatre itself. We made the plethora of new characters, and the blizzard of quick costume changes required, the means to generate a wild excess of its own. The production slowly overwhelmed the cast of actors who became adrift in the barely coherent joy of performing. The audience hoot with laughter, especially the young children. This vitality of style fuelled the exuberance of the story. The genius of Dickens's classic tale allowed us, as theatre makers, to access not just the deep and understood thrill of a seasonal festival, but the equally deep and impossible to define 'life' in performance itself.

Brave New Theatre

By Paul

Theatre and Science Fiction are not usually comfortable bedfellows. But two of my personal favourite TNT productions fall into that category: 'Fahrenheit 451' and 'Brave New World'. We have mounted these plays six times in total: five times on 8-month tours, and once in Costa Rica as a single theatre run. The productions use stylised settings and futuristic scores from Paul Flush that do far more than create an imagined world. They emotionally manipulate the audience.

Emotion is surely the key to creating good science fiction. It is why the Russian films of Tarkovsky, notably 'Solaris' and 'Stalker', remain not just my favourite sci-fi but have influenced TNT's aesthetic. Tarkovsky's future world is not about gadgets and laser swords; it's about our humanity trying to deal with a future where we have lost control, where time and space is melting.

It is one of the joys of Science Fiction that there is little that is culturally specific. So, TNT's 'Brave New World' could manifest as 'Mundo Feliz' (Happy World) in Costa Rica and have a similar impact to that of our European production performed in English. It is interesting that Shakespeare's one true Sci-Fi play is 'King Lear', set in a future that pretends to be the past (like 'Game of Thrones'). This allows the Bard to explore his most profound themes without historical or religious baggage.

In 'Brave New World', Aldous Huxley creates, as Phil points out, a convincing vision of our shared future. One where pleasure and technology combine to deaden true feeling, where absurd sport replaces literacy, where cold sex replaces love, where the state provides the drugs, the elderly are turned into compost and the workers are cloned and regimented. By accident, a rather shallow and selfish rebel discovers the last person on earth who cares for literature and love, hidden on a 'Savage Reservation' by the guilty high official who illegally spawned him. This survivor's name is John the Savage.

The first half of the TNT production explains and demonstrates the working of this society (helicopter billiards, anyone?) and sets up the narrative dilemma by bringing John back to this corrupt 'civilisation'. So far so normal for an adaptation. But the second half is rather different. In our production, John's progress is followed as if in a Reality TV show where the live audience are like guests in a TV studio.

When John the Savage is traumatised by his mother's composting, he throws away his drugs, rejects casual sex and falls in love with an 'Alpha' female whose heart he manages to touch. This story is presented by the *compère* of the 'show' as a thrilling reality. In a pain-free society John's anxieties are treated as a spectacle for us to enjoy. We want to see him read a book or speak poetry, but we do not want to copy him, just marvel at this relic of the old-fashioned past. This is classic grotesque. The audience are invited to laugh at horror. John throws his drugs (sweets) into the audience, cloned drone workers race around the audience handing out more sweets and tell the audience to take their soma drug. John follows shouting and screaming at the audience to spit out their soma. This is great fun, especially for a teenage audience, but it is also terrifying. So when John fails and collapses exhausted on the stage a wave of uncomfortable emotion replaces the hysteria in the auditorium (which is fully lit, no hiding in the dark here).

The finale of the play (and book, to which we remain faithful) is performed as if at an outside broadcast. John has failed to connect with his Alpha lover. Her social programming is too strong. He has come to despise all humanity. He is now whipping himself in public and crowds are gathering to see the spectacle. Our *compère* excitedly presents the scene to the audience. Several members of the public (our audience) are asked to comment on the whipping, asked if they find it exciting. John's lover pushes her way through the crowd. She has had a change of heart, she has also thrown away her soma drugs. She is ready to go with John back to the 'Savage Reservation', embrace her mortality and discover love. But it is too late. John's own heart has hardened, like Hamlet's. He has transferred his disgust from the many to the one. All he has are the words of Shakespeare to understand his pain. And his Alpha lover will have no more sympathy than Ophelia. As she climbs towards him, he knocks her to the ground. She dies. He then turns on himself and speaking Othello's death speech, ends his life. The *compère* comments throughout and her microphone is ever at the ready to elicit responses from the actual theatre audience. With the audience participating throughout, this is like an extended moment of raw energy, when the fabrication of theatre falls away to leave a stream of live energy bouncing between stage and auditorium, until the boundary between the two melts. At the moment of John's suicide, the audience falls silent, the *compère* acts as if stunned. This has surely gone too far? She looks hard at the audience and then, in a state of exhilaration, says: "I find this very, very…entertaining."

The worker-clones on stage applaud. The lights go down. The end. The audience applaud but things are not clear, divisions are not re-established: are the audience applauding as characters in the play? As other clones? Or as those people who arrived earlier to watch a play? They are trapped in an ambiguity of roles until they leave the theatre for the 'brave new world' outside. Then who are they?

The future setting of Aldous Huxley's 'Brave New World' is terrifying, not because of a corrupt authority we have nothing to do with, but because of our co-option into it, because of the corruption we see within our own lives, right now. It shows us the seeds of a horrific world based on generalised selfish pleasure. The fiction of the novel and the audience participation of our production co-opt us into planting these seeds in ourselves, and then they ask us 'do you really want to keep on doing this?'

Manufacturing humans in TNT's 'Brave New World'

This drawing in of the audience so that they become part of the theatrical event in a unified space is part of our aesthetic. It extends to our work on the classics. Let me give an example from our production of 'Taming of the Shrew', a surprising mainstay of our repertoire given its reputation for sexism. In a particularly doubtful scene we are able to recruit the audience in transforming the nature of the action. This is when Petruchio finally "tames" Kate on a journey to see her father in Padua. On the way they meet the father of another character, called Vincentio. Kate is asked to address him as if she has mistaken him for a young woman. She rebels, but eventually agrees to do so because her husband wishes it. Petruchio then mocks her for her 'mistake' and insists she apologise to the venerable old gentleman. When she does so "the game is won". So far so sexist – though soon to be undermined by our production – but that is the drama at this point.

Despite us setting this on a boat and having Vincentio on the river bank, the scene was not working. No one knew or cared about Vincentio. To create the river bank it was best that Vincentio was upstage, but that meant Kate and Petruchio turned their backs to the audience. In a funny play this was turning into an unfunny scene. So after an early performance in Singapore I suggested the following: cut Vincentio, throw the lights on the audience, and have Kate select an older man. She asks him to stand, praises him as if he were a young woman and says he will make a "fair bedfellow" for hers or any husband. Cue laughter.

Petruchio is suitably outraged and insists that Kate must be mad for this is not a "fair maid" but a man, "old and wrinkled". More laughter. Kate apologises heaping more back-handed compliments on the "venerable, old father". In countries as diverse as China and Germany there is no English Pantomime tradition, no breaking of the fourth wall of theatre, especially in the classics; yet the scene works. It is true to Shakespeare. Not one word is changed except for the name of Vincentio. But this is not just any laughter; the laughter is grotesque, our hallmark. The joke is not just on Kate; the whole audience is drawn in; for as we laugh we also feel Kate's humiliation as our own (through our representative "old father"). We squirm at Kate's mistreatment, physical and psychological, at the same time as we laugh.

In our early production, 'English Tea Party', the audience have a very specific role: they are part of the nightmare of the play. They attend on the trauma of the central character, Neil, a British tank gunner who is part of an attack on a village near Hamburg in which he kills a young German woman. Bent over her body his mind breaks down and he imagines himself back home in Britain. But that family home is a bombed out ruin. His father is there: "Dad" a northerner, always trying to avoid reality by cracking a joke. His mother is a life size dummy. Though the house is in ruins, an empty bird cage swings from a rafter. (Later, the German title for the play became 'Hitler Killed My Canary').

As Neil tries to make sense of his sudden return to his family, three things undermine him: his Dad's jokes which turn into full scale music hall routines, the dead German comes back to life and starts to take the role of his missing fiancée, and the audience, who make an appearance in his shattered house. Gradually Neil discovers that his mother is traumatised by the death of her canary in a bombing raid, his fiancée has run off with a GI and that his own guilt is so great that he cannot accept forgiveness for the killing of Anna, the German woman, despite the rather understanding attitude of the corpse at his side.

Neil attempts to make sense of all this by starting his own performances. He must assert control over the audience that have apparently invited themselves into his ruined house. So, he elevates his dad to the role of King and attempts to marry the dead German at a Royal Wedding – "since folk take so much more notice of *Royal* Weddings". The audience must perform the congregation at Westminster Abbey. Dad becomes the Archbishop of Canterbury and sets off on an extravagant music hall act of mass audience participation. Every 'serious' ceremony that Neil tries to organise is undermined by his comedian dad with the connivance of the public. Their laughter is his dad's chief weapon in the fight to avoid reality and the guilt that comes with it.

So the action is no longer a representation of something happening somewhere else, or something that once happened. It is happening right now, right here in the theatre, and, most importantly, it can happen only with the agreement and participation of the audience. At such a moment theatre is both art and ethics, and at the same time just plain excitement.

As 'English Tea Party' approaches its conclusion, there comes the 'killer line'; the apotheosis of the audience's role. In his frustration Neil bellows to his impossible father: "Shut up, Dad!! Sorry... I mean shut up, your highness." And then he turns to the audience and shouts: "Stop it! Stop laughing! Or I will wake up and you will all disappear!" There is no reality to represent; there is only the fiction of theatre. This is how the play ends:

NEIL: (To the audience) My father is going to be judge, and you, if you would, will be the jury. I am the accused and the prosecution.

DAD: Who's the defence?

NEIL: There is no defence.

DAD: All stand up in the king's court for the judge! Stand up!

(Gets audience to stand.)

NEIL: Please, sit down… please... he's got it wrong… it won't work, sit down…For Christ's sake, Dad, you've got no wig!!

DAD: Swearing in court. Fine – five pounds. Let's see your money!!

NEIL: Be serious!

DAD: I am serious. Get in the dock!

NEIL: I'm in the dock

DAD: Watch out for the banana boats!

NEIL: Call the first witness…

DAD: Call Anna Schwoorl! Call Anna Schwitz… Schmooo…. Schmertz… Shkoo(etc.)

NEIL: (Exhausted) Schwarz.

DAD: Oi! (To Anna, the corpse.) Get up, will you. (She rises from the dead and takes a position as if in court.)

NEIL: Anna, Anna. I want you… I want you to tell the court in your own words…

DAD: What about the oath?

NEIL: Sod the bloody oath

DAD: Good oath, carry on, counsel!

NEIL: Anna, I just want you to tell the court in your own words what I did to you on the last day of the war.

ANNA: Neil, you did what any other soldier would do.

NEIL: I foolishly imagined the allied fire to be German, even though I knew the enemy had ceased to oppose us. I was excited, I was elated. I attacked the farmhouse and I killed this young woman who was coming to welcome me with a cup of tea.

ANNA: Ahorn Kaffee eigentlich. Your honour, I could have hung out a white flag if I had thought. But I was distracted, thinking of my own fiancé out on the Eastern Front.

NEIL: Your honour, I took this woman's life.

ANNA: What life? There was nothing left for me to live for. The cities were destroyed. The people broken. I would have ended up a bitter old woman … begging amongst the ruins, nostalgic for Hitler…

NEIL: (Angry) Why won't you let me plead guilty?

ANNA: (Shouts) Why won't you let me alone?

DAD: Order! Order! Everyone was just following military orders!!

NEIL: Yes, that's right I was just following military orders, but I can still be judged. I am responsible: Coventry, Belsen, Dresden, Katyn, these are war crimes I was a part of and a party to – Auschwitz, Hiroshima, Nagasaki…

DAD: This is not what the public want to hear, Neil. They want more jokes, they want pretty girls dancing about the scenery, they want a story they can understand without having to think too much and most of all they want a good night out at the theatre – yes? (Audience agree).

ANNA: Joseph, Joseph, da bist Du, mein Geliebter. (She goes to embrace Neil as if he were Joseph, her boyfriend. Anna starts to sing 'Lili Marlene'. All sing as Anna and Neil dance slowly, then Neil pulls away and the song falters.)

NEIL: Joseph… I'm not your bloody Joseph. I'm the man who murdered you.

DAD: Christ, that's let the cat out of the bag!

NEIL: Let's just get on with the verdict.

DAD: All right, all right – the verdict! Silence in court! Neil Down, you have been charged with serious criminal conspiracy… to steal toast and jam from the kitchen table… (Neil grabs Dad.) Forget all this guilt crap, son…

NEIL: No. Without punishment there is only chaos!!

DAD: All right!! All right!! Get in the dock! (To audience) Shuttup… are you ready? Shuttup! Neil, I find you guilty of murder. I sentence you to be taken from this place to a place of execution and there in front of a military firing squad … to make us all a nice cup of tea.

NEIL: What!! I'll bloody kill you! (Neil chases Dad into audience where Dad hides.)

NEIL: (To the audience.) Please, please!! Please be quiet. Right. I am now going to pass judgement on myself. (Takes the judge's 'wig', a teapot cosy.) I, Neil Down, find myself guilty of murder. And I sentence myself to be shot to death in front of a firing squad. (Takes off wig. Hands Anna his gun.) Anna, you have the gun. Just think of me as the man that murdered your Joseph. (Neil ties himself to a wooden pole he has taken from the rubble of the house.)

ANNA: There are too many graves.

NEIL: No, there is still one empty.

DAD: Any, last requests? The joke about the Englishman, the Irishman and the Scotsman in a boat… no?

NEIL: Fire! Fire!

(Anna fires at Neil, but it is her that is hit by the bullet, it is her and not Neil that falls dead. Blackout. Torches.)

NEIL: Anna, Anna! I'm sorry – I'm still alive...

Chapter Sixteen: Israel

By Paul

Jerusalem. The audience for TNT's 'Macbeth' fills the impressive theatre built of the same golden stone as the old city. We cannot start on time, not just for the security checks that remind me of an airport but the number of elderly Israelis who slowly take their seats. The theatre has a hearing aid loop we are not allowed to ignore. I watch these ancient audience members as the tragedy unfolds onstage, they lean forward but they often shield their eyes. Are they rejecting the dance-like physical theatre with which TNT has illuminated the play? Then it occurs to me that this is perhaps the last audience in the world that listens to a play; that are an "audience" from the verb *audio*: to hear. Samuel Pepys writes in his diary of going to "listen to a play" and here they are, holding on to a long-lost tradition of the word. This audience is literally a dying breed. Most of them are Yiddish speaking holocaust survivors, some surely with tattooed numbers on their wrists. They bring with them the fabulous intellectualism of the lost world of European Jewry. A world view based on the Word; the Word of God and the words of the Torah and of the poets and the minds that illuminated our civilisation until we allowed barbarism to overwhelm and exile these people from our continent.

Our next tour to Israel will deal more explicitly with this genocide and its sad resonance in our own times. 'The Wave' is an idea as much as a book. It follows an experiment in an American High School in the 1970s when an idealistic history teacher tried to answer his students' question: how did young Germans become attracted to Nazi ideology? The teacher set up an organisation within the school called The Wave. It was not overtly fascist, nor did he reveal that this was an experiment. The Wave offered team-like solidarity, physical exercise, discipline, marches, drumming, banners and became an irresistible force in the school. In particular, it brought an outsider in the class into the group; it changed his life. The teacher lost his moral bearings and began to enjoy the hero worship of his movement. And then the discrimination began; Jewish and Black students became targets. The teacher realised with horror that he was not exploring how young people became Nazis, he was turning young people into Nazis. He disbanded The Wave. In doing so he destroyed the world of the formerly outcast pupil, and, in our play, a chilling modern parallel became possible: the mindset and motivation of the High School mass killer.

Phil Smith and I turn this story into a rather more complex play than the original book which documents the events. The production tours across Europe and is then invited to Israel, performing to both students and adults from Bathsheba in the south to Haifa in the north. Post-show discussions are often emotionally charged. Many of the audience have family members murdered in the camps. But now comes the second layer of meaning, and how it touches on the question that the reader might already have asked themselves: what of modern Israel? How do visiting artists feel about the great moral and political questions that arise out of Israel's occupation and treatment of the Moslems and Palestinians (not the same thing, by the by)?

The company's second producer in Israel is a formidable woman named Judy: an Israeli academic who was much taken with our production of 'Hamlet' at the Jerusalem theatre and offered to promote us throughout the country. Her verve and enthusiasm is as great as her stature is small. Judy is committed to bringing Arab, Druze and Jewish audiences together to see theatre. She devotes herself to this noble aim with such intensity that she gets results. Her base became our base; an idyllic town in the hills behind Haifa known as Zichron Ya'akov, a wine growing area first settled by European immigrants in the nineteenth century with funding from the Rothschilds. Cobbled streets, old villas and above all wineries make this one of Israel's most attractive small towns. Its Tishbi wine is one of the country's finest. Its theatre, however, is set in the middle of an outdoor military museum. We enter past tanks and rocket launchers. The nation's troubles are never far away. 'The Wave' is due to be performed to a mixed Arab and Jewish audience. We have already promised to take the kissing out of the teenage romance scenes. There is some opposition in the cast until Judy and I remind them that the two Arab teachers who bring groups to see TNT productions take a great personal risk with their reputation and even employment should we refuse to compromise.

We perform 'The Wave' to the audience with their three conflicting religions (the Druze are Christians). The Jewish students sit at the front, the Moslem boys middle left, the Moslem girls middle right and the Druze at the back. When we came to Israel we already knew that this play was not only about the past, that its power comes from its contemporary relevance: from the Beast being born again. So when one of the Arab teachers, in hijab and robe, stands up during the post-show discussion and says: "This play is not about the Holocaust, this play is about how we, the Arabs, are being treated by you Israelis now. But you cannot see it, you refuse to see that you treat us like the Germans treated you!" there is first a shocked silence, then a furious barrage of competing languages. It is clearly time to bring the proceedings to a pause. When the teacher is roundly criticised in the dressing room by our Israeli friends we do what we always do in Israel: nod. Are we cowards? I think it is impossible to be in Israel as anything other than the most superficial tourist unless you do two things: listen and know. Listen to learn about the complexity, read and research to know about the complexity.

I spent so much time doing this that, in 2017, I was asked to write a play about the Balfour Declaration that founded Israel. It was to be performed before the Knesset (Parliament). I wrote the play with Phil. It was never performed. I had said that I would write something that would explore the Balfour Declaration, not celebrate it. That if the producers wanted a play that was a nationalist tub thumper there were plenty of fine Israeli writers they could approach. The failure of the play to reach the stage is a symbol of the dilemma that underpins Israel: its wish to be accepted as a modern democracy and its failure to address the occupation of Arab land. When I turned up some fascinating facts about the sister of Chaim Weizmann, an admirable man we had placed at the centre of the play, a Professor of History at Jerusalem University first challenged our research and, then, when confronted with the facts stated in writing: "This may be so, but it cannot be performed as it will give comfort to our enemies".

Ramallah, Palestine. I would like to get a TNT performance through the 'Defence Wall' as I once got TNT through the Berlin Wall. The two walls look very similar, except the Defence Wall is taller. Crossing from Israel, once you are through the twin walls of the Defence Wall, the other side is a wild patchwork of graffiti and street art.

There is a fine theatre in Ramallah, run by the eminent director George Ibrahim. I am shown round the theatre and we discuss how it would be possible to bring a TNT production through the Wall, with our Israeli producer dropping us off on one side and the Palestinians picking us up on the other. I invite George and his female assistant to see our 'Macbeth' which is currently running in West Jerusalem. His assistant simply looks down at her desk as if ashamed. "She cannot go," he says, "She has no permit." So here they are, just like East Germans, locked behind a Wall. We failed, TNT never performed in Palestine. We were happy to perform for free, but we could not afford to pay to perform. The British Council would not support us, the Palestinians could not put us up for the night and the

Israelis refused to drive us to the checkpoint. This gesture was beyond our power.

I hesitated before our producer booked us to tour Israel, but ended up fascinated and charmed by this extraordinary land. In most countries the inhabitants shield visitors from their politics; talking politics in China is like drawing teeth. In Israel you buy an orange and the seller airs his grievance. I once had an Arab taxi driver in East Jerusalem switch off his meter and take me for a tour of the sites of the various abuses practised on the population. It was fascinating, but it was his idea, and it was not an option I could decline. Nor should I give the impression that this is a one-sided experience: I have been given a tour of Hamas rocket landing sites before a performance near the border with the Gaza strip. (We once tried to beam a Shakespeare into Gaza – no go). There are Israelis whose opinions are worth far more than mine, the novelist Amos Oz being one; but my best advice is to read Ari Shavit's masterful non-fiction: *My Promised Land*.

We were made aware of the conundrums of two people's rights to the same land by our first promoter, Hadar Shalgi, who worked for a production company with far bigger fish to fry than TNT. Indeed, they brought the Pope to Israel. We used to joke (just) that they organised the Mossad Christmas Party.

Hadar was tough. When a conscript, she opted for serious military training rather than typing and became a mortar instructor. However, she was no hawk when it came to politics and became a personal assistant to Shimon Peres, the last significant Labour Party leader and perhaps the last powerful voice of moderation and peace in this conflicted land. Hadar loved a night out on the town and showed us the wild side of Tel Aviv, truly a city that never sleeps; a secular city where the Sabbath is one long party. I and my wife, Angelika, used to stay with her by the square named after her Israeli political hero: Prime Minister Rabin who was murdered for proposing peace.

Trying to find a balanced approach to performing in Israel is rather like trying to set off blindfold on a tightrope-walk having not yet learned to walk. For moments, it could be amusing in practice. Zichron Ya'akov again. We have been delivered an especially tough audience for our production of 'The Tempest': Muslim students at 3pm and a large party from a particularly orthodox Jewish sect at 8pm. Both groups make certain demands before buying tickets: no alcohol references or drinking onstage for the Muslims, and no female solo for the sect(!). Those of you who know 'The Tempest' will recall that rather a lot of the plot revolves around a barrel of wine from the shipwreck on which the clowns float to safety. They then use the wine to persuade the monster Caliban that they are gods and proceed to drunkenly attempt to murder Prospero, rape his daughter and rule the island (and this is a comedy...)

It is remarkable that Shakespeare writes such grotesque comedy, with genuinely hilarious and out-of-control drunken scenes, in his final play. This kind of uncertain knockabout is right up TNT's street and our three fine actor clowns usually bring the house down with gags galore. So how can we stage the play without booze? We decide that humous is the answer. So it was that on that particular afternoon Stephano and Trinculo arrived safely on Prospero's Isle on a barrel of humous! Little wonder Caliban, who has lived on roots and berries, thinks they are gods! A lot of humous gets thrown about, some humous hits the audience. Some is eaten by the audience. We don't just change the actions, we change the words – replacing wine with humous and although it ruins the scan of the verse it doubles up the cast with contagious laughter. The performance is a great success; the rather fierce guardian teachers are delighted. I doubt our humous 'Tempest' will ever be performed again, but somehow we had delivered healing in this over-holy land.

There is one more tale to tell of TNT and Israel, one last tribute: Shimon Peres, now over 90, walks unsteadily into the family home of our producer Hadar. I had been invited to her wedding a few weeks before, but a premier prevented me going. Shimon is here to offer his condolences, because Hadar was killed on her honeymoon, not by a bomb or a rocket in Israel but a car mounting the pavement in Barcelona. Shalom.

Race

By Paul

Theatre has always been a unique forum for exploring where the personal and the public world, the private and the political, intertwine. From 'The Trojan Women' through 'The Merchant of Venice' to 'The Government Inspector' there is a strong line; one that has had a huge influence on our own work. Theatre is by its very nature public and private. In theatre we explore the deeply personal in a wide public space.

Race and racism, tolerance and prejudice, openness and hatred lie at the root of so much of our modern angst, our current political drama. Ideology seems to have given way to identity. In the 1980s TNT explored Fascism and Stalinism, Keynesianism and Monetarism. Then gradually, as the world changed, so did we.

With promptings from our producer, Grantly Marshall, we began to explore issues of race and reflect this not only in our texts but in our casting. 'The Wizard of Jazz' explored White musicians taking over Black art forms. It began with an extraordinary historical image: Al Jolson, a Lithuanian Jew, singing African-American spirituals in "black-face minstrel" make-up with a backing choir of Black Americans. The spirituals, of course, rooted in Jewish culture. The mix is a heady one. The play presents two conflicting versions of the American Dream: one of opportunity such as the Jewish immigrant Al Jolson seized (he being the first man to sing or speak in a Hollywood film) and the other of the racial supremacism of the Ku Klux Klan.

The musical fusion which is Jazz lies at the core of our production. An Al Jolson impersonator has persuaded his band to desert the British army and audition for a Hollywood biopic of Al Jolson on the eve of D-Day. But the mostly White jazz band turn against the Al Jolson impersonator, seduced by the clarion call of the charismatic Allan Johnson, a bigoted preacher from Alabama. Only the Indian guitarist breaks ranks. Whipped into a racist hysteria, the band lynch their own leader, acting as if he were genuinely Black. The singer's crime is to hold on to the vision of an inclusive racial melting pot, of which Jazz is the musical expression. The music dies along with the singer; the American Dream and the band are ruined.

In the last decade we created two popular pieces that directly confronted racial oppression, while celebrating the lives of those who overcame it: 'The Life and Death of Martin Luther King' and 'Free Mandela'. In both cases we attempt to escape the sentimentality with which Hollywood and mainstream media have presented these lives and themes; a sentimentality that depoliticises the issues of race. Indeed, there is an argument for suggesting that the saint-like status accorded King and Mandela arises not from the righteousness of their cause but for their willingness to forgive their White oppressors. Winnie Mandela and Malcolm X are far more challenging figures and both feature in our productions. We also try increasingly to avoid presenting Black history through White figures, and used first a mainly and then an entirely Black cast for the productions. White characters are presented in small pink masks.

Each play presents the heroism of its subject but then asks questions. We explored Martin Luther King's later years when he moved on from the clear cut Civil Rights victories in the Deep South to a wider political agenda: struggling against poverty and the war in Vietnam, failing in Chicago and troubled by the violent radicalism of Malcom X. We also explored King's personal failings, and how his sexual infidelities were ruthlessly exploited by the FBI. In 'Free Mandela' we gave Winnie as much theatrical space as Nelson. Her imprisonment and torture are routinely ignored, yet she was placed in solitary confinement for two hundred days and cruelly tortured. This changed Winnie. Her path became violent and her journey different from that of her husband.

Both plays are part triumph and part tragedy. Their nuances shocked many audience members, but we feel that we offer a deeper and darker fictional representation of astonishing lives. That "we" had to be an ensemble effort, where our direction and scripts had to earn the support of the casts who brought profound personal experience to the rehearsal room. The British Nigerian actor Eddie Muruako anchored both productions, whilst Adrian Carnegie played Martin Luther King with bright fury for three long seasons.

I find the phrase "colour blind casting" rather unhelpful. I prefer "colour provocative" casting, confronting an audience with their expectations. So that in casting a Black actor as Dorian in our 'Picture of Dorian Gray' we restored the frisson of danger to the piece that is often missing today, when Gay culture is increasingly widely accepted but racism is prevalent. Lord Henry and the painter Basil abuse and adore the beautiful Dorian and become metaphors for colonialism, desiring the exotic as long as it is on their terms. Dorian sells his soul, feeding off the society whose values will destroy him. The production was suddenly shocking and we encountered some resistance from unlikely quarters. Likewise a Black Nurse in 'Romeo and Juliet' raises the stakes. There have been numerous Black Romeos and Mercutios, so we claim no originality for our 2017 production. However, most of our touring is outside of the 'Anglo-Saxon' theatre world where such casting is common. Natey Jones's performance was stunning. Yet the show infuriated some regular venues; one Asian venue never booked us again. Even in France we were asked to send press photos with a White Romeo. Their justification was that old cliché: "I don't mind, but our audience are very conservative". We cast Eddie Muruako as Guy Montag, the hero in 'Fahrenheit 451'. Suddenly the audience had to deal with a character they presumed was White, but one with whom they had to feel an absolute sympathy. In Poland this even led to racial abuse in the theatre.

In this chapter I am dealing with the artistic decisions that we have made in an effort to expose and challenge racism through our work. However, it cannot ignore another dimension: how placing Black actors in leading roles in our ensemble exposes them to racism outside of the theatre. It is just a few days ago, late 2019, writing this, that I rang Adrian in Italy. He is performing as Bottom in 'A Midsummer Night's Dream'. I expected him to be enjoying southern Italy as most of our casts do. But he is angry and shaken. He cannot walk down the street without being met by catcalls and abuse. I doubt this would have taken place ten years ago. From East Asia to Eastern Europe and on to Southern France, the stories are depressingly similar: we ask our audiences to confront and comprehend intolerance on the stage but the actors themselves have to deal with this on the streets outside the venues. Sometimes this even spills into the venues. In Marseilles (as recounted in the 'Popular Theatre' section) a section of the audience started chanting "Kill the Jew" when Fagin was hung in 'Oliver Twist'. The actor playing the role of Fagin halted the action to call out (in French) the abusers and then refused to return to the stage to take his bow. The theatre manager reserved his anger for the actor not the audience.

In 'My Sister Syria' we extended our repertoire to explore not only the conflict in Syria but to encourage our audiences, especially younger audiences, to empathise with Muslims and especially Muslim women. We recruited three Arab performers, one of whose story (told above in 'The Gulf') is every bit as extraordinary as any of the fictional characters in our production: Lama Amine. Ignoring her lack of any work permit, she attended a TNT audition. I gave her the role and Angelika worked long and hard to get her the visas and permissions required to tour the EU.

When 'My Sister Syria' was performed in Munich, the artist Christian Schnurer gained permission to add an installation outside the theatre on the

City's grandest street: Leopoldstrasse. From the shores of the isle of Lesbos, Christian had collected several hundred of the discarded life jackets left by survivors of the crossing from the war zones of North Africa and created from them a vast pyramid between the theatre and the pavement. The play staged the sinking of a refugee raft, with huddled lifejacketed figures; a drowned child on the beach surrounded by callous photographers. We used six Lesbos life jackets in the play. They were not costumes. They were evidence. Outside the theatre our imagery broke from performance onto the busy shopping street. Experience became fiction, and then returned to reality.

Does all the above feel too 'worthy'? Are alarm bells sounding? That these shows were dull hours spent amongst audiences who arrived ready to agree with the authors? In answer, these productions are and were dynamic, popular and performed to a wide and often young audience, many as part of a school party. 'My Sister Syria' is a thriller based loosely on Conrad's *Heart of Darkness* and features some authentic Arab rap. 'Free Mandela' draws on Greek tragedy, using a chorus that sings and dances. 'Martin Luther King' follows the journey of a white journalist who turns from reporter to activist and then, in his disillusionment, is drawn into the conspiracy to murder his icon. The plays present questions not answers. They challenge ourselves as participating artists. All three plays are never able to answer that most troubling of questions: is it right to violently oppose violent evil?

Extract from 'The Life and Death of Martin Luther King':

(Sonny is a young radical activist. He and King are sheltering in a hotel room while outside a mob of white supremacists are stoning Black activists. Ralph Abernathy, a radical preacher, has been hit):

AIDE/SONNY: Get him inside – get him in!

RALPH: Christ, it could have been a bullet.

MLK: Hey, hey, Ralph, are you OK?

AIDE/SONNY: Hey sorry to spoil your dinner, Mr King.

RALPH: Now don't do that - he's a right to eat.

AIDE/SONNY: Yeah he's sitting there in his 'fancy pant' pajamas while we take the heat. He talks to the President and Time Magazine while we march and bleed. Bleed. Christ, look at all this blood! I wanna kill those white fuckers! (Waves fist outside.)

MLK: (Quietly, without anger.) Sometimes when the phone rings and they say they'll murder my children, rape my wife, I want to kill them too. Because we are only human we live with the temptation to take an eye for an eye, a tooth for a tooth, but if we ever did…. then that day we all end up blind and toothless.

AIDE/SONNY: (ranting): We're letting them kill us, man! We're standing there and they're arresting and beating five hundred of our school children every day…

RALPH: I want to keep to our path…

AIDE/SONNY: We don't have no path, they just smashed us off it! They just smashed your head!

MLK: We have a spiritual path, I have faith in ordinary decent white Americans, when they see the terrible things that have happened in Birmingham here, on their TV sets, they will rise up on our behalf…

AIDE/SONNY: But where are they? The TV isn't covering the Black churches the Klan are bombing five miles out of here! The Kennedys won't even answer your calls!

(MLK studying the letter, concerned.)

RALPH: Our friends in Washington can't do this alone, Martin. And we're running out of protesters here. The jails are full.

MLK: I know, I know…

AIDE/SONNY: You know what the young radicals are saying about you: they keep asking – where is this Martin Luther King? They want YOU there! Put yourself on the line! They're getting beaten, smashed up and -

MLK: I think I should have some say in the place and time of my Golgotha!

AIDE/SONNY: You're crazy!!! You think you're Jesus, as if Christ ate steak in his pajamas while the disciples were cut down.

RALPH: Crazy? – you're the loon, Sonny!

AIDE/SONNY: (to RALPH) You just follow every self-destructive idea that Martin has, Ralph!!! In love with the Kennedys! You're an Uncle Tom… you were probably planted by the FBI!

RALPH: Let me at him…

Martin Luther King confronts the National Guard during the desegregation of Birmingham, Alabama. Adrian Carnegie (centre) as MLK in the TNT production.

(Punches are swung and people are restrained by force).

MLK (calm): Brothers, brothers... we are doing their work for them. They beat us today and then you want to beat each other again tonight! We should be praying together, not fighting.... (He falls to his knees - they all pause).

RALPH: We should be drinking together!!! I ordered a crate!! You pray, Martin, while I get the beer. (Exits. MLK prays.)

AIDE/SONNY: I want to admire you, I want you to lead us. Lead us now. Don't wait for those lilly whites to get off their asses and vote in Congress because they don't like their TV dinners spoilt by bleedin' blacks. I want us to be the tide, the force and I want you to lead us, the negro nation. And if you need to feel like Moses to do that then go ahead. But I want us to smite them as David did Goliath, (crying now) I want to put a stone clean through their heads.

MLK: (Taking Sonny in his arms). I know, I know, Lord, that I am the least here ready to answer the call, the last in the march of the brave, the least able to think our way to victory, but Lord I am prepared to feel and suffer my way, to love and forgive my way, to cry and bleed my way... and if that is not enough, then, Lord, you must do the rest for I am offering my all... make us strong, make us wise, make us generous. Amen. (He takes out a cigarette and lights it.)

RALPH: (Entering mid-way thru speech with beer crate, transfixed) Amen! Beer?

Chapter Seventeen: Martin Luther King, General Fatima Kassab, and Winnie and Nelson Mandela

By Phil

While the ongoing war in Syria might seem a long way from the concerns of an early twentieth-century Russian theatre director, to understand why we have engaged with characters like General Fatima Kassab, a 'fictional' creation based on a former high ranking officer of the Syrian army turned rebel, it is necessary to return to the origins of TNT in the ideas and aesthetics of Vsevolod Meyerhold. While his theatre may at times have seemed other-worldly, it was the world that was his concern. At times he sought its transformation through the actions of workers and peasants, and at other times through a transformation of understanding by remaking the very mechanics of understanding itself. While his working life was mostly confined to Russia, he always thought globally, internationally.

When 'push came to shove', in 1917, he threw in his lot with those he thought were making a practical attempt at turning a rigid, inward-looking, hierarchical Russia into a fluid, outgoing and experimental one. When those agents turned on each other, and eventually on him, he dramatised the comi-tragedy in a subtle grotesquerie that tweaked the nose of a supreme dictator. It is remarkable that he and his theatre productions remained for over a decade immune from Stalin's anger.

By following Meyerhold's example, it was perhaps unavoidable that TNT should eventually engage in a series of plays with themes and events that are geo-political in nature. Stories that expand beyond their immediate locations to affect a much larger world and its audiences. Each of these plays – 'American Dreams and Nightmares: The Life and Death of Martin Luther King' (2014), 'My Sister Syria' (2017), 'Free Mandela' (2019) – has, as its basis, a wholly original script, based on our own readings of what we judged the most incisive and most reliable accounts and analyses of events, themes and, crucially, personalities.

If these were like any other previous productions of ours, then the clearest precedent was 'The Ghost of Illiam Dhone' (2013); set on the Isle of

Man, just off the northwest coast of England, during the seventeenth-century 'English Civil War'. The title character, often held up in local histories as the author of the island's independence, turned out to be a strangely empty, equivocal and mutable figure – not dissimilar to the shape-shifting 'zero' of the Woody Allen-directed movie 'Zelig'. But we found among the lesser-noted historical 'bit part players' an astounding figure of personal bravery, ruthlessness and charisma in the person of the Countess of Derby. She was as unflinching and consistent as Dhone was chameleon. The two make strange and intimate partners in their joint endeavour to keep the island loyal to the crown and in opposition to the Puritan Commonwealth. Illiam stands in for an absent and wastrel child in the affections of the Countess. They are sometimes like platonic lovers and sometimes like mother and son. The obtuseness of their unorthodox relationship, emotional and conventional, caught up in the unravelling of the English Civil War.

Crucial for the development of our more contemporary 'history' plays, is a 'discovery' (hardly an original one): that it was in the contradictory nature of the leading personalities and their uneasy grip upon the events they sought to shape – rather than any firm consistency between intentions and outcomes – that there was something revealing. Not just about themselves, but about the social and political circumstances in which they struggled to achieve their dreams or calm their fears. In 'The Ghost of Illiam Dhone', the moment that draws the contradictions tightest is when Illiam betrays the Royalist Countess to the superior seaborne force of Oliver Cromwell. In return, she tricks him into his own arrest and execution. Whatever the principles and loyalties in play, they do not find expression in any straightforward way, but are realised by compromise, betrayal, negotiation and misunderstanding – none of which are possible without some goodness, courage, generosity and self-sacrifice. In neither drama nor history is there much undiluted opportunism that finds happy success (see Iago, see Trump), but rather it is from the collusion and collision of different agencies, mixed motives, unpredictable anxieties and ambiguous desires that anything, good or bad, happens.

Historical documents do not provide us with characters. Occasionally, they provide us with accounts of private dialogue or records of public speeches. However, these are not always taken from those moments or in those contexts that we might want to include in our action. No matter how much we might wish to avoid distortion, we cannot swerve from invention. Our own chosen course has been to entangle a pared down documentary exactitude with a character complexity which together might illuminate the circumstances and the outcomes of momentous events. While we are sceptical that any single account can truly illuminate the multiple agencies in even the simplest social event, we are not minded to surrender everything to chaos; there is meaning to be had in all the mess.

All of TNT's historical dramas have, in some way, been tragedies. For even while the social movements our individuals are a part of may triumph, there is rarely any combination of political success and personal happiness. The personal costs of change are not trivial. Sometimes, they are so traumatic that they infect the success of the social movement. Equally, if not more so, the costs of stasis or reaction can be catastrophic, even genocidal. In all our dramas much is at stake. Civil War England has already seen a crazed massacre of civilians at the hands of the forces of the Countess of Derby's husband, apartheid South Africa is a rolling attrition on the Black majority population that threatens to turn into a mass slaughter on all sides, Syria is and continues to be a country divided by mostly undemocratic forces, in the Southern States of 1960s' America Black citizens were liable to casual murder and organised lynchings. In such situations doing nothing can be tantamount to suicide, while doing anything at all is recklessness; so, our history plays are about people trying to make right and wise choices when there are very few good and almost no safe options to be had.

Against a gameboard of clear moral divisions – against segregation and for diversity, against oppression and for equal rights, against war and for reconciliation – we have been privileged to play out the quandaries and paradoxes of making a difference. We have presented the toll of suffering on the minds of those who would assume some kind of power, national or local. We have shown the unsung and unacknowledged activists who have invested power in their movements and their movements' leaders. We have shown the distortions on the human psyche of those stressed by making life and death decisions with no resources but their own lives.

We have also shown the private misdemeanours and shortcomings of those who would later be hailed as saints for their social achievements. Not in order to forgive them or 'let them off'; but to show how the violence and ugliness of circumstances twist not only the reactionaries who seek to hold malevolence in place, but even those who seek to change it too. That there is a sort of chaos in the human psyche – something very close to that non-intellectual and visceral energy that theatre is always searching for – which cannot translate good ideas into good feelings, but must take a trip through the back streets, before re-emerging, sometimes unscathed and sometimes horribly compromised, into the public arena.

Our plays are set, simultaneously, in both that public arena and in those back streets. 'American Dreams and Nightmares: The Life and Death of Martin Luther King' shows Martin Luther King endangering the standing and prospects of the Civil Rights movement by his use of prostitutes, while 'Free Mandela' shows Nelson Mandela assuming much of a young partner 'abandoned' for 27 years to solitary confinement, physical torture and exile. And they show the brutality all of these characters faced, and the courage and compassion that they often demonstrated towards those who did nothing to deserve any such thing. Without stint they show the glorious unfolding of successful struggles against wrong, racism, malevolence, exclusion, segregation, discrimination, manipulation and constructed poverty.

These plays also show moments of unexpected variance within the struggle for better things and happier times. As we find our way through the labyrinth of war to the general in hiding in Syria we maybe do not expect the mystical Sufism she has embraced in the face of defeat, ambivalence and betrayal. Equally, in 'American Nightmares' we may be surprised to find that it is a local refuse workers' strike that brings Martin Luther King's campaign for civil rights into crisis, struggling to bridge the gap between a fight for racial equality and a wider campaign for social justice. Of course, we should be able to explore calmly the nuances of this conflation through the lens of historical events, but these particular historical events include the assassination of King and the effective cessation of the campaign of non-violent resistance. Once King was dead, riots broke out and the Black Panthers stepped forward. Detroit burned.

Without claiming anything approaching the poetry or the fluidity of feeling, we have learned something structural from Shakespeare. That having established the structure of events, what best reveals the likely reality of human response is not a schema, but a writing-devising-improvisation; an emotional and psychological riff through the bones and pillars of the historical architecture. This allows the representations of historical persons (and their actors) to explore the same contradictions as wholly fictional characters, within the constrictions of historical outcomes, revealing far more than any attempt to put human skin on social, political or moral principles. Indeed, it is the moral uncertainty even in the most just campaign that uncovers what might be right about it.

Perhaps oddly, for history plays, these are original plays. Whatever the actual outcome, within the drama of the play, the result and the worthiness (or otherwise) of it all are still at stake. As with 'Illiam Dhone', we were back to making a whole performance – as in our early days! These plays are rooted in the TNT style, and attending to contemporary issues of race and freedom. As the global political crisis – climate change, anarchy in the Middle East, economic malaise, the rise of populist authoritarianism, the returning threat of nuclear war – deepens, so we have been drawn towards more explicitly political stories. They are the themes towards which our (often young) audiences are also drawn: anti-racist, pro-ecology, pro-liberality and freedom, against wealth and power, for difference, for compassion, for the rights of all bodies and all individuals, for a free range of ideas. But not always. Certainly not always revolutionary. Most often our plays are exploratory, imaginative, connected; and always complicated with the joys and difficulties of divergent desires, of listening and hearing, of speaking and understanding.

No surprise then, that our (often young and serious thinking) audiences have connected to depictions of change or defence of difference, depictions that are complicated, compromised and downright mucky, principled and practical. Rather than being put off by the difficulties and imperfections, even betrayals, of those who agitated for civil rights or racial equality or simply for the security of minority communities, these audiences were often inspired – often demonstrating with long curtain calls and sometimes standing ovations – by difficulty and complexity. The successful implementation of good ideas by flawed people perhaps offers them the possibility of their own positive involvement.

These productions also signalled a cultural shift within the TNT company. In 'The Life and Death of Martin Luther King' and in 'My Sister Syria' (2017), the 'way in' to the narratives was, in each case, through a White journalist who 'undoes' and introduces the story: in one case, of the grass-roots campaign for civil rights in the USA, in the other of resistance against both dictatorship and foreign intervention in Syria. Then the White journalist 'closes it down', no matter how inadequately, at the end. In 'Free Mandela', however, there is no White interlocutor; the Black cast plays all the Whites; there is no White character with which an audience can empathise. Instead the audience must work their way through the complex sufferings and decisions of Winnie, Nelson, brave activists and police informants (who may be one and the same), in order to find their way of feeling elation in the defeat of apartheid.

It would be foolish to claim that there was ever any substantial or efficacious strategy or philosophy in these plays, but what they did was explore what it meant to be human not as a fixed set of qualities, but as a journey of inquiry and as always a work-in-progress.

Prisons, Palaces and Fragments

By Paul

Singapore Prison. Our intrepid local producer, Myriam Woker, has not only arranged a performance for us but a day of interaction with the prisoners. We are accompanied by journalists and government officials. We are guided around the prison which, given the scarcity of space in this island nation, is unsurprisingly cramped and claustrophobic. Even the yard is roofed and we feel as if we are entering a giant cage. We glimpse shaven-headed inmates squatting on the floors of long corridors. We are fed and watered by prisoners who speak of their contrition and desire to reform. Two coaches of female prisoners arrive from a nearby jail to swell this captive audience. We prepare our performance in a concrete hall. It is 'Romeo and Juliet', a tale of street crime and the fragility of love in the face of gang warfare. Warders patrol the audience. Before we begin the inmates are warned to remain seated on the floor. We give our play.

It's hard to say what causes more astonishment: the sword fights or the kisses. After the Prince speaks her bitter epilogue, chastising the gangs who ruined this precious love, the audience erupt. And stand. The warders look at each other, some raise truncheons. Have we and Shakespeare caused a riot? Tension mounts, cheers echo in the concrete hall and an officer takes the stage and blows a whistle. The audience bow their heads and return to their cross-legged, seated position. Silence falls. It is done.

After the performance we are interviewed by various journalists as the prisoners serve us tea. But none of our comments ever reach print. Someone somewhere silenced the journalists. Someone somewhere thought that prisoners having theatre was the wrong message to give to the world, or at least the electorate. The rest was silence. TNT's 'Romeo and Juliet' in Singapore prison never happened.

That night we perform 'Romeo and Juliet' in the theatre of the smartest hotel on earth: The 'Raffles'. That happened.

The Outer Hebrides. The Gulbenkian Foundation have funded TNT to take theatre and workshops to these remote islands. On Harris we arrive at a school that faces west towards the infinite ocean. As we enter the dining hall we are greeted by a choir of children who sing to us in Gaelic. A teacher explains that the pupils are in a state of great excitement; the first school trip to London will depart next week. Most of the children have never seen a shopping centre or an escalator. Many have never set foot on the mainland, a three-hour drive and a two-hour ferry crossing away. It is a glorious May day; we elect to run the workshop in the playground, a field that runs down towards the sea. The children chatter to each other in Gaelic and then switch effortlessly to English to speak to us unfortunates. After a few theatre games I have a sudden idea: I will adapt a TNT exercise to harness the "great excitement". Each pupil is asked to run around the field and return to the departure point and imagine they have just returned to Harris from London and are telling a rather deaf aunt about their recent trip. The deafness forces the child to enact, not merely describe, their journey. I play the aunt. The result is quite extraordinary: one by one the children hurl themselves around the field, startling seagulls in their wake, and arrive breathless at their deaf aunt's chair (actually a rock). Each describes London as a place of towering cliffs, huge seabirds, enormous waves and giant seals. No one laughs, no one mocks, each vies to describe London as a grander version of these remote isles on the edge of Europe. The least my deaf aunt can do is to learn the Gaelic for thank you: *tapadh leat gu mòr*.

That evening on the long drive back to our hotel in Lewis we stop at the stone circle of Callanish. Two thousand years ago the ancestors of those children raised these magnificent granite blocks and set them against the sea. It is late May and the sun is still high above the horizon. Beyond lie the Americas. We are alone. Gaelic melodies linger in my ear as we watch the sun slowly set in the endless west.

The Hebrides are almost as far north as St Petersburg and it was in that city that I cut my teeth as a director on a big stage: the State Comedy Theatre known as Akimov. This theatre lies on what may be the world's most impressive boulevard: Nevsky Prospekt, beloved of Dostoyevsky. For three years I not only worked at two theatres on this grand artery of imperial Russia, I slept there, either in a garret on the fifth floor of the Comedy or at the apartment of the Conductor of the Imperial Orchestra overlooking the Winter Palace Square. In February I watched gangs of workers with iron poles smash the ice on the pavements. In July the locals sunbathed by the banks of the Neva. One wet November day I joined the crowds as we celebrated the city's change of name from Leningrad to St Petersburg. On Sundays I would attend the sung mass at the Alexander Nevsky monastery at the top of the street, and each afternoon, in the breaks from rehearsals, I would use my free pass to enter the Hermitage Museum at the Winter Palace and choose a different place to read. My favourite was a small room with a *chaise longue* overlooking the palace square. The walls were studded with Gaugin's paintings of Tahiti. Nothing was destroyed in the Palace when it was stormed during the Revolution. In fact more people died remaking the event for Eisenstein's fabulous film than in the original Revolutionary charge. Eisenstein was Meyerhold's pupil. The street was loaded with history.

In the graveyard of the Monastery lay the tomb of Tchaikovsky, always draped in red carnations, even when the shops were empty of food and the Hermitage empty of visitors. One day I sought out an apartment just off the street, climbed the stairs and met Dostoyevsky. His rooms were left as on the day of his death. On his writing desk lay a pen and an open manuscript. In the hat stand a cane to help his laboured journey up the stairs. When I could afford it, I took dark 'Caravan' tea at the Literature Café and pictured Pushkin leaving the same room, setting out for his fatal duel. Opposite the Comedy Theatre stands a statue of Catherine the Great supported by her lovers. Chekhov sat down and wept on its base after the catastrophic first night of 'The Seagull'. Behind the Empress stands the Imperial Theatre, the Alexandrinsky. Shostakovich was in-house composer here. The last Tsar was a regular visitor. His Imperial box was fronted with armour plate cunningly concealed by laughing cherubs. I once hosted Andy Hay, director of the Bristol Old Vic, and he and I sat down at the theatre for a business meeting which began with Russian hospitality: vodka. It was ten in the morning. After the first few toasts we were relieved to be told that this was the last toast, only to find that the next filled glass was the toast after the last toast. We watched a dreadful 'Cyrano de Bergerac' and a marvellous production of 'Forest' by Alexander Ostrovsky. We never managed the collaboration. But I did work over the road at the grand Comedy Theatre, with its huge glass window overlooking Nevsky Prospekt, its chandeliers, its smell of theatre and its fabulous actors who brought passion and sparkle to every play in which they performed, even my own.

We succeeded in getting the company to Britain to tour a Russian language version of 'Charlie Chaplin Putsch'. In London, they admired Tesco's more than the British Museum. Where are they now? I cannot know because the days of British directors working and living on Nevsky Prospekt are long gone. Now tourists queue up to pay €50 to enter the Hermitage and Putin has stated that the purpose of art is to glorify the nation. So I won't be spraying a bloody hammer and sickle on a screen of *Pravda* newspapers in a clown nose any time soon. And I will never forget Nevsky Prospekt.

The Winter Palace was the first palace where I felt at home. A decade later and palaces became regular haunts for TNT. For the last twenty years TNT has performed every year, outdoors, on what our producer Grantly Marshall calls 'The Castle Tour'. This has now become the largest outdoor circuit of any theatre company. Every summer the company perform in over fifty castles and palaces in twelve or more countries from Norway to France, from Britain to Austria. Flexibility is once again the key to the venture. We travel with two vehicles: one van with the cast and costumes, the other is a ten-ton truck in which we load a theatre. The truck holds a full stage with adjustable legs to suit any surface; screens and steps, two lighting structures, a sound system including directional microphones, five hundred chairs and a box of rain capes. We can set up the stage and be ready to perform in three hours and take the whole thing down in about ninety minutes. However, many castles are designed to restrict access, so setting up can be challenging. This is especially true on the island castle of Chillon in Switzerland. Here the only solution is to draft the audience into the assault and have them carry their own chairs across the drawbridge to the inner courtyard where Macbeth is awaiting their entrance.

TNT's 'Taming of the Shrew' on the Castle Tour in Copenhagen, Natalia Campbell as Kate

The Castle Tour allows us to present Shakespeare as he intended, with the actors able to see the whites of the public's eyes. These castles and palaces generate a special excitement in the audience, even before the first actor climbs the steps to the stage. This is an energy that in turn fires the actors who, despite the hard work involved, relish the Castle Tour. Whatever the weather, we always perform; even in Bergen, the wettest town in Europe. Each year we return to this Royal Norwegian Castle despite the soaked costumes and August chill, and so do our audience, each one grasping their umbrella. Rain can strike anywhere. At the medieval castle of Orgueil on Jersey our cellist and violinist had to crouch under the stage to keep up their accompaniment to the storm in 'King Lear'. John Moraitis as Lear rose magnificently to the occasion. Drenched in rain he chided the elements for their cruelty and hugged his 'poor fool' as she sang: "The rain it raineth every day". Most of the audience stayed despite the wind turning umbrellas inside out.

The heat waves of the last few years may herald global warming and its horrific prospects, but for a while they are giving comfort to cold actors on the chillier evenings of the long summer tours (the Castle Tour runs from early June to mid-September). Is there any theatrical experience more wonderful than to sit outside on a balmy summer evening, surrounded by battlements and Alps, to see Hamlet melt into tears in the halls of Elsinore?

The 'Castle Tour' takes us back to Britain every year, chiefly to the Channel Islands and the Isle of Man. Indeed the Isle of Man gives us our last toehold on public subsidy in the British Isles. For over a decade we have performed outdoors in the summer at the great castles of Peel and Rushen and indoors each winter at the marvellous Victorian theatre in Douglas: The Gaiety. So it was that we were commissioned to create that production about the most famous figure in the Island's troubled history: Illiam Dhone who saved the place from Cromwell's anger and was repaid with a Royalist firing squad. As you might have gathered from our descriptions above, it seemed to Phil and myself that Illiam was a model for our own age, a man of few qualities and no convictions who attempted to navigate the extreme passions of the English Civil War with calm self-interest. In doing so, in the end, he so infuriated both sides he was shot for his pains. I created a role for myself in this play: the Bishop of the Isle, remembered only for his drinking songs. This was rather a gift and allowed me to steal a few scenes whilst proving that in order to survive it was prudent to pretend to share the passions of powerful men and women.

Many of the themes and dramas of our 'Ghost of Illiam Dhone' seem prescient now as Britain is once again sunk in bitter divisions. Brexit hangs over us in much the way that the execution of King Charles hung over that earlier time. As a company that works each year in every single EU country, Brexit threatens to be an unmitigated disaster for us. There is no such thing as an EU-wide work permit; so how will we tour a company of British actors from Finland to Portugal and back? As to those pro-Brexiteers who say that we need to unleash our imaginations and go global, we counter that we are already global! Brexit will not help us one jot in Chile or China. I have German dual nationality, John Kenny Irish. But what of our veteran actors, the core of our ensemble; what of our very identity as an authentic British theatre company? Phil comes from Coventry. Will he need a work permit to visit me in Munich?

Our last nationwide UK tour was 'King Lear', a tour that was not originally planned but gained its own momentum and was rather successful if measured in press reviews and audience numbers. The play is supposedly set in Britain's past but surely is in Britain's future. The kinds of forces 'unleashed' by Brexit are neatly embodied in the character of Edmund, who dismisses morality in the interests of a "natural" identity. In the play France offers hope but is defeated. The victors tumble into violent division, dragging the innocent with them into despair and destruction. "Why should a horse, a dog, a rat, have life, and thou no breath at all?"

Why or how should TNT theatre survive? If we do will it be by abandoning our British identity? That identity was always a fertile mix of the international with the native. Ken Dodd and Monty Python are our gods along with our dear Meyerhold and Pina Bausch. Like Shakespeare we could never resist a good gag. When John Lennon asked the posh folk in the audience to rattle their jewellery, then we knew what was best about Britain. Like John Lennon I was rewarded for my services to British culture with a 'gong' at Buckingham Palace. When I turned to leave, the band of the Royal Marines played the Monty Python theme tune. Had they been warned?

The staircase of Buckingham Palace reminds me of the grand stairwell of the Winter Palace, although no Revolutionaries have ever charged up its marble steps, yet. Is that a good thing? I want to hold onto the best of being British: to the band playing Monty Python, the gravedigger's gags and Lennon's 'pilchards climbing up the Eiffel tower'. But I feel it is slipping. TNT's journey to Buckingham Palace was a long one. It started in a Miner's Welfare Club in Calverton. Now there are very few miners left in Nottinghamshire or anywhere else in Britain. Identity, which used to be allied with solidarity, seems to have become little more than crude nationalism and a loathing of 'the other'. Theresa May, then British Prime Minister, accused people like me of being "citizens of nowhere". I would rather be a citizen of everywhere. Through theatre we become one.

What was it all about? What is it now?

By Phil

There have been moments in TNT performances over the past forty years when something was tapped into that is not quite explicable.

In 'Wizard of Jazz' an inebriated pub landlord, sent by an absconding group of army musicians to contact the singer Al Jolson, accidentally attends the preaching of the white racist US military preacher the Reverend Allan Johnson and returns to the band, spouting paranoid bigotry and, in a lilting high-pitched drawl, channels a malevolent Southern States belle. The effect was of some sickly demon uncannily manifest on the stage. In 'The Mystery', the actors stood around a tin bath, like strange glowing symbols, illuminated by the flames of their earnings as the banknotes from the night's takings were incinerated. In our Martin Luther King play, the entire cast appeared in chains, as both prisoners and protesters, imprisoned by unjust laws and yet bound to each other in solidarity. At the opening of 'A Midsummer Night's Dream', a love story, Amazons wildly attack their Greek male adversaries, biting off their genitals. The ghost of Hamlet's father appears inside a sheet of ectoplasm, trying to push its way out of its sac, no longer human but unable to entirely shake off its consciousness. At the end of 'Moby Dick', the drowning, flesh-and-blood crew of The Pequod sink as indistinct shadows into a white sheet; hard-working, hard-thinking creatures abruptly transformed into vanishing spectres at the flip of a whale's tail.

What did these moments mean? They were allusive and ambiguous happenings, but what was most powerful was what was more evident by 'feel' than rational explanation. More important than meaning was their exact force, their capacity in the immediacy of performance to grip an audience. Indeed to subject themselves to the same transforming energy as the characters on the stage were experiencing. In TNT, we were never very interested in the mystical or transcendental. While there has always been an awareness of the power of images, a legacy of the Symbolist part of the Meyerholdian aesthetic, we work more with the physical energy generated when comedy and tragedy *in extremis*, death and slapstick, rub up against each other. Yet the examples above seem to escape even that dynamic. They are moments when everything else (including any representation of 'real life') falls away and all that remains is a raw pulse of performance, a life-drive. Rarely exposed, this is the pool from which the actor derives their charisma, from where the play draws its intrigue. It is pre-moral; a kind of 'id' of the stage.

In later performances of 'The Murder of Sherlock Holmes', after the play had been performed many hundreds of times, moments of improvisation would occur among the seasoned actors that were more like free-form jazz than theatre. At these times it is hard to know exactly what play we are performing. If any. A kind of plasma kicks in; and nothing more is needed. Whatever the contexts or the linear narrative of the scene, whether happy or murderous, the effects of these moments are a life-affirming communion of actors and audience. For that last element is always essential for us. While the art and transformation of the actor might be wonderful things, they only have value in the TNT scales when the audience is in the weighing bowl with them.

The plasmic energy is what draws our audiences, and drives the stories of our plays and the desires of our characters, constituting and reconstituting their Stanislavskian objectives and super-objectives: Macbeth desires the throne, Winnie desires liberation, Iago lusts after the downfall of Othello, the soldier in 'English Tea Party' longs for absolution. But it does more than all of that; for it is only by this energy that we have the authority at times to make a difference. Even though we may make mistakes and suffer failures, while we still reverence and draw from that pool of plasma, we continue to be invited to castles, draw audiences of thousands in remote Chinese cities, and take alien ideas about freedom and ecology and multiplicity to audiences who do not agree with us, in countries where there are sometimes laws against what we portray. Somehow we continue with very little interference. Perhaps because many of those who may not be wholly or even remotely sympathetic to our philosophical ideas still recognise the raw power of 'life' when it sneaks under the stage door and pushes back the curtains. Only the extreme puritans or those ultra-ideologists who would embrace death rather than difference are wholly against us.

Let's be clear, however; chasing that raw energy easily leads artists into a compulsive realm of cheap thrills or to self-transcendence and self-destruction. The way we have skirted those temptations is a combination of that strange psycho-embodiment we call acting and the equally odd mix of philosophy and action we call dramaturgy. These hybrid skills together bring hundreds of audience members every night to engage with manipulation, liberation, peril, protection and extinction through the motions and emotions of (mostly) fictional characters. They allow us to explore, under the critical gaze of those hundreds, the complex of overlapping tendencies towards apocalypse in hypermodern industry and the green movement, the hard conundrums of waging peaceful or popular struggle against violent oppression, the fruits and costs of resisting war and poverty, the social and psychological mechanics of fascism, the value of books, the social consequences of a technological transition to a posthuman society and the rights of re-animated flesh. Part of the depth of the impact of these mass feelings-musings is how they cross borders; so our play about US civil rights and our #MeToo 'Pygmalion' both drew total audiences of thousands over successive nights in Istanbul, not despite but because of their content. Repeatedly, we have experienced audiences interpreting their own experiences through those of others. We have no detailed ethnographic evidence to support the idea that this encourages empathy with remote others; but we have experienced, and heard from actors many accounts of audiences, formally and informally, keen to discuss the details of distant events brought to them by theatre.

We have no verifiable quantitative data about what has been the effect on audiences of our plays exploring the consequences of populism and racism – 'Wizard of Jazz', 'The Wave', 'American Nightmares', 'Amerika! Amerika!'. However, just about every German adult under forty-five will now, mostly at a young age, have seen a TNT production of some kind and it is tempting to speculate that we might have had some influence on that country's generous response to the refugee crisis and the resistance of so many of its population to attempts to draw it into anti-immigrant sentiment. Equally, our eco-critical 'Dracula' may have played some part in the engagement of school students with the climate change actions led by Greta Thunberg; not least perhaps in Slovenia where school teachers organised their pupils to make a climate change-denial protest against our play? But who can say quite what the consequences, intended or unintended, of these clashes and exchanges might be?

Even a systematic ethnographic case study would struggle to establish a clear one-to-one relation between the effects of watching a play and a decision to do anything. That is not the way that plays work. Theatrically successful performances rarely have anything like a simple message or programme of action; their dynamic is often based upon the complexity of their messages, of how they shift from moment to moment, scene to scene; moving closer to the mutability of myths while still holding the coherence of their multiplicity. How they create complex webs of culture from which considered action and interaction emerges. Instead of hard evidence of effects – though there is plenty of anecdotal evidence here, from the interest of the Chinese Army Farce Troupe to advance their traditional craft through our aesthetic, to the young German women enthusiastically supporting Eliza through 'Pygmalion' – we offer what we have, which is the evidence of our invitations.

In country after country, we have made an offer to audiences, sometimes small and often large, to join us in considering the roots of poverty, the politics of climate destruction, the dilemmas of social movement leadership, the consequences of unbridled technology, the threat to books, the relationship of care and desire in the contest between romantic love and arranged marriage, the costs of selling one's principles, the morbid effects of commercialism, the manipulation of female identity, the rewards of generosity, and the production of a culture aboard a ship of whale-hunting Americans. Often the narratives and the dramatic mixes of our productions are fluid and extravagant in their means of engagement. It may be the thrill of being guided through a story by a series of ghosts. Or seeing a character constructed from pieces of dead flesh, and then hear it philosophise. It may be giving witness to a king gone mad on a moor, or a revolutionary unhappy in triumph; it may be the fun of seeing a scarily powerful Queen of the Fairies in love with a big-hearted donkey-headed oaf, or a young woman exorcising a spectre with her sexual power. Or joining a naive young radical lost in a nightmare US city on a mission to find the tower of a powerful economic entity approaching metamorphosis... sometimes the stories creep closer to the edge of the id pool.

Although some old photograph of me often appears in TNT programmes, I have never yet been recognised in an audience. Such anonymity is one of the pleasures of being a dramaturg; allowing me to sit in the midst of an audience as they react to actions I saw first as a stage direction, or hear their reaction to a joke I typed or saw first in a new draft from Paul. In those moments one feels very directly that theatre is not a product, but a long-term process; a work of many people, from the costume designer to the set builder, from the original commissioner to the bookers and the local promoters, from the agents to the road managers, from the literary managers to the legal departments to the stationery shop assistant, to the theatre caretakers and coach party leaders to actors and audience. Even if they come (and leave) with very different attitudes, ideas and prospects to ours, for the duration of a performance the audience gives up something of themselves to share in the collective self-deception of a fiction or a reconstituted history.

Working on the plays of William Shakespeare for twenty years – rather unexpectedly, given a background in alternative theatre – I am conscious of the way that his works often reference the popular theatre and pre-Puritan ritual of Warwickshire (my own county). As well as citing the exaggerated character of Herod in the Mystery Plays performed in Coventry (my home town) – "It out-Herods Herod. Pray you avoid it" – Shakespeare is alive to local folk traditions. Hence we see Puck in 'A Midsummer Night's Dream' and hear of Queen Mab in 'Romeo and Juliet'. While the clumsy amateur theatricals of the Mechanicals of 'Dream' continue today in the tradition of seasonal Mummers' Plays or Plough Plays; local and communal, ritualistic and yet pantomime. Both in our classic adaptations and Shakespeare productions and in our original work we seek something as simply communicative and richly allusive as these (at least) medieval traditions. At the same time we draw into our audience's collective gaze the complexities of hypermodern living and the mixtures of bitter violence and spectacular ennui of contemporary and recent politics. We hybridise a very old kind of performance with the challenges of a contemporary life that is inundated with representations. All this we do on a wounded planet; sometimes feeling as if we are characters shipwrecked in a time-travelling 'Tempest'.

However, that is only my impression. Each member of TNT, seasoned or temporary, will have a different story to tell. The same for every audience member and supporter, supplier and booker. That is as it should be. The point is that through the medium of live theatre, inflected by our experience of growing up European in the post-war century, and with all these years of making and travel, we are still weaving those different stories into performances, and entangling them with the ones running through the heads and nerves of the audiences. We have some rough blueprints, some of which we have shared in this book. Each time, however, we must reinvent the wheels. Otherwise they tend to come off the wagon of live performance.

Now we face a future with Brexit (the withdrawal of the UK, still our legal home, from the European Union). A Brexit that may finish TNT. At the same time we contemplate a future of ever more extreme global weather conditions with the consequent dangers for a travelling theatre. The more usual threats to artistic freedom – from authorities seeking to control the culture their publics can access – have yet to materialise. This, despite the rise (if patchy) of populism. Where the populists have gained power in parts of Europe it seems to have mostly stimulated an appetite for TNT's theatre rather than scared away audiences and bookers. Perhaps the populists have judged that the rise of social media and digitally streamed mass media makes live performance irrelevant?

We are used to being on the margins. We began work in 'fringe theatre'. And, while we have, and still do, play in some very prestigious and some very large venues, we are often somewhat aberrant presences there. Sometimes we are only welcome thanks to the indulgence of friendly protectors of the unconventional.

It would be pleasing to announce at the end of this book that this review of the experiment we began in 1980 has produced findings that unveil a clear way for us to place ourselves in the future. That is not so. Instead, it seems increasingly hard to predict the likelihood of political and social events, let alone their real nature or consequences. The all-encompassing reach of climate change and the bewildering possibilities of digital communications and illusion-manufacture (Virtual and Altered Realities) affect everything; just as the pall of nuclear threat and Mutually Assured Destruction (MAD) hung over us in 1980 as we were forming the company. Now, we are unclear whether malevolent and intelligent mini-robots, neural invasion by algorithms, self-obsession, thirst or drowning threaten us most.

Throughout this 40-year-long experiment of ours – called 'TNT Theatre' – we have not simply made findings (though there are plenty listed throughout this book) and applied them in further explorations of our crafts and their effects. We have also changed the method of our enquiry. In academic research, this is called "emergent design". Our "design" initially emerged from our bringing a barely regarded early twentieth-century innovation in theatre to the opportunities for experimental theatre in the UK at the end of that century. Today, in 2020, exactly as far from our beginning in 1980 as we were back then from the death of Meyerhold in 1940, our experiment is more precisely guided towards others.

In 1980, our work tested our hope to combine serious texts and physically trained performance as a means to release experimental theatre beyond a niche audience without destroying our core aesthetics. This encapsulated our first two research aims. At first this enquiry went little beyond testing our Meyerholdian methods in making a performance and surviving. After a decade of some small success (and some failures) on fringe circuits, we began to find a way, unevenly and with different collaborators, to sporadically break beyond the niche audience and attend to larger, more popular and more diverse audiences, with work still observably consistent with our founding principles. Later, and by now more confident in the flexibility of our aesthetics and the means we had discovered to bring consistency to their deployment, we began to address our third question: "how far and in what ways can such an aesthetic – combining experiment with popular forms – travel and develop and engage with a changing world?"

The answer to "how far" is "almost globally". While war zones and those societies that actively forbid live theatre are not accessible to our convivial methods, wherever there is sufficient infrastructure to facilitate travel, accommodation and performance, we are only restricted by the limitations of a small company funded by box office takings. Or, as Paul describes above, in 'Failure', when a combination of cultural and technical factors combined in India to make touring very difficult indeed.

When "theatre is a language", diversity and divergence of languages can be sensitively negotiated. Cultural differences generate intrigue, when fear of the 'other' is calmed and post-colonial legacies and other inequalities are openly addressed and owned up to. In cases where there are political or ethical challenges to any kind of connection at all, we have sought to navigate these as far as possible by what we have learned by direct engagement. This is not a simple opportunism. There are countries to which we toured previously, but which we have either elected not to go, or found the terms of going now unacceptable.

As to "what ways" we can "engage with a changing world", there are changes in our content. In the face of rising racism and nationalism, we have responded by developing content that addresses these issues explicitly and in 2020 we will revive our play about the roots of fascism, 'The Wave'. In response to climate change we produced 'Dracula and the Eco-Warrior'. Given the reach of our productions, playing to some 120,000 people every year in over 30 countries, while we cannot know in detail what the effects of complex, serious and entertaining productions engaging with the above themes might be, we can be confident in asserting that there will be effects.

However, we should be cautious in claiming to know exactly what those effects are. The stated subject matter of our performances can conceal other content. So, in 'Dracula and the Eco-Warrior' we used our body-based physical theatre styles to engage with the vampiric algorithmic invasions perpetrated through digital devices. In 'Pygmalion' a similar body politics was addressed, but through a critique of the manipulation of a woman's voice and posture. We have no grounds for claiming any universal quality for our body-centred Meyerholdian theatre aesthetics. However, we are moving towards an understanding of how their particular historical qualities – initially evolved in response to Fordist mass-production and against psychology-based acting and naturalistic appearance – are in some way helpful in making contemporary performance. Here I mean, in particular, in making a kind of performance that is resistant to the bodily disassociations of a digitised culture and which at the same time can model a more organically sound ethic in the face of a global industrial complex that is filling our bodies with micro-plastics as enthusiastically as it puts them in the seas.

In response to these more recent and therefore more tentative findings, part of our ongoing experiment and its unfolding methodology is to explore how we can better share our sustainable tapping of the plasmic 'life' of theatre. This involves testing new ways of engaging with our mass audiences and collaborating with our host organisations, as a means to thinking in the theatre together about how best to protect and develop the rights of bodies, and about how our bodies can best be in response to the challenges of hyperactive industries and climates.

Given that in the short life of our theatre company we have seen the fall of the Berlin Wall (at close quarters), the dismantling of Apartheid and the signing of the Northern Ireland Peace Agreement (all generally deemed impossible in 1980), not to speak of numerous expansions of rights and burgeoning diversities and freedoms, we have no grounds for pessimism about the prospects for future efficacious change. However, every day comes new empirical confirmation of the warnings by scientists of climate catastrophe and species extinctions; if anything, the evidence points to a situation that is worse and developing more quickly than most scientists have previously predicted.

The likely disruptions of human society by extreme weather and rapid changes in climate do not bode well for theatre. Theatre does not thrive in social chaos; its very form is a construct of a society with at least some resilient aspects. In times of Plague, live theatre was banned, travelling theatre was particularly feared (and, at the time of writing, our tours have been stopped by the Coronavirus outbreak, posing a threat to the future of the company). Today another Plague threatens us, one of images; its viruses are electronic ones. For the first time since the Puritan Reformation, there is an existential threat, not just to theatre, but to 'liveness' itself; from the twin menaces of an ecology inimitable to human bodies and a visual technology inimical to mental wellbeing.

The existential themes that we have always been attracted to – from 'Don't Look Back' via 'Frankenstein' to 'Le Petit Prince' – threaten to present themselves before us in un-theatrical form. In our 'Dracula', the vampires are real. Essence and existence are making their entrance as characters lost in an abject world. Can we survive? Can we rise, with theatre, to the challenge of a threatened world?

Some Conclusions?

By Paul

So why TNT? How did three unemployed actors in a borrowed Mini end up as a global force? And what does it mean? Maybe a list of possible causes is a good place to start:

- A strong aesthetic: combining the popular with the innovative for accessibility.
- Practical flexibility: "our only technical requirement is an audience".
- Chameleon-like ability to adapt, collaborate and develop.
- Attracting and keeping highly skilled performers.
- An early international perspective and a style that works without or beyond words.
- Risk-taking in terms of both geography and theatre.
- Gradual rejection of dependence on public subsidy (though we needed it to get going) with effects on both our repertoire and the development of the productions; opening up to larger and more diverse audiences.
- Switching of focus from a declining circuit in the UK to an expanding circuit in Germany.
- Recognition of the rise of English as a global language.
- The reunification of Germany and the opening up of Eastern Europe as a major opportunity.
- The rise of cultured East Asia resulted in a curiosity about, and a desire for access to, Western culture.
- Humility. Where appropriate, we shifted out of English to connect with audiences and artists. We learned from our audiences. We accepted failure as necessary.

- The worldwide explosion of interest in Shakespeare.
- A refusal to go into financial debt – poverty is acceptable, borrowing is not.
- Uniting with ADG Europe so our administrative base became secure and we could focus on making art not selling it.
- Good fortune. Though, like a wily gambler at the casino, we spread our bets.

And:

- To never hold grudges, never expend energy on revenge, to move on. Create.

And yet why create at all? And why does the audience want to go to the theatre?

As I write, there are, I think, seven productions out today from TNT/ADGE. (That was in late 2019; sadly by 2020, due to Coronavirus, there were none.)I don't even know where they all are. I shall go to our 'Christmas Carol' tonight, in Munich. There are two performances of the play today, so I suppose that is one thousand people. It is a classic TNT production, clearly popular but very experimental too. Hardly any carols, but songs composed to drive the story, in a style somewhere between Kurt Weill and Tom Waits.

Towards the end of the play, Scrooge is given a present by the Ghost of Christmas. Noises come from inside the sack, the cast cry aloud "Don't open the sack!" Scrooge is learning his lesson; he is keen to open the sack with its red ribbon and learn more: he has not had a present for decades. Inside the sack is a vicious skinhead, who gives terrible advice to Scrooge. Sitting on Scrooge's knee like a ventriloquist's dummy he echoes a scene from 'English Tea Party', when Dad attempts to turn Neil the solider into his puppet. But this time the manipulation is the other way around. The skinhead doll tells Scrooge to evict his poor tenants and pours contempt on Tinkers, Irish and Gypsies. Scrooge is terrified as the dummy quotes his own cruel lines back to him: "the poor are surplus population, let them die! Let them die!"

The skinhead dummy hops off the stage and the Ghost returns:

SCROOGE: Please, take it back! I don't want this present!

GHOST OF CHRISTMAS PRESENT: This isn't your present, but it may be your future.

SCROOGE: What is it?

GHOST OF CHRISTMAS PRESENT: His name is Ignorance. He is the child of mankind. Written on his brow is doom and destruction. Unless that writing is wiped away, all will be flames, all. Oh, city of London, this is your child. You have made him in your workhouses and refined him in your prisons. Unless you change he will come of age! Then you will not control him, he will control you and the city will sink in flames.

The speech is pure Dickens. The scene is true to the angry original. 'A Christmas Carol' is not just a charming seasonal entertainment, it is a passionate tale of poverty and redemption. TNT's production is very entertaining, but it is as radical in its own way as anything we have done, and it is performing, as I write, in Costa Rica, where Bob Cratchit dances to Salsa and the Teatro Nacional is as packed as the Munich Concert Hall.

Nor is it only the seasonal entertainments that are popular. Four hundred teenagers are today watching 'Free Mandela' in Salzburg:

CHORUS: We are the Xhosa! We are the Zulu!

We are the

Warriors farmers shamans healers brothers sisters that are one.

We grow from the land like trees, like mountains.

But we are not, we are not, we are not

We are Soweto

We live without light

We live without colour

We live grey in the black town.

We are Soweto.

We drink illegal liquor

Sing illegal songs, live illegal lives

No pass, no papers, no rights.

Some of us hate, some of us hope.

Most of us just survive.

Living grey in the black town

Soweto!

Why are these three theatres full? Munich, Salzburg and San José? I can suggest some answers.

Before a performance, we often address the audience: "Please turn off your mobile phones. They are destroying your brains; do not let them destroy our play." The laugh that follows is a laugh of recognition. We have noticed that the hunger for the shared live experience has increased as the world becomes more digitalised. Most of us spend all day looking at a screen for work and all evening looking at a screen for pleasure. We check our phones on average eighty times a day. We are like a dog running, breathless, behind a bicycle; "this is not what going for a walk was supposed to be" thinks the dog!

Virtual Reality on stage in TNT's 'Dracula and the Eco-Warrior'

But the traffic is not all one way. Ross Mullan is a TNT veteran; now a minor star as 'The White Walker' in 'Game of Thrones'. He attends conventions, signs autographs and is, I hope, handsomely rewarded. On a recent visit to Italy his taxi could not get into Lucca because of the vast crowds massing for his own Convention. These crowds need the live experience; I suspect it means more to them than watching the actual programme on a screen. Many dress up as favourite characters. They move from audience to participant, just as Grotowski dreamed might happen in the theatre.

But we are in danger. All of us. Not only of becoming overawed by technology, but of it invading even our most private spaces. Our identity as embodied humans is becoming secondary to our online identity. Theatre provides a forum and a shared experience to escape this vice-like grip. The future may be grim for Uber drivers and accountants, but no robot will ever self-drive a theatre performance. In cinema, the word 'CGI' has become as tainted as 'monosodium glutamate' is in cookery. The Rolling Stones make more money than any other band in the world, because they are the kings of Live Performance.

All I want is to sit in a space with five hundred people and laugh at Mrs Fezziwig and cry with Tiny Tim and sing along with a ghost. In our production, I even get to give a Christmas kiss to a stranger sitting beside me. Two hours with five hundred people who do not check their phones.

SCROOGE: Oh I will be a merry gentleman!

GHOST: And it was always said of Scrooge that he knew how to keep Christmas if any man alive possessed that skill.

BOB CRATCHIT: And Tiny Tim did not die!

SCROOGE: God bless! God bless us, every one!"

So is it a mystical thing? Does "God" bless our theatre and our audience? I do not believe so. In fact, I would suggest that religion is a metaphor for art, not the other way around. When I enter the ruins of the Parthenon in Athens I am not in awe of Zeus. It is the people who made this wonder that move me; their vision of beauty and humanity. In Chartres Cathedral I feel the same despite it being the functioning church of a powerful religion. I can even be moved by an Aztec temple, despite loathing the brutal sacrificial cult that celebrated there. Art makes sense of human consciousness. It is an ever-present impulse. To repeat: the first cave paintings are not representations. They are fiction, stories! We don't care that the 'Iliad' is a religious poem; instead we understand it as a foundation epic of Western civilisation. We are civilised not because of what is outside ourselves but what comes from inside us and travels outwards. Civilisation unites us as humans through shared artistic activity. Art unites the moral with the beautiful and is incapable of hate (or it soon ceases to be art and becomes persuasion). We see in the pain of the Trojan Women, the laughter of Tiny Tim and the wry smile of Harlequin something essential and right. I am often asked which line of Shakespeare's is my favourite; my contender is King Lear's speech when reunited with the daughter he so badly wronged:

Pray do not laugh at me,
For as I am a man, I think this to be my child, Cordelia.

We are all on two journeys: one inwards, one into the world. TNT has magnified these journeys, allowed one to inform the other.

Chile. The southern town of Puerto Montt, a thousand miles south of Santiago, the gateway to Patagonia. This grim town is chilled by the Antarctic Ocean. The cast of TNT's 'Macbeth' are walking along the seafront, picking smoked mussels from the street stalls. There is a performance tonight, but how it will be given is in question... Two days ago, thieves broke into the company van in Santiago and stole every last suitcase belonging to the group. Costumes, props, everything has gone. So here they are at the end of the world, with nothing but themselves and the text of Shakespeare in their heads and the moves of the play in their bodies. There are no knives to kill the King, no swords to finish Macbeth, no crowns, no robes, nothing to anoint the head of Malcolm.

The show will go on.

New friends rally round. A stranger brings a gift of two Burger King crowns that she has wrapped in gold foil. Sticks will do for swords. The show will go on. And so, here, at the furthest point from Nottinghamshire that TNT has ever performed, we have arrived with nothing. We are a truly poor theatre. Not travelling towards one; we *are* one. We have become what we have always been; and that will be enough.

The shows begins, the story travels back and forth between actors and audience. This is our journey, to end here beneath wheeling gulls, beside an ice cold ocean. "Poor players who strut and fret our hour upon the stage and then are heard no more."

Epilogue

On Friday 13th March 2020, all TNT's tours from Mexico to Poland were cancelled owing to the outbreak of the dreaded virus. Six casts, seven productions and 28 actors were suddenly out of work. March 2020 was the most important month of the year for the company in terms of bookings and income. Three of the productions were new and had no time to recoup their rehearsal costs. It is hard to imagine any other event that would have closed a global touring company, usually able to respond to problems in one market by shifting to another. We cannot read the runes, all we can do is attempt to stay solvent, honour as many debts as we can and rely on the generosity of supporters (such as the newspaper owner Dirk Ippen) who have held out a helping hand. Last season TNT increased its touring by twenty per cent. We hope these audiences will return to the theatre with renewed enthusiasm once these dark times are over. It may be that the effects of the virus and Brexit combine to force the company to restructure and indeed uproot from Britain. We live in hope that this tragedy may still end with a smile on our lips. The tragedy of Romeo and Juliet hinges not on love or hate but this:

FRIAR JOHN: Going to find a bare-foot brother out
Here in this city visiting the sick,
And finding him, the searchers of the town,
Suspecting that we both were in a house
Where the infectious pestilence did reign,
Seal'd up the doors, and would not let us forth;
So that my speed to Mantua there was stay'd.

FRIAR LAURENCE: Who bare my letter, then, to Romeo?

FRIAR JOHN: I could not send it,--here it is again,--
Nor get a messenger to bring it thee,
So fearful were they of infection.

FRIAR LAURENCE: Unhappy fortune!

About the Authors

Paul Stebbings was born in Nottingham. He studied Drama at Bristol University and trained in the Grotowski method in Britain and Poland. After directing and acting professionally he founded TNT Theatre with Phil Smith in 1980. The company expanded rapidly, achieving funding from the UK government. TNT began its international touring in 1981 and gradually became a global theatre company.

In 1993 TNT began its collaboration with Grantly Marshall's ADG Europe. Paul gradually shifted from actor-producer to theatre director and writer. He began directing Shakespeare's major works in 2001. He has also directed independently in theatres as diverse as the St Petersburg State Comedy Theatre, the Athens Concert Hall, the Shanghai Dramatic Arts Centre, Teatro Espressivo de Costa Rica and the Munich Glyptothek, all in languages other than English. Paul is the author or co-author (with Phil Smith) of over thirty plays or adaptations of novels. TNT performs around the world, giving more performances in more countries than any other theatre company. In 2014 Paul was awarded an MBE by Queen Elizabeth for services to British culture. Paul lives in Munich and is married to the TV producer Angelika Stebbings.

Phil Smith is a performance-maker, writer and academic researcher, specialising in work around walking, site-specificity, mythogeographies and counter-tourism. With artist Helen Billinghurst, he is one half of Crab & Bee, who completed, in 2019/20, an exhibition and walking project called 'Plymouth Labyrinth (funded by Arts Council England), a short walking project in the Isles of Scilly, a residency at Teats Hill slipway and the pamphlet 'She Is The Sea'. They are currently engaged in researching their forthcoming book, 'The Pattern'.

With Tony Whitehead and photographer John Schott, Phil published in 2019 *Guidebook For An Armchair Pilgrimage* with Triarchy Press. He is currently developing a 'subjectivity-protective movement practice' with Canada-based choreographer Melanie Kloetzel. With Claire Hind and Helen Billinghurst, he co-organised in 2019 the 'Walking's New Movements' conference at the University of Plymouth. As company dramaturg and co-writer for TNT Theatre (Munich), he most recently premiered 'Free Mandela', co-authored with TNT's artistic director Paul Stebbings, about the end of apartheid in South Africa.

Phil is a member of site-based arts collective Wrights & Sites, who published *The Architect-Walker* (2018). As well as *Walking Stumbling Limping Falling* (Triarchy Press, 2017) with poet Alyson Hallett, Phil's publications include *Making Site-Specific Theatre and Performance* (Red Globe/Macmillan, 2018), *Rethinking Mythogeography in Northfield, Minnesota* (2018) (with US photographer John Schott), *Anywhere* (2017), *A Footbook of Zombie Walking* and *Walking's New Movement* (2015), *On Walking* and *Enchanted Things* (2014), *Counter-Tourism: The Handbook* (2012) and *Mythogeography* (2010). He is an Associate Professor (Reader) at the University of Plymouth.

Phil Smith (left) and Paul Stebbings

About the Publisher

Triarchy Press is a small, independent publisher of books that bring a wider, systemic or contextual approach to many different areas of life, including:

Acting and the Theatre (including *Before the Curtain Opens* – a book about Alexander Technique in the actor's life – and *Body and Performance* – about somatics, movement and drama).

The Money System

Government, Education, Health and other public services

Ecology, Sustainability and Regenerative Cultures

Leading and Managing Organizations

Psychotherapy and Arts and other Expressive Therapies

Walking, Psychogeography and Mythogeography

Movement and Somatics

Innovation

The Future and Future Studies

For more information, please visit:

www.triarchypress.net